Ethical
Dimensions of
International
Management

▧ Sage Series in Business Ethics

Series Editor: Robert A. Giacalone
The E. Claiborne Robins School of Business
University of Richmond

▧ Editorial Board

Stephen J. Carroll
Martin J. Gannon

Ethical Dimensions of International Management

SSBE
Sage Series in Business Ethics

SAGE Publications
International Educational and Professional Publisher
Thousand Oaks   London   New Delhi

For information address:

SAGE Publications, Inc.
2455 Teller Road
Thousand Oaks, California 91320
Phone: 805-499-0721
E-mail: order@sagepub.com

SAGE Publications Ltd.
6 Bonhill Street
London EC2A 4PU
United Kingdom

SAGE Publications India Pvt. Ltd.
M-32 Market
Greater Kailash I
New Delhi 110 048 India

Printed in the United States of America

Library of Congress Cataloging-in-Publication Data

Carroll, Stephen J., 1930-
    Ethical dimensions of international managment / Stephen J.
Carroll and Martin J. Gannon.
        p.   cm.—(Sage series in business ethics)
    Includes bibliographical references and idex.
    ISBN 0-8039-5543-X (acid-free paper).—ISBN 0-8039-5544-8 (pbk.:
acid-free paper)
        1. International business enterprises—Management—Moral and
ethical aspects.   2. Business ethics.   I. Gannon, Martin J.
II. Title.   III. Series.
    HD62.4.C365   1997
    658'.049—dc20   96-25308

This book is printed on acid-free paper.

97 98 99 00 01 02 10 9 8 7 6 5 4 3 2

Acquiring Editor:	Marquita Fleming
Editorial Assistant:	Frances Borghi
Production Editor:	Sherrise Purdum
Production Assistant:	Karen Wiley
Typesetter & Designer:	Andrea D. Swanson
Indexer:	Cristina Haley

Contents

This book is dedicated to our parents and teachers who especially exemplified principles of integrity and ethical behavior and by so doing served as models of emulation for us and many others: Helene Carroll, Stephen Carroll, Sr., Catherine A. Gannon, Leo W. Gannon, Marvin Dunnette, George England, James Jenkins, Thomas Mahoney, Donald Paterson, George Seltzer, Dale Yoder, the late Brother Bernard Rodolf, S.J., and Clarence C. Walton.

Preface

It is difficult to identify two topics that have been more frequently discussed—and either directly or indirectly accorded prominent attention—in very recent years in business schools and business itself than those of ethics and culture. Ethics, of course, has been an important topic since ancient times and, although such writings as Plato's *Republic* and Aristotle's *Nicomachean Ethics* are still widely read and discussed, ethics in business is of more recent vintage. We now have courses on ethics in business schools, laws governing ethicality in business behaviors, codes of ethics in companies, and even some journals focusing on business ethics at both the academic and the practitioner levels. With the ever increasing globalization of business, we also have a renewed interest in national cultural differences and their influence on international business operations, which is reflected in a significant increase in the number of academic courses and journals devoted to these topics.

This book examines the issue of the relationship of national cultural differences to ethical behaviors. One might legitimately ask: Why is an investigation of the relationship of cultural differences to ethical differences important? Perhaps the best place to begin the search for an answer is to analyze why it is important to study ethical behaviors at all. One reason for doing so is that ethical behavior in a society has a significant influence on critical social and economic outcomes. Societies must have some degree of trust before they will cooperate with one another in any type of extended relationship. Predictability is necessary for cooperation and for social and economic investments that will not provide a payoff for many years, and clearly predictability is associated with a perception that certain ethical standards of behavior are a given in a society and across societies.

Such ethical norms or standards of behavior may be incorporated officially into the laws of the nation but they may also be unofficial in the sense that they consist of the internal standards that govern daily behavior. One of the reasons why there have been so many difficulties in moving from collectivist to market-oriented economies in the former Soviet Union and Eastern European economies is that ethical systems currently operating appear to be insufficiently supportive of the development of trust. Also, the ethical standards of a nation are related to other economic factors, such as the willingness of organizations from other nations to invest in that country or to join in partnerships with that country's enterprises. Furthermore, a nation's ethical standards and behaviors can be associated with the amount of internal conflict or social turbulence in that nation, which can directly affect the country's quality of life.

Thus, we feel that the relationship between national cultures and ethical behaviors may help to account for some of the variation that we can observe among nations in terms of their economic progress, their political stability, and the quality of life of their people. Also, studying the relationship between cultural factors and ethical standards and behaviors can help us predict how the ethical norms of a nation may change over time in response to alterations in culture. Knowledge of the manner in which culture affects a society's ethical standards and behaviors can also promote a better understanding of the nature of other societies, which, in turn, can reduce ethnocentrism, racism, stereotypes, and other cognitive biases that militate against human understanding and cooperation in general.

This book is structured around a model of culture and ethical behaviors of managers (see Figure 1.1). In Chapter 1, we explain our research approach for validating this model. We point out that because of the absence of data on ethical behavioral or decisional differences among managers in different nations, we must use an eclectic approach that combines several sources of data, which include surveys, actual published cases on unethical decisions by managers in many countries, and published descriptive information on the many characteristics of nations around the world that we wish to compare.

With respect to the structure of the book, the remainder of the first part, dealing with ethical differences, includes two chapters, one that compares managerial ethical practices across nations, and one that analyzes differences among nations with respect to values and other cultural characteristics. The next part of the book describes primary influences on ethical behavior, such as parenting and educational systems, and secondary influences, such as law, human resource management or HRM systems, and organizational cultures. In the third part of the book, we then provide in-depth treatments featuring case studies of the ethical systems of the United States and Japan. Our original plan was to discuss two additional nations, but space limitations prevented us from doing so. (However, we do present extensive information on specific countries throughout the book.) Thus, we chose two nations that are quite different culturally to discuss this issue of national managerial ethical orientations in some depth. Part III concludes with an analysis of the degree to which ethical systems of different nations may converge or diverge in the coming years.

Given the sensitive nature of the topics addressed in this book, we feel strongly that the reader should understand our backgrounds and values. Neither of us can be described, or has ever been accused of being, radical partisans in any area, including politics and education, but we do react negatively to true believers who feel that their viewpoint represents the only valid truth. We have taught on the same faculty for 28 years, have had extensive consulting experiences in a large number of business firms and governmental agencies, and have traveled, lived with, and taught students and managers in several nations. Most important, we were both attracted to the field of management because it provided an outlet for pursuing many significant and diverse but interrelated intellectual topics, and we have published extensively in the areas of human resource management, business strategy, organizational behavior, and cross-cultural management. Given our close intellectual interests and friendship, we welcomed the opportunity to work together on this book, as we believe strongly that ethics—particularly the development of trust among people of all types—is central to human existence. This book has given us the opportunity to explore our mutual interests in management and ethics in some depth, and for this we are grateful.

There are several distinctive features of this book, and these include the development and justification for the basic model, presented in Chapter 1, around which the book is structured; the very large number of short cases (at least 200) that can be found in every chapter; the numerous short examples that we use to illustrate our points; the extensive and intensive review and summary of the relevant research literature; the focus on a large number of nations; and the direct comparison of two very different nations, Japan and the United States, in terms of their ethical orientations. We have attempted to make the book reader-friendly not only through the use of case studies and examples but also by presenting discussion questions at the end of each chapter and starting each chapter with short cases.

We would like to thank several individuals for their help with this book. Bob Giacalone has been a patient and helpful Series Editor, as has been our

Sage editor, Marquita Flemming . . . and so on. Of course, we accept responsibility for any errors that might have occurred and would be grateful if the reader would bring them to our attention.

Stephen J. Carroll, Jr.
Martin J. Gannon

Culture and
Managerial Ethical Behaviors

Bid Rigging in Japan

On May 25, 1992, the Administrative Vice Minister of Construction in Japan called upon the heads of seven construction industry associations to remedy precontract, bid-rigging collusive arrangements known as dango. The Construction Ministry also decided to exclude 66 Japanese building contractors from bidding on some public works projects for 1 month for violation of the Anti-Monopoly Law in Saitama Prefecture. The Asahi Evening News, *an English-language newspaper, said that these punishments involved only a "symbolic wrist slap."*

Asahi Evening News
("Companies Receive," 1992)

Embezzlement and Bribery in China

Shen Haifu, 39, president of the Great Wall Machinery and Electronics High-Technology Industrial Group Corp., was put to death on charges of embezzlement and bribery. Executions in China are by a bullet to the back of the head.

The Washington Post
(" Fu," 1994)

Fraud in Europe

All over Europe, execs are in trouble with the law. Whistle-blowers and prosecutors have launched a slew of probes into shady practices, which they claim are on the rise in European business. Among the cases *publicized recently are those of four German executives under investigation for a $1-billion credit fraud, a Belgian executive jailed for financial fraud, a French executive charged with insider trading, a German developer being sought for falsification and tax evasion, a Spanish executive charged by his former employer with theft of corporate secrets, a famous Italian banker under investigation for financial irregularities, and a Spanish executive accused by a bank of using questionable accounting practices to inflate company profits.*

Business Week
(Barnathan, Galuszka, & Del Vallue, 1994)

Massive Layoffs in the United States

AT&T announced that another large group of its employees (40,000) would be laid off to make the company more competitive. More than 100,000 AT&T employees have lost their jobs in recent years.

Washington Post (Church, 1996)

Throughout the world, examples of problematic or unethical behaviors among managers are routinely highlighted by the media and concerned citizens. Bribery, sexual harassment, patent or copyright infringements, lying and deceit about product performance and safety, deliberate use of harmful substances, intentional environmental pollution, discrimination, dangerous working conditions, violations of promises, and other similar types of behavior are widely discussed and frequently condemned.

Certainly, part of this widespread interest in ethics and allied topics of morality and the law reflects the fact that they are central to human existence. Humans are social animals, and commonly held notions of what is acceptable or unacceptable behavior constitute the glue that holds societies together. Since time immemorial, Plato, Aristotle, Confucius, Kant, Spinoza, Moses, Jesus, Muhammad, Gandhi, and many others have lectured and written about the principles of conduct governing individuals and groups, or the standards of behavior that constitute the focus of ethics.

There is some evidence to suggest that interest in the specific topic of business ethics has slowly been increasing in recent years. Certainly, one reason for this has been the very large number of publicized cases in which unethical behaviors have cost businesses sometimes not only millions but even billions of dollars. Obviously, unethical behavior can be very costly.

On the other hand, is there any evidence that being unusually ethical is related to exceptional economic performance? There seem to be few such studies of this relationship, and some of the research results have been mixed. However, one major study showed that an investment of $1,000 in each of 30 companies with higher than average ethical values produced, after 30 years, an investment 4.7 times greater than a similar investment in a Dow-Jones composite of companies (Aguilar, 1994). Interest in international business ethics or comparative business ethics seems to be quite a new area of concern and is obviously related to the globalization of the world's economy. The typical large company must now operate in many countries around the world and must face a myriad of laws and customs or norms of behavior that can be quite confusing, to say the least. What is considered unacceptable or problematic business behavior in one nation might be quite acceptable in another. This is a particular bone of contention in the United States, which has more laws legislating ethical behaviors for its managers than any other nation. From 1977 to 1992, the United States either jailed or fined more corporate officers and prominent businessmen than all other capitalist countries combined (Vogel, 1992).

Today, it is quite common for government officials and executives from some nations to severely criticize another nation for widespread acceptance of a particular managerial behavior deemed to be unethical by them. For example, recently commentators in the United States have harshly criticized China for violating the human rights of its prisoners, who are frequently used as slave labor in manufacturing plants. The Chinese government, however, reacted negatively to this criticism, as it felt that such treatment was justified for criminals, especially because China is at an early stage of economic development and needs to produce effectively if its economy—and the concomitant well-being of all citizens, including prisoners—is to grow. An enormous amount of media coverage in the United States and Japan in recent years has been given to charges and countercharges of the ethicality of various management practices in both nations. Thus, this high interest in international business ethics reflects the recent trends of creating a global economy and rapidly internationalizing management. It is now apparent that what is done in business all around the world affects all of us.

▨ BASIC DEFINITIONS AND APPROACH

As the title indicates, this book focuses on the relationship between culture and managerial ethical behaviors. For *culture,* we accept the common definition of this term as the patterned way of thinking, feeling, and reacting that exists in a particular group, organization, profession, subgroup of a society, nation, or group of nations (Tosi, Rizzo, & Carroll, 1994). Operationally, the concept of *widely shared* is central to the concept of culture, and culture allows its members to "fill in the blanks," or behave automatically without having to specify everything in detail. When cultural values are violated, there tends to be an emotional reaction and, in extreme cases, complete disregard or even banishment of those who have committed the violations.

The word *ethics* is derived from the Greek *ethos,* which refers specifically to the "character" and "sentiment of the community." Specific definitions include "the principles of conduct governing an individual or a profession" and "standards of behavior" (Shea, 1988, p. 17). Ethical means "conforming to the standards of a given profession or group. Any group can set its own ethical standards and then live by them or not" (Toffler, 1986, p. 10). Ethical standards, whether they are established by an individual, a corporation, a profession, or a nation, help to guide a person's decisions and actions. Given such overlapping perspectives, we will use the commonly accepted definition of ethics as "rules or standards that govern behaviors" (Toffler, 1986, p. 10). Our definition, however, moves beyond a purely consensual perspective by recognizing the importance of a normative perspective, that is, some acts are so evil and reprehensile that we should seek to extirpate them or at least control them as much as possible (see Chapter 8).

Because the book focuses on managerial ethics, we are primarily concerned with managerial decision making. This is the type of behavior that managers are paid to do, in all or almost all countries of the world. They must make choices from among alternatives and these may vary in terms of their perceived ethicality. Decision making is the process of reasoning before behavior or of calculating the pluses and minuses or the "goodness" or "badness" of various alternatives with which an individual is confronted before making judgments or choices. It is a cognitive process, and the study of such cognitions is the primary emphasis in psychology today. Thus, any discussion of ethical decision making can make effective use of current knowledge and perspectives from the field of cognitive psychology.

Because this book emphasizes culture and its relationship to the ethical choices of managers, we want primarily to emphasize those cultural antecedents of the managerial decisions that have ethical implications. Culture has been specifically recognized as one of the determinants of ethical judgments in the models of ethical behavior proposed by Bartels (1967) and Hunt and Vitell (1986). Also, various factors influenced by culture, such as a society's laws, values, and religious beliefs, have been identified as key influences in ethical decision-making situations (Bartels, 1967). Furthermore, organizational culture and the decision maker's past experiences, as molded by national culture, have been identified as significant influences on ethical judgments.

As Donaldson and Dunfee (1994) point out, in the past there have been various approaches to the study of business ethics. Two contrasting approaches they highlight are the *normative,* with its extensive historical roots in philosophy, and the *empirical,* which today often draws upon psychological research in moral behavior. Using these two approaches, we often have a contrast between how managers should make choices (if they possess certain characteristics such as rationality) and how individuals are influenced when making ethical decisions, although the two approaches can be compatible. This epistemological conflict is a disagreement of long standing in academic circles.

With respect to normative theories of ethical behavior, we often contrast deontological theories to theories of utilitarianism, as proposed by writers such as Jeremy Bentham and John Stuart Mill, which emphasize the consequences of decisions. Deontological theories, such as the Categorical Imperative of Immanuel Kant, stress the essential correctness of the action or rule itself without regard to consequences. In actual human decision making, it seems likely that some combination of ends and means considerations is used, given the actual complexity of many of the ethical dilemmas facing individuals in real life. Examples of moral duties include such rules as the duty of fidelity, or telling the truth and keeping promises; reparation, or righting previous wrongs; nonmalfeasance, or avoiding harm to others; justice, or appropriately rewarding merit; gratitude, or recognition of past services; and so on.

Some would also argue that the principle of relativism, which emphasizes the concept or principle of right or wrong or justice and injustice in terms of the values and goals of particular groups, is important. Of course, the merits of the relativistic perspective are a matter of some long-standing disagreement. A very recent criticism of the principle of relativism has been cogently made by James Q. Wilson (1994), who argues and extensively documents the point that human beings have a natural moral sense that is the product of innate dispositions and early family experiences. He indicates that such a universal moral sense is in fact necessary for human survival, and that is why it exists. Wilson feels that only a very small percentage of the population does not have a well-developed inner moral sense and thus is prone to commit crimes and other social transgressions. He also highlights the importance of the four moral senses of sympathy, fairness, self-control, and duty, which combine to form this general moral sense. However, one could argue that Wilson's concepts are so abstract and vague that they do not establish any universal sense of what is or is not ethical. In any society, sympathy may exist for some people (insiders) but never for others (outsiders, etc.) and, consequently, one can have two standards of ethical behavior. The sense of duty may cause an individual to murder thousands when asked to do so by higher authorities, and so on. For the purposes of this book, let us emphasize that there is some evidence that all of these considerations (ends, means, and moral principles) are used in the making of judgments in ethical situations (Mayo & Marks, 1990; Vitell & Hunt, 1990).

In schools of business, the case method has long been used and still is emphasized in the study and teaching of business ethics and all business subjects, for that matter. Cases have always been used in professional schools both because they relate to the actual behaviors or situations that professionals face and because they are readily available as sources of information. Because cases are real-life events, it is difficult to apply the scientific method of hypothesis testing to them to represent a sample of a population; and because they typically have many unique aspects, it is difficult to produce valid generalizations from their use. Nevertheless, cases are being recognized as a useful research tool and a very valid source of hypotheses. As Yin (1989) points out, although cases cannot be generalized to a larger population, they are generalizable to theory and they can provide an effective research methodology that permits the examination of a wide body of evidence. Also, when there is a significant number of cases, they can be a valid indicator of the behavioral tendencies of a larger group. Furthermore, cases in some ways involve both the empirical and the normative approaches to the study of ethics and other subjects, because students are typically asked to make a diagnosis and evaluation of the case situation to identify more general or normative principles or conclusions. This book, both of necessity and for educational purposes, will make very heavy use of cases in its analysis of the relationship of culture to managerial ethical decision making.

Our approach, then, in discussing the subject of cultural influences on ethical aspects of managerial decision making, will be an eclectic one. We will combine relevant empirical research with published management ethical cases, factual descriptive data on cultures, and appropriate conceptual writings. We feel that this is the best approach to the subject, given the present low level of knowledge in this area. Also, this approach reflects a management orientation that tends to be issue-oriented rather than method- or discipline-oriented. In

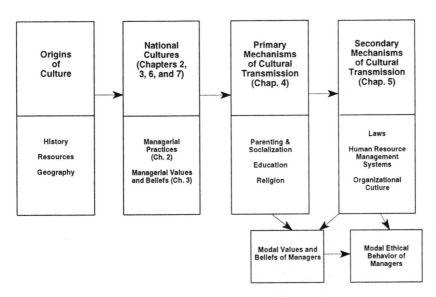

Figure 1.1. A Model of Culture and Ethical Behaviors Among Managers

addition, it is important to point out that in examining the characteristics of nations and cultures, one finds that most of the research available focuses on differences in values and beliefs rather than on actual behaviors or decisions. We and others who have worked in this area recognize that values and beliefs may not necessarily be translated into behaviors or decisions but that they do significantly overlap. For example, the theory of reasoned action and the research derived from it indicate that attitudes, beliefs, and values often do affect behavioral intentions and subsequent behaviors (Ajzen & Fishbein, 1980; Fishbein & Ajzen 1975; Tosi, Rizzo, & Carroll, 1994).

Of course, part of the problem of predicting behavior from individual characteristics is that situational factors influence and may overwhelm individual propensities or inclinations in a particular situation. We have recognized, since at least the 1930s, that behavior is a function of both individual and situational characteristics. Indeed, there is presently a good deal of attention to this interactional perspective on behavior (Miner, 1988) and to the subfield of interactional psychology (Schneider, 1983; Terborg, 1981). This perspective is reflected in the relationship of culture to managerial ethical behavior or decision making as described in our model (see Figure 1.1).

Before describing the model in more detail, we want to stress the usefulness of the psychological expectancy model for examining the critical variables in all choice situations, including ethical decision making. In this model, choices are asserted to be the result of an individual's expectations about achieving a goal or outcome and the degree of desirability associated with it, considering all of its consequences and their meaning for the individual decision maker. The consequences are a function of individual factors and environmental factors. For example, in deciding to do something that is unethical, the individual must first calculate whether it is possible to do it. Obviously, management controls or surveillance procedures might make an action impossible and therefore, in that situation, the action would be avoided. If the action is possible because of some opportunity, and the individual has the capability of doing it, the next calculation is whether the pluses and minuses make it worthwhile. The pluses and minuses of an unethical act may include the possibility of making money, the individual shame experienced by doing something unethical, the social rewards or punishments given by one's peers, the probability of getting caught and paying a penalty, and so on. Thus, the weight given by the individual will depend on personal characteristics such as personal ethical standards or values with respect to that particular action, risk-taking propensities, importance of or need for money or the rewards in the situation, need for social acceptance, and so on. Obviously, these will vary from one individual to another and furthermore are likely to vary on an average or *modal* basis from one culture to another. One can see from this expectancy model that a particular reaction to an ethical situation in which an individual finds himself or herself will be affected by a wide variety of individual, group, work environment, and societal factors. These include personality, values, needs, beliefs, laws, HRM practices, organizational culture, professional group standards, and societal cultural expectations. In this book, the primary emphasis will be on the contribution of national cultural factors in managerial ethical decisions or reactions; however, many of the cultural transmission factors in Figure 1.1 can independently influence the ethical decisions of managers.

▧ A MODEL OF CULTURE AND ETHICAL BEHAVIORS

Figure 1.1 describes the model that we will use throughout this book. This model begins with the origins of cultures themselves, and we emphasize a culture's or nation's history, geography, and natural resources. For example, Italy has been a unified country only since 1861, and it was ruled for centuries by other countries. Historically, Italians have feared outsiders who may be sent by their rulers to infiltrate their cultural groups. Italians hated to pay taxes to such rulers and devised elaborate schemes for avoiding them. Today, these historical factors still play a prominent part in the ethical practices of Italians, because they tend to trust only people in their cultural in-groups and flagrantly violate the tax laws.

Geographical location also plays a major role in understanding differences in managerial ethical behaviors. Once again, Italy serves as a prime illustration, as it has historically been victimized by overwhelming natural disasters: volcanoes, floods, famines, and earthquakes. As a result, Italy exudes an aura of "precariousness" (Haycraft, 1985). Italians tend to accept insecurity as a fact of life, which helps to explain why they are able to enjoy life more for the moment and are willing to accept events as they happen (Gannon & Associates, 1994). Sometimes, Italian businessmen will make extravagant promises that they know have only a slight chance of ever being actualized, and this behavior is in accord with their view that all life is precarious and subject to chance. Just as a mountain is beautiful before being destroyed by an earthquake, so too an extravagant promise is acceptable if there is any chance, however slight, that it can be fulfilled.

Natural resources also influence managerial ethical behavior. Japan, for instance, is a small island nation that has few natural resources. It imported the practice of rice farming from China, at about the 7th century A.D., because this type of agriculture provided at least a subsistence level of living for all Japanese. However, for each village to survive, it was necessary that all contribute and work hard at rice farming. Thus, harmony in working toward the common good became the chief value underlying the Japanese perspective; it was the first article in the country's first constitution, written by Prince Shotoku in the 7th century. Behaviors that tend to destroy this sense of harmony are frequently classified as unacceptable or unethical.

This perspective is in sharp contrast to that in the United States, where life, liberty, and the pursuit of individual happiness predominate. In the United States, the abundance of natural resources and land helped to strengthen this ideological perspective. Americans in the 17th and 18th centuries had almost unlimited resources and they tended to develop practices that were wasteful and careless of resources. Even today, this wastefulness is a problem in the United States, as we shall document in later chapters.

The next element in our model is the national culture itself, and we will focus on two overlapping aspects of it: the management practices in such areas as bribery and issuing false reports, and the basic values that lead to such clear differences in these practices. In Chapter 2, we describe such practices in detail to give the reader some understanding of the wide differences in this area. Then, in Chapter 3, we describe in detail the dimensions of national cultures or their basic values that lead to such practices or different ethical behaviors across nations. According to a number of investigators of national culture, the most important dimension or value across cultures may well be individualism-collectivism, that is, the degree to which the individual feels that he or she is integrated into a group, even to the extent of making decisions only if they are acceptable to the group. Research has indicated that members of collectivist cultures tend to be very cooperative with other members of their in-groups but uncooperative and hostile to members of out-groups (Brislin, 1993). Such a zero-sum or winner-loser perspective has obvious ramifications for defining acceptable managerial behaviors. For instance, a manager should always try to help members of his or her culture or in-group and act in an honest and trusting way toward them. However, this same manager may well lie to members of the out-groups and even view them as "less than human." Some Japanese managers, for instance, believe that they need to be honest only when speaking Japanese, and so they sometimes use the English language when dealing with non-Japanese managers if they want to deceive them or avoid being held to a commitment (DeMente, 1991).

Primary and secondary influences on values and behaviors constitute the third element in our model. Parenting and socialization represent such a primary influence. For example, for the first few years of life, Japanese children are strapped to the bodies of their mothers, who encourage them to look at their faces, thus developing a relationship of dependency. These children also sleep with their parents until the age of 6 or 7, which strengthens this sense of dependency. Such parenting practices are consistent with the emphasis on harmony. By contrast, American children are strongly encouraged to explore the world about them as early in life as possible. Such patterns strengthen either a group-oriented style of ethical decision making, as in the case of Japan, or an individualistic style, as in the case of the United States.

Education is also an important primary influence on values and behaviors. In Germany, children are separated into different types of schools at the end of fourth or sixth grade; other European countries make similar assignments at the end of eighth grade. Some of this separation is class related, because only the wealthier parents can afford to hire tutors to help their children pass the rigorous examinations required for admission to the schools that lead to a university degree and a prosperous life. Tutoring of 4-year-olds is quite common. Such educational systems reinforce the belief that there are natural and definite social class barriers in society. Although sheer ability is sometimes sufficient to overcome such barriers, in many instances individuals are born with special rights and obligations. Although it is difficult to precisely identify cause and effect, it may well be that the United States punishes more of its managers for unethical acts than all other developed countries combined, partly because of the more open educational system that exists in the United States. Some citizens, including managers, do not automatically have special rights and obligations different from those of other citizens.

Religion is a third primary influence. Many of the citizens in several developing countries believe in astrology, and some of their businessmen will not undertake a course of action until it is approved by an astrologer; even the president of India has used astrologers. Also, some of the major religions, particularly Catholicism and Confucianism, tend to have an antibusiness bias, thus making major business activity in and of itself immoral and unethical. For example, the Catholic theologian and philosopher, St. Thomas Aquinas, argued that a price should be "just," that is, just sufficient to cover the costs of labor and materials. However, his approach was antithetical to charging interest, which is a major foundation stone of modern economic life. Clearly, there are instances of companies charging a usurious rate of interest, and any American paying an interest rate of 22% on a bank credit card balance while receiving only 3% for money invested in bank certificates of deposits can easily sympathize with the concept of the just price. Still, as Max Weber has persuasively argued, it was the Protestant ethic and its emphasis on relating worldly success to divine salvation that was a major precondition for modern capitalism and its high standard of living. In Chapter 4, we will compare and contrast two religious theories, the Confucian ethic and the Protestant ethic, that are related to radically different managerial and ethical behaviors.

There are also secondary influences on values and behaviors that are not as direct as the primary influences, and these include laws, organizational cultures, and human resource management (HRM) systems. They still, however, exert a powerful influence. Thus, Title VII of the Equal Employment Opportunity Law and its extensions have changed life dramatically in the United States for many groups, including women, African Americans, and the disabled. There are various HRM policies in the areas of recruitment, training, performance evaluation, and reward systems that exert a powerful influence on ethical practices. For example, Sears, Roebuck and Co. recently changed its policy of paying its employees in auto services on a commission basis, because some of them deliberately charged customers for services that were never rendered. In Japan, where the customer is considered king, it would be hard to imagine a similar situation occurring at a prominent company.

Also, IBM had a no-layoff policy until recently and it supposedly led to a more conservative approach to decision making and, by extension, what was acceptable or ethical behavior. Similarly, many large Japanese organizations guarantee lifetime employment to a core set of managers and employees and, although this has led to an increase in feelings of company loyalty, it has also been accompanied by conservative decision making and the treating of some employees performing approximately the same jobs in radically different ways. An employee who has been guaranteed lifetime employment may receive twice the salary of his short-term counterpart.

Organizational cultures also represent a potent secondary influence. Thus, in Japan, the Sony Corporation has a more innovative and risk-taking organizational culture than that of many older and more established companies such as Mitsui, partly because Sony was established about 300 years later than Mitsui, when conditions were quite different. Sony needed experienced managers and so it did not follow the practice of "maturing" managers and hiring them directly from schools and universities. Rather, Sony started to hire managers away from other Japanese companies. Still, Sony and Mitsui are more similar to one another in terms of their organizational cultures than to such American companies as Xerox or RCA.

There is, however, a trend for large companies in one nation to implement changes in their organizational cultures that make them more similar to companies in other nations. Honda, for many years, followed the Japanese emphasis on harmony, which led to a slowing down of the decision-making process in the organization. Managers did not want to openly criticize the ideas of their peers and superiors, and frequently problems were not even discussed until it was too late to solve them. Recently, however, Honda has encouraged such American-style practices as openly confronting a problem at a meeting, even if some loss of face occurs, and rewarding successful managers much more than in the past. This abrupt change in the management systems has been difficult for many of the Honda managers to accept, especially because what was previously unacceptable and unethical is now considered acceptable and ethical.

Figure 1.1 indicates that the primary and secondary influences have significant effects on the values and beliefs of individual managers. It also shows that individual values and beliefs are then related, although imperfectly, to subsequent behaviors or decisions. As the figure indicates, it should be recognized that these secondary influences can overwhelm individual behavioral propensities, as previously indicated; for example, tight management control systems decrease unethical behaviors. Thus, these secondary influences not only reflect the culture but also exert independent pressures on individuals to behave in certain ways.

As Figure 1.1 suggests, we emphasize *modal* behaviors found in a nation, that is, points in a statistical distribution of a nation where large clusters of individuals can be found. It is impossible to identify and describe the behaviors of every individual within a nation, and we make no attempt to do so.

Throughout this book, we will use this model as a framework for organizing the presentations. In the remainder of this first part, we will discuss actual managerial practices as they relate to ethics (Chapter 2) and the influence that values exert on ethical behaviors (Chapter 3). The next part examines the primary and secondary influences on ethical behaviors (Chapters 4 and 5). In the third part of the book, we contrast the ethical systems of Japan and the United States to address the final and important issue of this book, namely the possible convergence or divergence of national ethical systems in the future as they apply to managerial behaviors.

◩ DISCUSSION QUESTIONS

1. In the past 15 years, the United States has jailed and fined more managers than all other developed countries combined. Does this suggest that American managers are more ethical than those in other developed countries? Why or why not?

2. It has been persuasively argued that, by and large, government should not place major restrictions on the activities of corporations in capitalistic societies, and that the use of voluntary industry codes of conduct are sufficient to handle any problems that may occur. How do you feel about this argument?

3. What are the differences between consequential, deontological, and relativistic ethical systems? If you had to combine these systems, how would you do it?

4. How are ethics and law related to one another? Is the law just a substitute for ethics? Why or why not?

5. Do the Ten Commandments represent a moral code or an ethical code? Why?

6. Describe the differences between the normative and the empirical perspectives on ethics. Which offers the must useful guides to behavior? Why?

7. What is culture? Is this definition more compatible with relativistic ethics than with consequentialist ethics and deontological ethics?

8. How do you feel about *enforceable* universal laws and codes of business ethics that transcend national boundaries?

9. A distinction between primary and secondary influences on managerial ethical behaviors is emphasized in the model that will guide the discussion in this book. What is the distinction? Can you think of any other primary and secondary influences that are not explicitly described in this model?

2

Comparing Managerial Ethical Practices and Propensities Across Nations

United States Expels Japanese Bank From the Country

The Federal Reserve Board in the United States has given Japan's Daiwa Bank Ltd. 90 days to leave the country. The bank was accused of concealing false records of more than $1 billion in trading losses. Supposedly, the bank's top managers in the United States and in Japan not only helped to conceal these and other losses from U.S. bank regulators but also lied to the Federal Reserve about organizational structural changes. The case illustrates the problem that nations have in managing foreign firms within their borders whose ways of doing business are different from those in the host country.

The Wall Street Journal (Wilke, O'Brien, & Shirouzu, 1995)

A Peril of Global Marketing: A Beer Tampering Scare in China

It was reported that some consumers fell ill when home brewed beer was poured into empty Pabst beer bottles and resold in China. The incident illustrates a major problem for foreign consumer products companies in China, where illicit imports of products and counterfeiting of brands are common.

The Wall Street Journal (Smith, 1995)

AUTHORS' NOTE: Nance Lucas, a doctoral student at the University of Maryland, provided research assistance and coauthored this chapter.

As we have seen in Chapter 1, one of the major reasons, if not the major reason, why there are clear national differences between ethical practices is the degree to which individuals either see themselves as isolated persons whose fate is in their own hands or see themselves as part of and embedded in social groups. When an individual takes actions without any regard to the feelings of others in a group with which he or she is closely associated, he or she is expressing a high degree of individualism; when action will be taken only if it is in total conformance with the group's norms, the individual is expressing a high degree of collectivism. Nations differ significantly from one another along the individualism-collectivism dimension and this accounts for some of the variance in ethical propensities. For example, it is not surprising that the Chinese character for *I* is often paired with other characters that are somewhat derogatory in connotation, because China is a collectivistic nation, and that there is really no word for *privacy* in many languages.

The three ethical systems we described in Chapter 1 reflect such differences in individualism or collectivism. Deontological ethics, with its emphasis on protecting the value and worth of each individual, tends to flourish in individualistic countries such as the United States, Germany, England, Australia, and the Netherlands. More collectivistic or group-oriented countries, such as Japan, African nations, and South American nations like Colombia, emphasize pluralistic utilitarianism, that is, maximizing the greatest good for the greatest number who are in-group members (Pratt, 1991). In such group-oriented countries, relativism is also an important ethical perspective, because ethics tend to be context-specific or situation-specific, and members of the in-group are treated in a radically different manner from those in the out-group, even to the extent of considering out-group members as less than human.

In this chapter, we will examine some actual ethical behaviors among managers against this backdrop of individualism-collectivism. Our focus is on the degree of individualism in a nation, but we recognize that a person can be highly individualistic in a group-oriented nation, and vice versa. We are basically interested in the general patterns that can be found in a nation. We will begin our discussion by focusing on group orientation, after which we shall examine the issues of bribery, false information of all types, gender, and dealing with competitors.

◼ GROUP ORIENTATION

A group-oriented culture needs mechanisms that strengthen the relationship between individuals and the group. As we have seen in our discussion of Japan in Chapter 1, parenting is one mechanism that is very effective, as the child learns quickly to follow rules and engage in behaviors that are in conformance with *amae,* that is, looking to others for love and affection and, as a consequence, fostering mutual dependence among all members of the group. Perhaps the most effective mechanism is *face,* which is an unwritten set of rules by means of which people in society cooperate to avoid unduly damaging others' prestige and respect. Although face is generally associated with Asian societies, it is important in all group-oriented societies. In bargaining, for example, the winner should allow the loser some minor tactical reward to save face, especially when all observers can ascertain the identity of the vanquished. If a father's business becomes bankrupt and he dies suddenly, frequently his sons will work to pay off the debt to maintain face for the family. Among the Chinese and the Japanese, when an individual loses face, he or she tends to adopt a stony or blank expression as if nothing has happened; generally, face is forfeited through loss of self-control or a display of frustration and anger (Bonavia, 1989, pp. 73-74; Gannon & Associates, 1994, p. 326).

Also, group-oriented societies tend to grant their leaders much more freedom of discretion than do individualistic societies. For example, a subordinate in Japan will tend to react more positively to a manager who chastises him harshly than will his American counterpart, because the manager's behavior is seen as a sign of genuine care and *amae* (Bond, Wan, Leung, & Giacalone, 1985). Such a manager may also engage in behaviors that would be considered acceptable in Japan but unethical and illegal in the United States.

Individuals in Japanese organizations tend to be motivated "not by their personal needs, but by the need not to lose face" (Cohen, Pant, & Sharp, 1992, p. 691). The Japanese will close ranks and protect the integrity and image of their groups as a way of saving face. It is not uncommon for Japanese workers to cover up for their bosses as a way of showing loyalty and protecting the reputation of their enterprise.

Failure, according to Confucian thought, is dishonor and is characterized as losing face (Dollinger, 1988). The strong dedication, loyalty, and respect by the Japanese to hierarchical systems motivate employees to protect the company, the superiors, or both at all costs. To dishonor a company or superior is a serious breach of the Japanese value of loyalty in business organizations. These conflicting ethical perspectives—individualism and collectivism—are highlighted in the reactions of individualistic Americans and the more collectivistically inclined Japanese to whistle-blowing, which is an act of telling the public about the illegal or immoral behavior of an employer or organization. The United States recently passed legislation to protect the employment rights of whistle-blowers and to prevent retaliatory actions against them. Some American businessmen have compared whistle-blowing to civil disobedience, which was prevalent in the 1960s (Shaw & Barry, 1989). Americans are more inclined to allow moral obligation, such as reporting a wrongdoing or injustice, to override loyalty to the company.

In Japan, however, workers are discouraged from expressing ideas or opinions that run counter to the practices, or the harmony, or both of their organizations. Whistle-blowing is considered a taboo action in Japan because it violates the high value that the Japanese place on loyalty to the company (Taka & Foglia, 1994). Similarly, in collectivistically inclined Peru, it is not uncommon for workers to be fired for whistle-blowing (Donaldson, 1985).

Given the distinctive perspective of group-oriented societies, it is not surprising that they manifest different attitudes toward honoring kinship ties and fostering nepotism than individualistic societies, although there are also differences among the individualistic societies. Nepotism, showing favoritism to relatives and close friends in such areas as hiring and promotion, is widely practiced by Nigerian rulers and political figures (Amadi, 1982). Kinsmen are appointed to well-paid jobs and positions of high stature in Nigeria. It is also pervasive in Saudi Arabia (Donaldson, 1985). In underdeveloped countries, nepotism is a result of clan and family loyalty and does not necessarily arise directly from economic needs.

Arguably, nepotism and other forms of in-group behaviors constitute a rational and functional response to an uncertain world. When individuals begin to feel that the administration of laws is unjust and that some groups are unfairly treated, it is natural that they would respond by encouraging trust within an in-group, and nepotism is one way to solidify such trust. Putnam (1993) demonstrates quite convincingly that Sicily and other areas in the south of Italy witnessed the rise of the Mafia because of the effective but highly autocratic rule of King Federico in the 11th century. Power was only vertical; everyone was totally subordinate to the king. As his successors gradually became weaker and more corrupt, there was a dramatic need for justice, the normalization of life, and an intermediary between the king and the common person, and the Mafia families fulfilled this role. These families and those directly and indirectly dependent on them encouraged in-group behaviors such as nepotism. Unfortunately, the Mafia itself became corrupt over time and impeded normalization of life and economic growth. In the north and center of Italy, there was never a period of autocratic rule but, rather, significant citizen involvement in the life of society. As a result, guilds thrived, as did many other types of voluntary associations, and consequently the north and the center of Italy have been not only more democratic but also more economically successful than the south.

Furthermore, widespread nepotism is quite common in family-owned American businesses and in labor unions (Shaw & Barry, 1989). In the United States, labor unions have been described as organizations run by families, with relatives of high-ranking officials holding prominent and high-paying positions. Still, research indicates that Americans tend to give job recommendations to individuals who are competent to perform the work. In group-oriented societies, there is a tendency to recommend a family member or a friend for a position, even if he or she is not qualified for it.

Even the performance evaluation systems of individualistic and group-oriented societies tend to reflect these patterns. Group-oriented societies rank or rate employees in an absolute sense to save face; for example, Jones is a superior or good performer. American corporations, however, usually rank or compare employees to one another; standards are relative and not absolute; and an employee who is performing in a satisfactory manner may well be replaced when someone else ranks higher than him or her. Such a practice is frequently viewed as both immoral and unethical in group-oriented societies.

China represents an interesting modern paradox. Its Confucian tradition emphasizes group orientation, and the Communist regime that assumed control in the late 1940s has strengthened this emphasis. Under the Communists, the concept of the "iron rice bowl" was and still is popular; that is, everyone should share work, food, and basic rights; however, public shaming of a manager or employee for poor job performance or ideological infractions is common. This reinforces the group orientation of the Chinese. Today, however, China is privatizing its economy and, as it does so, it must reorient its priorities, even in the sense that behaviors that were once considered immoral, unethical, and illegal are now quite acceptable, including the pursuit of large profits.

▧ BRIBERY

In the early 1970s, it was reported that Exxon Oil Corporation paid $59 million to Italian politicians to pave the way for achieving its business goals in Italy. Prior to the passage of the Foreign Corrupt Practices Act of 1977 in the United States, it was estimated that approximately 400 American companies paid about $300 million in the form of bribes to foreign officials for business or political favors (Shaw & Barry, 1989). The Foreign Corrupt Practices Act prevents American corporations from exchanging money or material goods for something in return, which is a form of bribery. John Graham (1984) offers convincing evidence that this act is not detrimental to U.S. business. Moreover, it must be realized that bribery affects citizens, because it raises the costs of goods sold, leads to perceptions of unfair treatment of some companies and groups at the expense of others, and decreases the level of trust across groups. Different forms of bribery also lead to differential perceptions that can further decrease trust. For example, some Americans decry outright payoffs to obtain business contracts, but some foreigners see large financial contributions by interest groups to American political campaigns as much more damaging than a modest financial payment that is straightforwardly offered and accepted.

Shaw and Barry (1989) define bribery as "remuneration for the performance of an act that is inconsistent with the work contract or the nature of the work one has been hired to perform" (p. 303). American executives found guilty of bribery have been fined heavily and frequently sent to prison (Vogel, 1992). In Malaysia, which is significantly influenced by the Moslem proscriptions against bribery, execution of executives for the offense of bribery is legal.

Despite American regulations against bribery, many parts of the business world consider it to be an acceptable or normal practice, regardless of whether it is considered legal. Bribery seems to be more extensive in developing nations and those stressing a high degree of collectivism. Table 2.1 lists the countries where it is reported bribery is so pervasive that it acts as a disincentive to trade and the countries where it is not. Asian, African, and Middle Eastern nations seem to consider bribery an acceptable or normal practice, regardless of its legality. In the Swahili language, the terms for bribery, *chai* and *zawadi,* are used in respectful tones and are a part of the Swahili's expectation of doing business and closing a deal. In a number of African nations, bribery is such a strong and common norm that it overrides the law. Historically, the benefits

TABLE 2.1 The Differential Impact of the Foreign Corrupt Practices Act (FCPA)

Countries where FCPA reported to be a disincentive to trade (improper payments common)	Countries where FCPA not mentioned as a disincentive to trade (improper payments uncommon)
Argentina	Bahrain
Australia	Belgium/Luxembourg
Austria	Chile
Bangladesh	Ecuador
Egypt	Finland
Indonesia	France
Japan	Germany
Kenya	Ghana
South Korea	Iceland
Kuwait	India
Liberia	Iraq
Mexico	Ireland
Netherlands	Jamaica
Nigeria	Jordan
Oman	Lebanon
Philippines	New Zealand
Saudi Arabia	Norway
Singapore	Qatar
Syria	South Africa
Turkey	Switzerland
United Arab Emirates	Spain
Venezuela	United Kingdom

SOURCE: U.S. Department of Commerce (1980, pp. O-6 to O-14).

reaped by bribery or extortion in Africa were considered "communal heritage" and were shared throughout the community. In collectivistic countries such as Kenya and Indonesia, bribery is viewed as a way to meet communal obligations by distributing the wealth to members of the community's inner circle. Most of the Middle East recognizes bribery as a tradition centuries old (see Shaw & Barry, 1989).

In countries such as Thailand and India, government workers have low salaries. High-ranking government officials can become wealthy or can supplement their salaries through widespread bribery, which appears to be a common and acceptable practice (Kohls & Buller, 1994). Bribery also seems to be an acceptable and open practice among poorly paid and low-level Peruvian government officials, who consider income from bribes a significant contribution to their compensation (Cohen et al., 1992).

Even individualistic countries such as Canada and the United States, however, differ among themselves as to the manner in which they view and condone bribery. For example, Canadian law permitted Exxon and General Motors to make large political contributions, which were considered illegal in the United States (Benson, 1992).

Some nations' tolerance of bribery in conducting business is higher than others. Japan, although having a partial code against bribery, seems to maintain a high tolerance level for this practice (DeGeorge, 1986). Bribery in Japan is an "open kind of activity which is culturally accepted" (Wicks, 1990, p. 197). Also, one study shows that American managers are more concerned about bribery as an unethical act than German and French managers (Becker & Fritzsche, 1987). Universally, bribery is not accepted as an immoral, illegal, or unethical business practice despite the American desire to level the playing field and assert a utilitarian ethical approach to replace all forms of bribery internationally with competition based solely on the merit of the products and services offered by nations (DeGeorge, 1986).

Still, there is frequently a gap between the intended meaning of the law and its execution. In Venezuela, payments and commissions to public entities and unlawful gifts and payments to civil servants are viewed as the most condemnable type of behavior (Perdomo, 1990). Nevertheless, as in the case of Japan, this type of corruption appears to be quite common in Venezuela.

Because bribery is a standard way of doing business in many countries, the United States made provisions for corporations to either use or succumb to small bribes, which are required to travel or work in less developed countries. *Cumshaw* and *baksheesh* are terms used to describe these small payments, which are commonly referred to as "grease payment"; the Foreign Corrupt Practices Act stipulates that American employees and managers can legally be reimbursed for such payments.

Furthermore, although many countries have legislation prohibiting bribery, few actually seem to enforce violations or confront individuals involved in bribery. Bribery "is a way of life" for many foreign business professionals and government officials (Graham, 1983, p. 90), It is frequently expected that key government officials will not accept bribes but they are motivated to actively solicit them because of their extremely low salaries. The United States's strict Foreign Corrupt Practices Act, which is seriously enforced, is not in line with many other countries' written, yet loosely enforced, policies and laws.

▧ FALSE INFORMATION

One serious detriment to the expansion of international business is the degree to which various nations condone the practice of falsifying information. If a corporation in one country cannot trust the information provided to it by a corporation in another country, it is difficult for them to transact business. Areas in which false information is a problem include lying and deception, false or deceptive advertising, taxes, and padding one's expense account.

Lying is a particularly complex phenomenon. One definition indicates that a lie must be false, and the person engaging in a lie must believe that it is false. Most important, the person lying must intend to deceive the person with whom he or she is communicating (Agar, 1994). However, lying or other forms of deception must also be evaluated in terms of the *specific* intentions of the person. Thus, collectivistically inclined individuals are more likely to deceive others when the deception is related to group or family concerns. Individualists, on the other hand, are more likely to lie or deceive to protect their privacy and that of others, regardless of membership in the in-group or out-group. For example, American businessmen engaged in a joint venture with Mexicans accused them of lying and deception when the Mexicans promised to complete a project within a specified period of time, even when they knew that it was impossible to do so. To the collectivistic Mexicans, such deception is a mechanism for smoothing relations between in-groups and out-groups and protecting the interests of the in-group (Agar, 1994).

Similarly, individualists and collectivists use different forms of expression when saying "no." Germans and Americans tend to be very direct in expressing the negative. Japanese, however, will usually say such things as "maybe" or "that would be difficult" in the same situation. In some collectivistic societies such as Ghana, businesspeople may give a negative answer by not showing up for an appointment.

Although the simple expression of the negative might be a minor issue in many instances, it can become a problematic ethical issue when individualists are expecting a definite response and collectivists fail to provide it. For instance, the U.S. Chamber of Commerce of Thailand spent 1 year finding a suitable American partner for a Thai entrepreneur interested in establishing a joint venture in Thailand, but when the American showed up with his lawyer and a complex written contract for the first dinner meeting with his Thai counterpart, the Thai was so offended that he immediately walked out. Apparently, such rigid, contract-focused behavior was too unacceptable and even unethical to the face-saving Thai.

In the area of advertising, nations seem to differ in their reactions to deception. Such differences in reactions do not seem to be associated with the individualism-collectivism dimension. In collectivistic Hong Kong and Malaysia, managers tended to view deceptive advertising as ethical, and managers in the individualistic United States and the United Kingdom did not view it as a major problem (Robertson & Schlegelmilch, 1993). In Venezuela, however, fraudulent advertising is considered a very grave problem in the business world but not highly unethical when compared to the ranking of other ethical issues (Perdomo, 1990). In Canada, false advertising was rarely discussed in companies or addressed in corporate ethical codes (Lefebvre & Singh, 1992).

One of the most widely publicized cases of deceptive advertising is the marketing of baby formula in Africa and some other developing nations by the Swiss multinational Nestle; this is commonly known as the "international infant formula controversy." The advertising campaign used to promote Nestle's powdered breast-feeding substitute product led uneducated consumers in Africa to believe the formula was safe and a better alternative to breast feeding. Nestle distributed free samples of the product and actively encouraged women to use it. Many women did use the formula but were faced with the dilemma of not being able to afford the formula when the free samples ran out (Henderson, 1992). Warnings or cautions about the problems of lactating that the samples produced, and also about the possible contamination from the water needed to mix with the formula, were missing from Nestle labels on the infant formula containers (Baker, 1985); contaminated water is a widespread problem in Africa.

When consumer action groups and international activist organizations in Africa and the United States protested Nestle's marketing strategy, the company launched a public relations campaign and initially made only limited efforts to correct the problem. It has been claimed that the decline of breast-feeding in underdeveloped countries caused widespread nutrition and health problems among infants who were feeding from breast milk substitutes (Baker, 1985). It took the Nestle Company years to address the problem.

The sale of pharmaceuticals such as antibiotics to Third World farmers to produce healthier livestock is another example of deceptive product advertising. Many people have died or have become seriously ill due to the passage of dangerous strains of bacteria to humans from meat and dairy products (Baker,

1985). As a result, some countries have banned certain antibiotics in the feed grains of livestock. There are many other countries that still permit this dangerous practice.

Although the degree of individualism among nations does not predict ethical reactions to deceptive advertising, to some extent it does so for falsely reporting taxes and padding expense accounts. False tax reporting in some countries is not even considered deceptive. In Italy, which tends to be more group-oriented than many countries such as the United States and England, there is even an apparent paradox: Submitting a false and favorable tax return is acceptable but submitting an accurate one is considered deceptive (Kohls & Buller, 1994). This is in part related to the fact that Italy was ruled for centuries by foreigners who taxed them mercilessly (see Chapter 1). In the United States, corporations are expected to avoid false tax reporting and to adhere to the strict laws governing taxes. Corporations or individuals in the United States who submit false tax returns tend to be viewed as deceiving the state governments, the federal government, or both. In Italy, the opposite is true. American banks in Italy have been encouraged by Italian lawyers to submit false tax statements that underrepresent actual taxes due (Donaldson, 1985). One American bank with operations in Italy, upon receiving this advice, discovered that this was viewed as a common corporate negotiating strategy with the Italian Internal Revenue Service. Submitting false tax information in Venezuela occurs frequently in business environments but is not considered to be among the most serious ethical violations (Perdomo, 1990).

Falsifying reports, according to Hong Kong managers, is a highly unethical practice. Malaysian managers also consider falsifying reports highly unethical. In Canada, many corporations stress the integrity of books and records (Lefebvre & Singh, 1992).

Furthermore, abuse of one's expense account was considered more of an ethical issue among employees of American firms than of United Kingdom firms, even though both nations are classified as highly individualistic (Robertson & Schlegelmilch, 1993). Padding one's expense account was considered by Hong Kong Chinese managers and Malaysian managers as one of the highest ranked unethical practices, presumably because it hurt other members of the group (McDonald & Zepp, 1988). In collectivistically inclined Nigeria, however, public officials and business managers commonly inflate budgets, illegally stash money in hidden accounts, and inflate contracts as a means of abusing or padding financial accounts (Amadi, 1982). Nigerian chief executives pad discretionary or contingency accounts, which only they are allowed to use without being accountable to others. One explanation for this behavior may well be that Nigeria has yet to develop a mature political and economic system that could curb such abuses.

◩ DEALING WITH COMPETITORS

The manner in which companies compete with one another in international markets is a vital issue. If companies feel that some nations do not provide a level playing field for all competitors, they are less inclined to do business in them, all other things being equal. Two overriding concerns are violations of patents and copyrights and obtaining information about competitors.

Outright violations of patents and copyrights that occur in some nations tend to impede international trade. A Thai businessman, for example, reacted to the sharp criticism of an American businessman, who repeatedly pointed out such violations in the products offered for sale by Bangkok stores, by telling him that, "America is a big and rich country, and Thailand is only in an early stage of development in which such practices must be condoned." Although the stage of economic development may explain some of this differential reaction to the protection of copyrights and patents, the degree of individualism among nations is also predictive of differential responses, particularly in the area of software piracy.

The ADAPSO, an antipiracy trade association representing 750 computer and software companies, promotes awareness and understanding of copyright law in the spirit of "Thou Shalt Not Dupe" (Swinyard, Rinne, & Kau, 1990, p. 655). The International Trade Commission estimated that the United States alone loses $40 billion annually in sales and royalties from the theft of intellectual property (Kohls & Butler, 1994). Asia, which is more collectivistic than the West, has been accused of the most serious offenses of software piracy. The Lotus Development Corporation estimates it loses $200 million annually from software piracy committed in Taiwan. A 1986 raid on a Hong Kong shopping center produced $130,000 worth of pirated U.S. software.

Copyright law and similar protective legislation are a Western phenomenon, especially in the United States (Swinyard et al., 1990). This protection reinforces the ownership of individual creative developments, which are honored and rewarded in the United States. In Asian culture, the Chinese proverb of "He that shares is to be rewarded; he that does not, condemned" (Swinyard et al., 1990, p. 656) implies that Asians are to communally share their individual developments. Americans are more influenced by laws and legalities than Asians, who tend to focus on the impact of actions on the family and community (Cohen et al., 1992).

In Asia, a student masters the teacher's knowledge and talents through copying. Asian calligraphy is an example of a student spending numerous hours tracing the pen marks of his or her master until the student's work is identical to that of the master. In Asia, artwork is signed by the school that produced the work and not by the individual artist. It is a high compliment and honor to a creative individual in Asia when someone imitates his or her work (Cohen et al., 1992).

Piracy is still considered legal in Indonesia, Malaysia, and Thailand, although software copyright protection legislation has slowly been passed in Japan and the Philippines. In 1987, Korea passed copyright legislation protecting intellectual property rights and, 2 months later, its government signed the Universal Copyright Convention document. Korea and Japan's agreement to pass copyright legislation occurred largely because of the urging of the United States. Despite the legal aspects against piracy in Japan, a high tolerance level still exists for software piracy activities in this country (Swinyard et al., 1990).

Asians tend to follow a utilitarian ethic in making moral decisions, which looks at the consequences of their moral behavior for members of their in-groups, but their American counterparts tend to emphasize the deontological or rules approach in making moral decisions (Swinyard et al., 1990). Copyright protection runs counter to the cultural value of sharing individual creative work in Asia. Although Asians' involvement in piracy activities can be considered illegal, Westerners should not necessarily view it as immoral (Cohen et al., 1992). The West's negative views on Asian's software piracy behavior are an excellent and clear example of ethnocentrism, and they underscore the differential influences on behaviors and business practices present in collectivistic societies, such as Asia, and individualistic nations, such as the United States.

Still, it is hard to imagine a complex international economic system in which trademark and patent protection is not legislated and implemented. Without such protection, companies would be less motivated to develop new products, and the level of trust among nations and their corporations would be significantly lowered. The slow but steady passage and implementation of copyright and patent laws in nations such as Japan and Korea seem to confirm this perspective, even when collectivistic values are deemphasized.

Another concern of international companies is the degree to which various nations seemingly condone industrial espionage or obtaining information about competitors illegally. In 1982, for example, 16 senior-level employees from Hitachi, Ltd., and Mitsubishi Electric were indicted for their concerted effort to obtain proprietary information from IBM. Millions and perhaps billions of dollars may be lost because of such illegal activities. Douglas K. Southard, a deputy district attorney in Santa Clara County, California, estimated that between 1977 and 1982, more than $100 million in electronic technology and products had been stolen in the Santa Clara County area alone ("Japan's High-Tech Spies," 1982).

There are, however, many ways for obtaining information about competitors, some of which are not overtly criminal even though they may well be unethical (Flax, 1984). These include the following:

- Milking potential recruits who have worked at competitors, even for a short period of time
- Picking brains at conferences
- Conducting phony job interviews
- Hiring people away from competitors to obtain information
- Interviewing competitors under false pretenses
- Debriefing design consultants who have served as consultants to competitors
- Encouraging key customers of competitors to talk about the products that the competition will produce
- Grilling suppliers
- Infiltrating customers' business operations
- Studying aerial photographs of a company's plant
- Taking plant tours

As this discussion suggests, gaining information from competitors is frequently a gray ethical area, and managers from different countries—whether individualistic or collectivistic—seem to accept such practices as a fact of doing business in a fast-paced and fast-changing world. Thus, gaining competitor information was considered ethical behavior by Hong Kong Chinese managers and Malaysian managers (McDonald & Zepp, 1988; Zabid & Alsagoff, 1993) and not a problem for U.S. and U.K. employees (Robertson & Schlegelmilch, 1993).

⬚ GENDER EQUALITY

Perhaps the one area in which individualistic and collectivistic nations differ most significantly is that of gender equality. Although nations such as Sweden, the United States, and Denmark have made significant advances in this area, most if not all of the collectivistic nations have supported few if any major changes. What is considered to be acceptable and ethical treatment of women in some nations is viewed as reprehensible in others. For example, in the late 1980s, female students were picketing a Japanese law school because its dean had told them it was a waste of time for females to attend law school. One of the female students held a sign inscribed with, "For women Sweden is heaven and Japan is hell."

Title VII of the U.S. Civil Rights Act of 1964 protects its citizens from employment discrimination, and various extensions of this law now cover race, color, national origin, religion, sex, age, and disabilities. Until 1991, U.S. multinational corporations were not required by law to follow Title VII regulations with respect to American expatriates. Supposedly, some companies took advantage of this exclusion, even to the extent of taking some executives to London under the false pretense of a business trip and terminating them there to avoid an age discrimination suit. In 1991, Congress passed legislation requiring Title VII to apply *extraterritorially*.

Laws protecting discrimination against women in the United States are commonplace and have been in place for decades; however, the United States does limit women from working in a few selected areas. For example, most U.S. women in the military experience some combat zone restrictions during a war.

The United Nations 1948 Declaration of Human Rights promoted the concept that "all human beings are born free and equal in dignity and rights." But, as we might expect, "unequal ethical terrain" exists internationally in the areas of gender and racial equality (Mayer & Cava, 1993, p. 701).

Japan and Saudi Arabia are nations that seem to emphasize gender inequality favoring men over women, especially in important positions or leadership roles in business organizations (Mayer & Cava, 1993); however, they do not use the word *inequality* in explaining such actions. In Japan, a sense of homogeneity has been stressed historically in the workplace. Some commentators argue that the increase in the workforce participation rate of Japanese women threatens the established male community (Taka & Foglia, 1994).

Because of their collective inclinations, the Japanese have a tendency to be somewhat resistant to newcomers in their communities, including women in the workforce. Women in Japan experience discrimination in most if not all areas of economic opportunity. Japanese superiors actually reprimanded an Irish businessman working in Japan for showing sympathy toward a Japanese woman who was consistently passed over for promotion and treated by Japanese male coworkers as the lowest ranking member, despite her seniority over them (Dollinger, 1988).

Korea, still influenced significantly by Confucian attitudes, perpetuates separate and better employment opportunities for men, even when the women are more skilled and talented (DeMente, 1991). Although attitudes toward Korean women are changing positively, there still appears to be a deeply ingrained cultural perception of women as inferior. The use of amniotic fluid to test the sex of unborn children, and the resulting abortions of female fetuses, underscore the realism of male chauvinism in several Asian countries such as Korea and India. Although Korean women are perceived as stronger and more clever than Korean men, they still are expected to protect the male egos in business corporations, which accounts for the low number of Korean females who supervise males or hold public positions of power (DeMente, 1991).

In Japan, women are expected to maintain domestic responsibilities while men dominate in the area of work or employment opportunities. When there is an economic recession, the female employees are terminated before all or most of the male employees. In addition, the females, even if they are college graduates, are often offered corporate positions designed to make the office more comfortable. They are "office ladies" who are expected to be pleasant, cheerful, and helpful, but they are not taken as seriously as their male counterparts (Mayer & Cava, 1993). Japanese culture places high values on stability and comfort. The Japanese seem to fear that this sense of security would disappear if Japanese women stopped tending to the home in favor of work or career opportunities. Although Japanese men today are contributing time to household chores, working women still put in 4 to 5 hours a day compared to the 8 minutes their husbands devote to domestic responsibilities.

Saudi Arabia has laws prohibiting women from traveling alone, working with men, and working with non-Muslim foreigners. These laws also apply to female expatriates. An Islamic male was quoted over National Public Radio during the Persian Gulf War as follows: "If women are allowed in the workplace, the forces of social decay would soon send the divorce and crime rates skyrocketing" (Mayer & Cava, 1993, p. 705). Islamic notions of gender inequality are supported by the concept of the *Qur'an*, a divine decree of social ordering that places women lower on the totem pole than men.

Working women in Australia tend to find employment in occupations limited to "women's jobs" or the tertiary sector, but men earn the highest pay, work in white-collar jobs, and have more opportunities for promotion than women (Bottomley & DeLepervanche, 1984, p. 12). Sexual harassment of women is not uncommon in the Australian workplace. The general perception of Australian women is that they belong in the home. There was actually some public outcry against the federal government's protection against sexual discrimination, which was viewed as a threat to the maintenance of the traditional family.

In ancient Nigeria, women were denied leadership positions due to the belief that they could not keep secrets. In modern Nigeria, women have proven themselves as capable leaders, but sexual discrimination still exists (Amadi, 1982). Women are likely to be excluded from important government and political leadership positions. Men rationalize the lack of women in leadership by claiming there are not enough women to fill these positions. Paradoxically, the jobs that are "fit for women" are predominantly occupied by men (Amadi). Meanwhile, a significant portion of Nigerian women prefers to be homemakers rather than pursue occupations. Nigerian feminists blame this attitude on the lack of educational opportunities for women. Overall, Nigerian women are valued primarily for their child rearing roles and responsibilities and are not encouraged to pursue careers (Brenkert, 1992).

In the United Kingdom, women are protected by equal opportunity legislation; however, during employment interviews, women are often asked about plans for starting a family and about child care arrangements (Davidson & Cooper, 1993). Although there is positive support for hiring women for all types of occupations in the United Kingdom, there are few provisions in the workplace for child care, maternity leave, and other support systems for women. Still, there is little blatant sexual discrimination found in the United Kingdom. Men and women generally are afforded the same occupational opportunities.

France has experienced a significant transformation in the workforce in recent years, with growing numbers of women entering the world of work and showing a desire to combine domestic and professional roles. Gender equality is recognized in France through laws and other measures. In comparing types of occupations, women are found more heavily in the following positions compared to men: child minder (100%), secretary (98%), nurse (92%), unskilled worker in clothing industry (92%), clerical worker (78%), primary-level school-teacher (77%), and shop assistant (78%). Women in France have made significant progress, with an increase of 20% in middle management positions between 1975 and 1989. Still, only 10% of women are in managerial positions in business corporations and only 18 out of 100 companies had more than 25% of women in managerial positions (Davidson & Cooper, 1993). France passed laws for equal pay in 1972 and for professional equality for men and women in 1983.

In Spain, women have been protected under equal opportunity polices since 1983. Women increased their involvement in the labor force by 27% from 1984 to 1990, but men's involvement increased by 5%. The traditional attitude toward women as homemaker or mother is rapidly diminishing. Women personnel managers in public administration increased by 245% from 1984 to 1990, but their presence in top leadership positions in the public and private sectors is scarce. Women in Spain still believe they are implicitly, and at times explicitly, denied promotion to top positions. The denial of promotions and pay raises reported by women compared to men is attributed to the belief that women will take time away from work to raise children. Men believe that women have less time for work due to supposed family obligations (Davidson & Cooper).

Only 30% of women in Italy work, which is a lower percentage than in other European countries, and only 3% are in upper management positions (Davidson & Cooper, p. 161). Some commentators have identified the Catholic church's position on gender equality as a major reason why the majority of Italian women marry and stop working after bearing children. In 1977, Italy passed the Equal Treatment of Men and Women Act (ETA), which provides equal opportunities for both sexes in the corporate environment. As in the case of other European countries, women in Italy still face discrimination and negative attitudes from men, and they report that their greatest source of discrimination emanates from male prejudicial attitudes in the workplace (Davidson & Cooper, 1993).

Another dimension of gender equality is the treatment and perception of female expatriates. American women who work overseas account for 5% of American expatriate managers (Ball & McCullough, 1990). A major disadvantage encountered by American businesses who employ American female expatriates is that some clients in foreign countries often refuse to do business with them, especially if they are single. Ball and McCullough identify Saudi Arabia and Pakistan as presenting the greatest risk to American businesses employing female expatriates. Still, many foreigners tend to view U.S. businesswomen as Americans first and women second, and can easily transact business with them (Jelinek & Adler, 1988).

However, even though the degree of individualism among nations is very predictive of attitudes toward gender equality, there are differences among nations stressing individualism. Some American expatriates note that British males are uncomfortable with female managers, probably because of the tradition-based and conservative nature of British society; however, Chinese businessmen appear to be less uncomfortable with women managers than American businessmen (Ball & McCullough, 1990). Such changing attitudes among the more collectivistically inclined Chinese may be a harbinger of the changes that we can expect in the treatment of females in international firms. Still, what is acceptable and ethical treatment of women in the workplace varies greatly by nation, especially along the individualism-collectivism dimension.

◣ UNIONS, THE ENVIRONMENT, INTERESTS, AND INTEGRITY

This chapter has highlighted several managerial practices in which there are national variations in acceptable or ethical conduct. Although we cannot touch upon all managerial practices, we have highlighted many of them that are important. In this section, we briefly mention a few additional areas that deserve attention.

One of the most interesting areas is that of managerial acceptance of unions. Although there has been a dramatic decrease in the percentage of the American nonagricultural workforce that is unionized, from 36% during the 1950s to 16% in 1994, the right to organize a labor union is protected by federal law. One major reason for the decline of unionism is that most of the rights of workers are now incorporated in general laws, such as Title VII, and many workers do not feel that they need to be unionized to protect their rights. American labor unions are more pragmatically focused than their European counterparts, which tend to be aligned to political parties and socialist ideals.

In the United States, unions tend to employ strategies that create an adversarial employment environment clearly separating management and labor. In Japan, unions assist Japanese management in building "support for and loyalty to the company" (Kelley & Shenkar, 1993; Lincoln, 1989, p. 101). Unions in Korea are termed "company unions"; the union of each corporation is considered a distinct, separate organization composed of members only from that specific company (DeMente, 1991, p. 103). Some unions in Korea are known as "Employee Friendship Associations" and work to maintain harmonious relations between employees and employers. Australian unions are similar to American unions in that they use aggressive methods to advocate for workers' rights and encourage and support strikes against corporations (Bottomley & DeLepervanche, 1984).

As this discussion implies, the more collectivistic countries, such as Japan and Korea, tend to emphasize a unionism that seeks to bridge the gap between management and labor, but in both countries the unions are subservient to management. Some of the European nations, such as Germany and Holland, advocate a more equal sharing of power. For example, Germany practices "co-determination," whereby the boards of directors of private companies include representatives from the federal government, labor unions, and management.

In the other areas under discussion, we have more limited information and have difficulty generalizing across the individualism-collectivism dimension. For example, managers from several countries responded to a critical incident describing a situation in which they could sign a desirable contract that presented a clear conflict of interest (Becker & Fritzche, 1987). A high proportion of managers from the United States, France, and Germany would not sign the contract; however, managers from New Zealand and Denmark were more inclined to sign such a contract (Lysonski & Gaidis, 1991).

In response to a critical incident involving a firm polluting or harming the environment, managers from France and Germany tended to argue that the pollution would not harm the environment, but the U.S. managers would not approve of actions that posed a threat to the environment or released illegal pollutants (Becker & Fritzche, 1987). Only the Danish responded that they would release illegal pollutants, but the French and Americans stated they would not approve such a plan (Lysonski & Gaidis, 1991).

The last behavior examined in these studies was personal integrity, which included elements of whistle-blowing behaviors. Managers from Denmark, New Zealand, Germany, France, and the United States expressed the belief that they would report their company, or blow the whistle, if there was a chance that their firms, through producing defective products, could endanger consumers or others (Becker & Fritzche, 1987; Lysonski & Gaidis, 1991). The French and American managers were more likely to blow the whistle than German managers.

Throughout this chapter, we have described managerial practices and their ethicality along the individualism-collectivism dimension. Although this dimension is considered to be the most predictive of values and behaviors across nations, our analysis suggests that it is incomplete and that we need to examine in depth the values that motivate people in different nations to behave in differing ways. In the next chapter, we reverse the emphases of this chapter as we devote much more attention to values and how they influence specific managerial behaviors.

▨ DISCUSSION QUESTIONS

1. What is face? Is it applicable only to Asian nations? Why or why not?
2. Do you feel that international trade can be expanded even if several major nations refuse to accept copyright and patent laws? Why or why not?
3. How do American and Japanese reactions to whistle-blowing reflect individualism and group orientation?
5. What is *baksheesh*? Is it or its equivalent prevalent when American companies do business with one another in the United States? Why or why not?
6. Identify the managerial practices that the degree of individualism in a nation can predict across nations, and those that it cannot. Please defend your answers.
7. Why are copyright law and similar protective legislation considered a Western phenomenon?
8. Which aspects or practices of industrial espionage do you feel are unethical, and which ethical? Why?

3

National Values and
Ethical Situational Predictions

Widespread Corruption in Italy

*In an operation known as "Operation Clean Hands" in Italy, by March
of 1993, 34 members of Parliament and three cabinet ministers were
under investigation for corruptions. Also implicated were more than 200
businessmen, ranging from officials of the state-controlled energy group to
dozens of top managers in blue chip companies in such industries as
automobiles, chemicals, and agriculture. The managing director of the
Benetton fashion group said that an entire system is ending rapidly. It's a
system in which you had to pay the political parties to get work.*

Business Week (Rossant, 1993)

Did IBM Unit Bribe Officials in Argentina?

*A judicial inquiry here was attempting to determine if a local subsidiary
of IBM paid kickbacks to Argentine government officials to land a
$250-million contract to modernize the nation's largest bank, which is
state-owned. The scandal has already resulted in the loss of jobs for IBM
Argentina's three top executives, several senior government officials, and
five directors of the bank. IBM said that neither the company nor its
executives engaged in illegal activities but that certain fundamental
business practices and controls were not followed.*

The Wall Street Journal (Friedland, 1995)

There is a clear relationship between the cultures of nations and the ethical behaviors of their managers not only in the attitudes and values that are manifested but also in the formal expressions and statements that are proclaimed. Langlois and Schlegermilch (1990) analyzed the formal codes of ethics of 196 corporations based in the United Kingdom, France, West Germany, and the United States and found startling differences (see Table 3.1). Although only 55% of the American corporations mentioned employee conduct, 100% of the corporations from the other three countries touched on this issue. Also, although 60% of the German corporations highlighted innovation and technology, only 20% or less of the corporations from the other three nations addressed this issue. Similar striking differences were found in the areas of community and the environment; customers; shareholders; suppliers and contractors; and political interests.

Although culture represents the patterns of thinking, feeling, and acting that are found in an identifiable group or community, it is difficult to capture its essence. Writers tend to use such metaphors as a tree or an iceberg to convey the essential meaning of culture; that is, many of the essential features of culture are hidden from view. A more modern metaphor is the computer. All human beings are hardwired in a similar manner, but culture is the *interaction* between the operating system—similar to a specific operating system such as DOS, WINDOWS, UNIX, and so forth—and the software programs such as Word-Perfect and Lotus, compatible *only* with a particular operating system that permits the hard drive to operate. If the operating system is established in such a way that it cannot link the software program to the hard drive, failure occurs (Fisher, 1988; Hall & Hall, 1990).

TABLE 3.1   Subject Addressed in Corporate Codes of Ethics Across Nations
            (in percentages)

	U.K. (n = 35)	France (n = 15)	West Germany (n = 30)	United States (n = 118)
Employee conduct	100	100	100	55
Community and environment	64	73	63	42
Customers	39	93	69	81
Shareholders	39	73	60	NA
Suppliers and contractors	21	13	20	81
Political interests	12	20	17	91
Innovation and technology	6	20	60	15

SOURCE: Langlois and Schlegermilch (1990, p. 627)

A related way of viewing culture is to examine its levels (Schein, 1985). The most visible level is that of artifacts and creations, that is, those things we can see, hear, and feel. A second level, which is only partially observable, is that of values, or those features of a group or community that its members prize and consider so important that they will attempt to mold their behavior in accordance with them. Such features typically are expressed as things that all of us *should* or *ought* to do, and many times they are not even overtly expressed, although members of the culture frequently react to their violations with surprise, anger, and even banishment of the offender. Finally, there is a third and deeper level of culture that also represents values but can be termed *assumptions* in that it represents the general manner in which we perceive and approach reality. For example, some cultures have a much more positive view of the essential goodness of all people than do others.

As this discussion suggests, the levels of assumptions and values overlap with one another, and both of them are expressive of underlying values that cannot be directly observed.

In this chapter, we describe several major studies of values and value assumptions. When possible, we indicate when we are emphasizing either assumptions or values, but we clearly recognize the overlap between these two levels.

We begin by analyzing the essential dimensions of culture, after which we attempt to make them a palpable reality or to provide some substance to them through our discussion of cultural metaphors. Next, we focus specifically on managerial values and on those values that seem to give rise to the seven cultures of capitalism. The chapter concludes by revisiting the topic of managerial practices, the main focus of Chapter 2, as they relate to values.

▨ DIMENSIONS OF CULTURE

Examining the dimensions of a community's or nation's culture is one of the most popular and fruitful approaches to identifying value assumptions. Florence Kluckholn and Fred Strodtbeck (1961) have been most influential in this area. They compare cultures across six dimensions. They point out, however, that philosophers, social scientists, and commentators interested in understanding cultural differences have focused attention on these dimensions for hundreds of years. These six dimensions are established by the following questions:

- What do members of a society assume about the nature of people—that is, are people good, bad, or a combination?
- What do members of a society assume about the relationship between a person and nature—that is, should we live in harmony with or subjugate nature?
- What do members of a society assume about the relationship between people—that is, should a person act in an individual manner or consider the group before taking action (individualism to groupism or collectivism in terms of such issues as making decisions, conformity, and so forth)?
- What is the primary mode of activity in a given society? Is it *being*, accepting the status quo, or *doing*, changing things to make them better, setting specific goals, accomplishing them within specific schedules, and so forth?
- What is the conception of space in a given society—that is, is it considered *private* in that meetings are held in private, people do not get too close to one another physically, and so on; or *public*, having everyone participate in meetings and decision making, allowing emotions to be expressed publicly, and having people stand close to one another?
- What is the society's dominant temporal orientation: past, present, or future?

Kluckholn and Strodtbeck note that each society has a dominant cultural orientation that can be described in terms of these six dimensions, although other, weaker orientations may exist simultaneously in its different geographical and racial and ethnic groups.

A more managerially focused approach to the dimensions of culture was developed by Geert Hofstede (1980, 1991). His work is based on a large questionnaire survey of 117,000 IBM employees, supervisors, and managers working in 53 different countries. Hofstede's work is especially significant because the type of organization is held constant, and it is the only large-scale, cross-cultural study in which the respondents all worked for a multinational corporation that had uniform personnel policies. He developed empirical profiles of these 53 countries across four dimensions (1980)—and, after his work was extended by Michael Bond and his associates (see the Confucius Connection, 1987)—an additional dimension was added, producing the following basic cultural values:

- *Power distance,* or the degree to which members of a society automatically accept a hierarchical or unequal distribution of power in organizations and the society

- *Individualism,* or the degree to which individuals perceive themselves as separate from others and free from group pressures to conform
- *Masculinity,* or the degree to which a society looks favorably on aggressive and materialistic behavior
- *Uncertainty avoidance,* or the degree to which members of a given society deal with the uncertainty and risk of everyday life and prefer to work with long-term acquaintances and friends rather than with strangers
- *Time orientation,* or the degree to which members of a society are willing to defer gratification of wants and needs in order to achieve long-term objectives and goals

The beauty of Hofstede's work is that he was then able to rank order societies on these five dimensions. His work has been enormously influential in many areas of business research. For example, advertisers can use this work to develop ads that touch on these dimensions; accounting researchers have studied differences in accounting practices across nations through the use of these dimensions; and organization design specialists have taken these dimensions into consideration when constructing organizations that are suitable for different types of national cultures.

Hofstede's dimensions overlap with those developed by Kluckholn and Strodtbeck in such areas as individualism and time orientation. This overlap is a perfect illustration of why the levels of assumptions and values stipulated by Schein are not separate from one another, and why we have chosen to use the terms *value assumptions* and *values* rather than just assumptions and values. However, it is clear that Hofstede's dimensions are more managerially focused not only because of the nature of the types of cultures that were examined but also because of the resulting dimensions. Uncertainty avoidance and masculinity, for instance, are dimensions of cultures with which managers immediately relate, because they focus upon the degree of risk that individuals are willing to accept and the degree to which individuals want to be aggressive and materialistic.

▧ CULTURAL METAPHORS

In an effort to provide some substance to these dimensions and to provide a richer and deeper understanding of value assumptions and values across a wide range of nations, Martin J. Gannon and associates (1994) have developed the concept of the cultural metaphor, that is, a unique or distinctive activity or phenomenon in a nation with which its members immediately identify and value greatly. They then use three to six characteristics of the metaphor to describe the values, attitudes, and behaviors of the nation's culture. For example, they use American football to describe the United States; its three characteristics are competitive specialization, huddling, and ceremonial celebration of perfection. For Japan, the metaphor is the Japanese garden with its characteristics of *wa* (harmony) and *shikata* (ways of doing things); *seishen* or spirit training through such activities as martial arts that help individuals gain some measure of internal control over their relations with the external environment; combining droplets or energies in a crowded and geographically small nation that is made possible because of the emphasis on *wa, shikata,* and *seishen* training; and the unique Japanese sense of aesthetics that is highlighted most clearly in Zen Buddhism. Other metaphors include the Chinese family altar, the Italian opera, the Indian Dance of Shiva, the traditional British house, the German symphony, the Swedish *stuga* or simple summer home, the Russian ballet, Belgian lace, the Spanish bullfight, Irish conversations, the Israeli kibbutz and moshav, and the Nigerian marketplace.

More recently, Martin Gannon, Edwin Locke, and six doctoral students— Pino Audia, Barry Goldman, Amit Gupta, Charles Osmund, Sabrina Salaam, and Jeffrey Thomas—have developed short cultural statements and metaphors for six nations, which have been incorporated into questionnaires that are being distributed only in two countries at a time. The general hypothesis is that members of a given nation should select that nation's cultural metaphor and statement over its twin in terms of a 10-point scale. The instructions are as follows: Please indicate, by filling in any single number between 0 and 10, the degree to which you agree with each statement or description; use 0 for do not agree at all, and 10 for totally agree, or any number in between. For the Taiwanese the cultural metaphors and culture statements or descriptions are:

- *Most people in my country* would agree that a family shrine or altar clearly reflects the basic values of the country's culture because of its emphasis on respecting and praying to ancestors, seeking harmonious relationships in the family and kinship group while safeguarding everyone's dignity, and building for the future while maintaining solid traditions.

- *Most people in my country* would agree that the nation's culture is based on strong, patriarchal, and conservative families and kinship groups which greatly value hard work and planning for future generations. In this culture, living family members show great respect for elder and deceased family members, and they pray to their deceased family members to help them with their problems, thus emphasizing the continuity and structural completeness of the family over many generations. Relationships between family members—for example, husband and wife, and older brother and younger brother—and the responsibilities flowing directly from these relationships are critical, and the goal is to achieve harmony for all while safeguarding their dignity. Because relationships are so close and specific, if there is a family business, it is difficult for family members to integrate nonfamily individuals into it.

The Chinese metaphor and statement were paired with their English equivalents:

• *Most people in my country* would agree that a stone or brick house is an appropriate metaphor for this nation's culture because of its projection of stability, fortitude, sense of order and permanence, traditions, a glorious history, and stable social identification.

• *Most people in my country* would agree that the nation's culture emphasizes the development of a strong, patient, and publicly unexcitable personality. There is a preference for individuals who mostly adhere to tradition, but harmless eccentric individuals are accepted. Emotional outbursts are generally frowned upon, psychological distance between individuals is prized, and patience is held in high honor. Playing fair is stressed, encouraging the underdog rather than favorites is viewed positively, and shunning abstract theory in favor of previously used practical solutions is favored. This nation's culture also emphasizes modesty, wry humor, communication that is circumspect, politeness, and phrasing questions and issues so as to avoid confrontation.

As these examples of cultural metaphors and culture statements suggest, the objective is to give content or substance to the value assumptions and values of a nation and its people.

In the area of ethical behaviors, this approach is especially helpful. If, for example, Americans tend to view life and reality as a football game, they would experience difficulty interacting with the Japanese, with their emphasis on the Japanese garden, or the Swedes, with their emphasis on the *stuga* or the relationship between nature and self-development. Cultural metaphors offer an approach that allows individuals to see the essence of a nation's culture quickly, although they are designed for accomplishing only that outcome and not for stereotyping every individual within it.

◳ MANAGERIAL VALUES

There have been several important studies of managerial values. We have chosen to describe the well respected and seminal international study completed by George England (1975) for several reasons. It is clearly managerially focused in that it examines in depth the importance of goals of organizations (productivity, industry leadership, organizational stability, profit maximization, employee welfare, organizational efficiency, social welfare, and organizational growth), groups within organizations (employees, customers, coworkers, superiors, subordinates, stockholders, etc.) and the personal goals of individuals. Also, this study categorizes the primary orientation of the managers as pragmatic, moralistic, affective, or a combination of these three. In addition, the sample size is large and consists of managers from a contrasting cross-section of countries: Japan, the United States, Korea, Australia, and India.

England provides the following descriptions for these three orientations:

• The *pragmatic* mode of valuation suggests that an individual has an evaluative framework that is primarily guided by success-failure considerations: Will a certain course of action work or not; how successful or unsuccessful is it apt to be?

• The *ethical-moral* mode of valuation implies an evaluative framework consisting of ethical considerations influencing behavior toward actions and decisions that are judged to be "right" and away from those judged to be "wrong."

• The *affect or feeling* evaluation suggests an evaluative framework that is guided by hedonism; one behaves in ways that increase pleasure and decrease pain.

England profiles the American managers as follows:

- Possess a large element of pragmatism
- Have a high achievement and competence orientation
- Emphasize traditional organizational goals such as profit maximization, organizational efficiency, and high productivity
- Place high value on most employee groups as significant reference groups

The profile of the Japanese managers includes the following:

- Very high element of pragmatism
- A high value on competence and achievement
- The most homogeneous managerial value system of the countries studied

For Korean managers, this profile includes the following:

- Large element of pragmatism
- A low value on most employee groups as significant referent groups
- An intended egalitarian orientation

For Indian managers, this profile includes the following:

- High degree of moralistic orientation
- High valuation of stable organizations with minimal or steady change
- High valuation of a combination of organizational compliance and organizational competence
- Low valuation of most employee groups

The final group was that of Australian managers, whose profile includes the following:

- High degree of moralistic orientation
- High level of humanistic orientation
- Low valuation of organizational growth and profit maximization
- Low valuation of such concepts as achievement, success, competition, and risk

As Table 3.2 indicates, there are clearly some major similarities and differences between these managers. Thus, 67.4% of the Japanese managers and 57.3% of the American managers had pragmatic value orientations, but only 34.0% of the Indian managers and 40.2% of the Australian managers fit

TABLE 3.2 Primary Orientations of Managers in the Five Countries (percentage)

Country	Pragmatic	Moralistic	Affective	Mixed	Total N
Japan	67.4	9.9	7.0	15.8	374
United States	57.3	30.3	1.2	11.2	997
Korea	53.1	9.0	8.5	29.4	211
Australia	40.2	40.2	5.4	14.2	351
India	34.0	44.1	2.2	19.6	623
International Sample	52.9	24.4	5.1	17.6	750

SOURCE: From George W. England, *The Manager and His Values: An International Perspective From the United States, Korea, and Australia*, p. 20. Cambridge, MA: Ballinger Publishing Co., 1975.

into this category. Also, only 9.9% of the Japanese managers but 30.3% of the American managers and 40.2% of the Australian managers were moralistic.

As England points out, Japanese managers had higher scores on the pragmatic orientation than did managers from other countries, followed by U.S. and Korean managers; the least pragmatic managers were Indian and Australian. On the other hand, Indian and Australian managers were more moralistically oriented than the other managers, followed by the U.S. managers, and then the Japanese and Korean managers. England also notes that the affective orientation is a minor orientation for managers from all five countries: less than 10% of managers in any country were so classified.

England's work overlaps with that on cultural metaphors. American football, for example, is representative of a pragmatic orientation in its stress on specialization and competition, and the Indian dance of Shiva is reflective of a moralistic orientation. His research highlights the importance of religious values, which we treat in Chapter 4 as a primary influence on ethical behaviors.

◩ THE SEVEN CULTURES OF CAPITALISM

Charles Hampton-Turner and Alfons Trompenaars (1993) have examined the manner in which values of different types of capitalism influence the ethical behaviors of managers from nations in which values are dominant. Their analysis is based on the questionnaire responses of 15,000 managers from 12 nations.

They theorize that without the following seven fundamental valuing processes or dimensions, wealth-creating organizations could not exist:

- *Universalism Versus Particularism.* When no code, rule, or law seems to quite cover an exceptional case, should the most relevant rule be imposed, or should the case be considered on its unique merits?

- *Analyzing Versus Integrating.* Are managers more effective when they break up a problem or situation into parts or integrate the parts into a gestalt or whole?

- *Individualism Versus Communitarianism.* This dimension is approximately equivalent to that of individualism and collectivism.

- *Inner-Directed Versus Outer-Directed Orientation.* Should a manager be guided by internal standards, or should he or she be flexible and adjust to signals, demands, and trends?

- *Time as Sequence Versus Time as Synchronization.* Should managers get things done as quickly as possible, regardless of the negative impact that their actions may have on others, or should they synchronize efforts so that completion is coordinated and the negative impact minimized?

- *Achieved Status Versus Ascribed Status.* Should individuals be judged primarily or solely in terms of achievement or on status, as determined by age, length of service, and the like?

- *Equality Versus Hierarchy.* Should subordinates be treated as equals and allowed to exercise discretion in decision making, or should they be strictly delimited by the hierarchy?

Hampton-Turner and Trompenaars employ a dilemmas methodology to identify the scores of managers from 12 nations on each of these seven dimensions. They combine several items to create a scale for each dimension. After presenting such dilemmas, the authors summarize their results by profiling the scores of each of the 12 countries on these seven dimensions.

We will provide one item for each of the seven dimensions to give the reader a sense of the research findings. For example, in the area of universalism versus particularism, they employed the following question:

While you are talking and sharing a bottle of beer with a friend, who was officially on duty as a safety inspector in the company you both work for, an accident occurs, injuring a shift worker. An investigation is launched by the national safety commission and you are asked for your evidence. There are no other witnesses. What right has your friend to expect you to protect him?

    a. A definite right
    b. Some right
    c. No right

Striking differences are apparent in the answers from the 12 nations. The percentages of managers who answered (c) were as follows: United States, 94%; Holland, 92%; Austria, 91%; Canada, 91%; Germany, 89%; United Kingdom, 82%; Belgium, 67%; Japan, 66%; Singapore, 59%; Italy, 56%, and France, 53%.

For the analyzing-synthesizing dimension, the researchers asked the managers to choose one of the following: (a) The only real goal of a company is making profit; (b) A company, besides making profit, has a goal of attaining the well-being of various stakeholders, such as employees, customers, and the like. The percentages of respondents choosing profit only were as follows: United States, 40%; Austria, 35%; Canada, 34%; United Kingdom, 33%; Italy, 28%; Sweden, 27%; Holland, 26%; Belgium, 25%; Germany, 24%; France, 16%; Singapore, 11%; and Japan, 8%.

For individualism versus communitarianism, the researchers posed the following dilemma:

Suppose you, as a manager, are in the process of hiring a new employee to work in your department. Which of the following considerations are more important to you?

    a. The new employee must fit into the group or team in which he or she is to work.
    b. The new employee must have the skills, the knowledge, and a record of success in a previous job.

Ninety two percent of the U.S. managers chose individual capacity or (b). The other percentage responses were as follows: Canada, 91%; Austria, 91%; The Netherlands, 88%; Germany, 87%; United Kingdom, 71%; Belgium, 69%; Italy, 62%; France, 57%; Sweden, 53%; Japan, 49%; and Singapore, 39%.

For inner direction or the degree to which individuals feel that they control their own destinies, the researchers asked the managers to choose one of the following: (a) Unfortunately, an individual's worth often passes unrecognized no matter how hard he or she tries; (b) In the long run, people get the respect they deserve in this world. They also asked several related questions in this area to confirm their results. The percentages of managers from the various countries who chose inner direction or (b) were as follows: United States, 68%; Germany, 65%; Canada, 64%; Austria, 61%; France, 60%; The Netherlands, 55%; United Kingdom, 51%; Italy, 49%; Belgium, 48%; Sweden, 45%; Singapore, 42%; and Japan, 41%.

The researchers addressed the issue of achievement versus ascription in the following questionnaire item: (a) Becoming successful and respected is a matter of hard work; (b) It is important for a manager to be older than his subordinates, and older people should be more respected than younger people. The percentages of managers choosing (a) or achievement were as follows: United States, 63%; Austria and Canada, 62%; Sweden, 61%; United Kingdom, 60%; Belgium, 59%; Germany, 58%; France, 57%; Italy, 53%; The Netherlands, 50%; Singapore, 44%; Japan, 42%; and Korea, 37%.

To measure time as sequence versus time as synchronization, the researchers employed Thomas Cottle's Circles Test. We will provide the instructions and suggest that the reader complete this test before reading further.

> Think of the past, present, and future as being in the shape of circles. Please draw three circles on the available space (a half sheet), representing past, present, and future. Arrange these circles in any way you want that best shows how you feel about the relationship of the past, present, and future. You may use different size circles. When you have finished, label each circle to show which one is the past, which one is the present, and which one is the future.

The results of this test are dramatic. The Dutch managers separated the past, present, and future completely, and the size of the circle increased from past to present to future. American managers had only a small circle for the past, and it was separated by some distance from the larger present and still larger future, which touched one another but did not overlap. For the Japanese managers, the past and future circles overlapped with the present, and size increased as time went from past to present to future.

We use the Circles Test in our classes and management development seminars and have found that many Asians, particularly those who are Buddhists, tend to have the circles within one another, with the past being the smallest circle and the future the largest circle. Such a time orientation is a stark contrast to that of Westerners, who tend to perceive time as linear, going from past to present to future.

As we discussed in Chapter 4, such psychological and religious conceptions in a nation's culture can frequently determine how it will view the relationship between individuals and the external world, and what is considered acceptable or ethical behavior once such a perspective is widely implemented.

For the seventh dimension of equality versus hierarchy, the researchers provided the following dilemma:

> There are people who believe the work of a department can best be done if the individual members and the company agree on objectives and it is then left to the individual to decide how to attain these goals. Other people believe the work of a department can best be done if the manager sets the objectives and also directs the members of the department in completing the various tasks that need to be done.

The percentages of managers who selected hierarchy or freedom within earlier agreed objectives were as follows: France, 88%; The Netherlands, 81%; Japan, 76%; Germany, 73%; United States, 71%; United Kingdom, 67%; Spain, 66%; Singapore, 60%; Sweden, 57%; and Italy, 52%.

The overall summary of the results is instructive, because it goes beyond looking only at one dimension at a time and examines dimensions simultaneously that overlap with one another. For example, the researchers classify the United States as individualistic and Germany as communitarian or group-oriented, although both nations tend to have high scores on inner direction. Recognition of such similarities and differences helps to enrich our understanding of national differences and similarities, because this profile is multidimensional rather than unidimensional in intent and execution. Furthermore, this research is important because it specifically focuses on various types of capitalism and the dilemmas that managers face when making ethical decisions. Although some Americans would like to believe that there is only one form of capitalism, the research indicates that different forms exist, and that what is considered acceptable or ethical behavior under one form may be seen as quite unethical under another form. Thus, Hampton-Turner and Trompenaars have provided a new perspective on the study of values and how they influence ethical behaviors.

◪ MANAGERIAL PRACTICES REVISITED

In the previous chapter, we emphasized managerial practices within the background of individualism and collectivism. We return to this emphasis in this section and look at ethical dilemmas facing managers in a manner that is different but compatible with that developed by Hampton-Turner and Trompenaars.

More specifically, Carroll and Ramamoorthy (1995) conducted a study to test whether future managers from various countries actually do react differently to the same ethical situation. In this study, conducted among 403 MBA and upper-level undergraduate business students at one public and one private business school in the United States, these future managers were asked to rate the ethicality of a manager described in 12 different ethical scenarios. The ethicality ratings of these future managers from different countries for each scenario were then compared statistically; the primary research question was to determine whether nationality differences were associated with differences in reactions to ethical situations. One unique aspect of this study is that all the foreign students were studying business in the United States. This meant that differences in educational experiences were largely controlled because all had received exposure to the same business ideas, including ethics, in their courses. This meant that only nationality was varied here. Thus, this is a stronger test of nationality or cultural ethical perspectives than previous studies similar to this in method. Significant differences among the nationality groups studied were found for 7 of the 12 ethical scenarios, indicating that indeed there did seem to be differences in ethical perspectives among those raised in different cultures.

Table 3.3 presents the mean or average rating score of each of the nationality or cultural groups for each scenario. The students were divided into five groups: Japanese, American, European, Chinese, and South American. Of course, because the study was carried out at two American universities, there were many more U.S. students in the sample than from other countries; however, the statistical procedures used take this into consideration and still provide us with information on whether there are some national cultural differences in reactions to ethical situations that appear to be real rather than just chance differences. In this study, the business students were asked to react to each scenario as they felt the average manager in their country would react. They were then asked to rate the behavior of the managers in the scenarios on

TABLE 3.3   Reactions to Ethical Scenarios by Japanese, U.S., European, Chinese, and South American Students: Analysis of Variance Results

Scenarios	Mean ethicality ratings provided by subjects from [a]					
	Japan	United States	Europe	China	South America	Sig. Level
1. A manager tells his or her boss that two other managers told him or her that they want to ruin the boss's career.	5.9	6.7	5.6	6.2	6.4	.04*
2. A manager complies with a request to develop a plan to sell possibly harmful pesticides in less-developed countries.	4.0	3.8	4.1	3.6	3.4	.92
3. A manager asked to reduce his or her budget lays off several long-term employees who were told they would always have jobs as long as their performance was good.	3.7	5.0	2.8	4.4	4.5	.002**
4. A manager agrees to stop doing business in a country under boycott edict in order to avoid losing business to the countries conducting the boycott.	5.8	7.0	7.3	6.7	5.4	.06***
5. A manager decides not to provide information to a customer that the equipment he or she is selling may not work well in the customer's country.	3.3	4.2	3.8	4.3	4.6	.56
6. A manager decides to inform the company president that his or her own boss has been giving large gifts to a government contractor that the company sells its products to.	6.0	6.4	6.1	6.9	6.3	.48
7. A manager uses reverse engineering to copy a product from another country without permission.	3.7	4.7	5.3	5.3	4.3	.16
8. A manager confronts another fellow manager and tells him to stop his sexual harassment of a subordinate secretary.	3.7	4.7	5.3	5.3	4.3	.007**
9. A human resource manager agrees to hire his or her niece after a request to do this from his or her brother even though the niece did not score as well as some other candidates.	4.9	5.2	4.6	5.7	5.5	.12

(continued)

TABLE 3.3 Continued

| Scenarios | Mean ethicality ratings provided by subjects from [a] | | | | | |
	Japan	United States	Europe	China	South America	Sig. Level
10. A manager conspires with his or her boss to benefit from inside information in stock purchases.	4.0	5.0	4.4	6.2	5.4	.002**
11. A manager does not tell a joint venture partner that his or her company does intend to copy a new technology created by the joint venture partner and thus lies.	6.1	5.0	4.8	5.9	3.4	.003**
12. A manager wants to change the suppliers' contract terms agreed to previously, because the economic situation has changed.	5.7	6.1	7.1	5.5	7.2	.007**

a. High score = higher perceived ethicality.
$*p < .05; **p < .01; ***p < .10.$

the basis of their own concepts of ethicality. In this way, a social desirability factor could be controlled. Actually, it was found that the individual ratings and national ratings were quite similar although, as anticipated, a social desirability factor was present.

There are some advantages to this approach of using ethical scenarios to determine whether international or cultural differences in reactions to ethical situations exist. First, each scenario is standardized and we are not faced with the difficulty of trying to compare ethical situations across cultures that may be different in important respects. Also, such things as the variability in responses within a cultural group can be identified. Such within-culture variability is very likely, although this may vary from one culture to another.

As indicated in the table, Scenario 1 focuses on the issue of a manager's breaking a confidence to tell his boss about a plot to damage his career. Thus, the issue is that of loyalty to one's boss versus breaking a confidence. There were significant nationality differences in response to this ethical situation. The situation described in this scenario is difficult for a young manager to be in and has obvious career implications whatever is done. All groups seem to feel that they should tell the boss about this political plot against him, with the U.S. student-managers scoring significantly higher on the ethicality of doing this. The acceptance of higher authority and obligations to higher authority are probably a highly salient issue here for all managers, given the role realities of the manager's job and the types of individuals selected for management.

Scenario 2, which involves a plan to sell possibly dangerous products to Third World countries, is perceived to be unethical by all national groups. The South Americans and Chinese seem to feel this is especially unethical. This finding is perhaps not surprising, considering that their countries are probably going to be the recipients of such products; however, there were no significant nationality differences. Perhaps most managers in the world would see this as an especially clear-cut case of unethical behavior. Still, there were a few students who thought this practice of selling pesticides to Third World countries was ethical. Examining the open-ended comments justifying their ethicality ratings showed that such students seem to be taking a strictly business interest point of view. What is good for business is good per se.

Scenario 3 describes a layoff decision. All nationalities except the Americans felt it was unethical to lay off employees to whom some oral promises on job security had been made. The Americans rated this layoff action significantly higher in terms of ethicality than the other nationalities. Most of the countries of the world except the United States do discourage layoffs at the present time. Even in the United States, however, the employment-at-will doctrine allowing complete authority to firms to lay off employees has been increasingly challenged successfully in the courts (Ledvinka & Scarpello, 1991), although most U.S. students are probably unaware of this trend. As the table indicates, the Europeans tended to be especially negative about the layoffs described in this scenario. As the comments section indicated, many of the Europeans felt that to lay off these employees would violate a trust and a promise.

In Scenario 4, we have some agreement among the different nationalities that to participate in an economic boycott, such as the one imposed by several Arab nations on Israel, is acceptable for business reasons; however, the U.S. and European students rated participating in this boycott significantly higher on ethicality. This figure includes the American business students who may be unaware that this is an illegal practice for U.S. firms. If they were aware of this fact, they would probably rate the ethicality of this practice differently, because illegality is related to perceptions of unethicality.

In Scenario 5, we have a manager withholding information about a possible product deficiency in the country in which it is to be used. Most see this as unethical, with the Japanese especially so inclined. There were no statistically significant nationality differences here. In their open-ended comments on this issue, most of the respondents cited pragmatic reasons for their unethical rating of this behavior, such as the bad effects on customer relations.

In Scenario 6, we have a situation where a manager reports on his boss who is engaging in bribery or gift giving for the purpose of currying favor. There were no statistically significant nationality differences in ratings of the ethicality of this practice. Most of the business students from all countries reacted to this in the same way, believing it is somewhat ethical to report on a boss when he or she is perceived to be doing something wrong; however, the reasons given for the ratings varied between nationalities. The Americans tended to see the boss's actions as unethical because of moral reasons, but the Japanese cited more pragmatic reasons, such as the possible future effect of these actions on the company. Of course, the Japanese are probably more concerned with the future of their companies than are Americans because of the lifetime employment situation they are in. If the company fails, they in turn will be in deep personal trouble.

Scenario 7 is a product copying case. There are no significant nationality differences here and some may have been expected. Certainly, the Chinese in particular have been accused of this activity frequently in recent years, and the Chinese culture is such that individual rights over creations are not absolute by any means. If the copying were more clearly illegal in this scenario, as in copying something for which a copyright or a patent existed, then the nationality differences might have been greater.

Scenario 8 focuses on the ethicality of one manager telling another to stop a sexually harassing activity. Almost all saw this as quite appropriate except for the Japanese, for some reason. Perhaps this activity is not so uncommon in Japan and therefore has acquired some legitimacy. Or perhaps organizational or cultural rules are such that one is not confronted directly about the behaviors that might offend the moral sensibility of another. It is quite possible that sexual harassment may not be considered illegal and therefore troublesome in some countries. Actually, only fairly recently has it been considered a problem for management to deal with in the United States.

Scenario 9 focuses on a nepotism case. Here there were no significant nationality differences. The Chinese were somewhat more inclined to believe this to be ethical than the other groups, citing the fact that it is not an uncommon activity. Given the high priority of the family in the Chinese culture, and the Chinese reputation for having this problem, it is surprising that the Chinese ratings were not even higher than they were. The fact that the data were collected in the United States may have had an effect on this outcome.

Scenario 10 deals with the use of inside information in stock transactions. Only the Chinese seemed to find this behavior ethical and they scored significantly higher than the other nationalities on this issue. Obviously, trading in stock is a very new activity in China and even in Taiwan. Insider trading probably is actually a very common activity in many countries and is not even illegal except in a few countries such as the United States. The open-ended comments of the business students showed, however, a rather deep division in attitudes about this issue. They seem caught between the illegality of this in the United States and their own strong desires for material gain.

Scenario 11 involves lying to a joint venture partner of another nationality about your company's intention to take advantage of a partner to obtain a promising new technology. There were significant nationality differences here. Perhaps they revolve around the issue of lying. The Asian students seem to feel it is not unethical to lie in this situation, but the Western students are more inclined to view this as unethical. Communication styles and practices are one of the biggest differences found among nationalities, and the varied reactions to this scenario perhaps reflect such differences.

Scenario 12, the final ethical case, focuses on changing an agreement because a situation has changed. There were significant differences here among the nationalities. Most of the nationalities thought this was ethical, with the Europeans and South Americans scoring significantly higher on the perceived ethicality of this action. Actually, the comments made by the business students in their open-ended responses indicate that they had a lot of difficulty with this scenario. The business students seem to believe that contract adherence is important and that agreements should be upheld. On the other hand, they also seem to believe that one must be flexible and that it is good for businesses to adapt to new conditions.

One conclusion that can be drawn from this study, and this was the most important question asked, is that cultural/nationality differences in reactions to some ethical situations do appear to exist even among foreign students living in the United States. There were statistically significant nationality differences in 7 out of the 12 situations described. Also, as indicated earlier, virtually all of these questionnaires returned were completed in the United States by the foreign respondents. The nationality differences would probably have been even more pronounced if the questionnaires had been completed by the business students while residing in their own countries, as indicated earlier. The data also do show, however, that there is a lot of variance within countries. The same behavior may be viewed as ethical or unethical by managers or prospective managers within a culture. Still, the study does show that there are differences in reactions to ethical situations by future managers with different nationalities and from different cultures. This finding is congruent with other somewhat similar studies showing nationality differences. These studies included comparisons of U.S. and Israeli students (Preble & Reichel, 1988), U.S. and British students (Whipple & Swords, 1992), Australian and U.S. students (Small, 1992), Austrian, Indonesian, and U.S. MBA students (Davis, Johnson, & Ohmer, 1994), and Taiwanese and U.S. students (White & Rhodeback, 1992). Although these were business student samples, there is some evidence that such students and practicing managers are quite similar in their sensitivity to ethical issues in business decision making (Lysonski & Gaidis, 1991). Thus, the evidence seems consistent over quite a number of empirical studies that there are cultural variations in reactions to different ethical situations. As in the present study, however, these differences were not so large as to be opposite to one another and there was variance within the samples. Obviously, a number of factors other than culture influence ethical decision making, including the state of the economy and the stage of economic development.

▨ DISCUSSION QUESTIONS

1. What level or levels of culture do the cultural metaphors describe? Why?
2. What are the seven cultures of capitalism? How do they relate to one another?
3. Compare England's work to that of Hampton-Turner and Trompenaars. What are some major differences and similarities?
4. How are the managerial scenarios described by Stephen Carroll expressive of both values and managerial practices?
5. Do you feel that the ethical differences across a wide variety of nations are greater than those within the United States or another developed nation such as Japan?
6. Several metaphors of culture are presented at the beginning of the chapter. Select or develop your own metaphor and describe the values that it encompasses.

4

Transmitting Cultural Values
Socialization, Education, and Religion

Culture of Jamaica

Jamaica was a British colony for 300 years and the middle and upper classes but not the lower identify with modern Western culture. Fathers in many Jamaican families are peripheral but mother-child bonds are strong. However, children are often raised and taught by their grandmothers, because their mothers work. Sometimes, the mother's sister or other relatives play a role in child rearing, which encourages an emotional identity with many family members. Independence in children is discouraged in favor of dependence. Parents stress obedience, submission, and respect for elders. A characteristic of the personality of the individual in this community is the tendency to believe that others are responsible for what happens to the person, and it's not what the individual himself caused.

Wedenoja (1995)

Cultural Adjustment

A study of 826 international students in attendance at a U.S. university was completed to determine their degree of adjustment or resistance to the U.S. culture. Those high on American cultural adjustment made decisions primarily on the basis of internal values, and highly valued work and happiness. Those high on cultural resistance were low on these same indicators. It was found that acceptance of the American culture was associated with being single rather than married, speaking English at home, and having close American friends. Those resisting the American culture were opposite. Speaking English at home was especially predictive of cultural adjustment. Previous research has shown that fewer contacts with home country relatives and more relationships with new country residents are related to acceptance of the new culture and rejection of the old.

Kagan and Cohen (1990)

The model underlying this book indicates that parenting and socialization, education, and religion may constitute the three most important primary influences on cultural values and beliefs. Of course, they are interrelated to some extent, even though we treat them separately. The manner in which parents raise their children, and related aspects of cultural socialization that can occur either within or outside the family, are critical in explaining subsequent behavioral propensities of individuals in a society, including their reactions to situations with ethical implications. Such cultural socialization is supported and strengthened by the educational system of a society. Admittedly, religion is more important in some nations such as Ireland and Poland, where church attendance is quite high, than in others such as Russia and China. Still, each specific religion can provide a framework of basic beliefs against which actions can be considered as ethical or unethical.

▨ PARENTING AND SOCIALIZATION

There seems to be a vast distance between the manner in which children are parented and socialized and their later behaviors as adults. The distance, however, might be quite small.

Ordinarily, we would not make sweeping generalizations when comparing Westerners and Asians, but they seem to have quite different styles of parenting, and in this area the generalizations seem warranted. As a general rule, Asian mothers closely watch their children and are physically close to them, even to the extent of strapping them to their bodies during the first year or two of life. It is also quite common for such children to sleep in their parents' bedroom until they are 6 or 7 years of age. Asian mothers tend to encourage their children to focus on their faces, and discourage an exploration of the external environment. Also, because many Asian mothers do not have occupations outside the home, they are able to devote large amounts of time to raising their children and are expected to do so.

Until the Asian child is 5 or 6 years old, he or she is treated specially, and even pampered, and this is particularly true of boys. For example, in Thailand and other nations, it is quite common for an 80-year-old man or woman to give up a seat on a bus to a child. This pattern of treating the Asian child in a pampered way extends to the first few years of education, but an abrupt reversal then occurs as even the schools become more regimented.

Western mothers, by contrast, even if they are at home full time, encourage their children to explore the world around them. Although these mothers also want the children to smile at them and look at their faces, their primary goal is to make the children inquisitive and independent.

Such contrasting patterns are directly related to the cultural dimension of individualism and collectivism (see Chapters 2 and 3). That is, the child's self-concept in Asian countries is built on his or her relationship with the mother and extended family, and he or she begins to see reality primarily from this perspective. There is a definite overlap between the child's self-concept and what the parents expect of him or her. The parents, particularly the mother, support this orientation, and it is often said that the primary motivation among Asians as a consequence is a sense of shame that the individual has let down the family. In contrast, the primary motivation among Westerners, because they are actively encouraged to be independent, is responsibility for one's own actions (see Benedict, 1946).

There are some striking illustrations of this approach to socialization. Japanese high school students take an examination that is particularly critical, because it determines both the quality of the university or college to which they can be admitted and their placement after college. Mothers of many of these students accompany their children, particularly their sons, to the test sites and wait for them to complete the examination. It is hard to imagine such a pattern in the United States. Similarly, suicide is quite high among young adults in Japan compared to many other nations, at least in part because some of them seem to feel that they have dishonored their families due to their poor showing on this important examination.

Furthermore, the overriding importance of the family is connoted by the physical living arrangements. Asians very frequently live in a compound with several houses, each for a different family member and his or her immediate family. The family is a palpable presence at all times and there is intense and frequent interaction among the members of the various homes.

According to Robert Christopher (1983), this pattern of socialization can retard the adult developmental process, particularly among men who as children receive not only an excessive amount of love from their mothers but also its withdrawal if they do not live up to familial expectations. Thus, throughout their lives, they look to others for love and approval, and their psychological well-being is critically dependent upon it. Various Asian nations use different words to express this concept—for example, *amae* in Japan and *krengchai* in Thailand—but the meanings are similar. Because, however, the Asian socialization process tends to emphasize great adherence to rules and expectations, there is a tendency for Asians to appear very calm when, in fact, powerful emotions are welling up that are not overtly expressed. This is a particular problem in dealing and negotiating with Asians, because this repression of emotions erupts in unpredictable ways, for example, becoming furious and negating all agreements that have been made. This pattern has been identified among not only the Japanese but also the Chinese (see Bonavia, 1989; Christopher, 1983).

Still, there are great variations within Asia, and we must be cautious about generalizing too much. For example, a Chinese Thai woman—herself a very successful businesswoman—was discussing why she married a Chinese Thai professor and business consultant, and she explicitly pointed out that she rejected her mother's suggestion to marry a Chinese businessman from Hong Kong because "the Hong Kongese are too aggressive." Also, Asians and other non-Westerners frequently criticize Westerners for their lack of patience in developing relationships and negotiating, which, to them, signifies childish, immature behavior. Thus, there seems to be some validity not only to the arguments advanced by Christopher and Bonavia but also to those put forth by Western critics.

Such outbursts and the attendant ethical problems frequently revolve around the Asian concept of face, which is "an unwritten set of rules by which people in a society cooperate to avoid unduly damaging each other's prestige and respect" (Bonavia, 1989, p. 73). Unlike the Western concept of a "good loser" who quietly withdraws, Asians stress the concept of a "good winner" who allows a loser in a negotiation or battle to save face by offering a small tactical advantage or favor. If the winner does not behave as expected, he or she is seen as not acting properly or ethically.

Looking to others for love and dependence is a phenomenon found in most if not all Asian societies, and to violate the unwritten rules surrounding these dependency relationships can cause undue harm when Asians and Westerners are interacting. Some Chinese businessmen have finalized negotiations with their Western counterparts, but they are astounded when the Westerners will not help their children who are seeking admission to major American universities. Given the Chinese emphasis on family, dependency, and face in which business relationships become personal and involve the fulfillment of such nonbusiness requests, it is not surprising that many business deals have come apart, even when written contracts have been signed.

It should be emphasized that we have been talking about Asians and Westerners, but the concepts of dependency and face also operate in many non-Asian societies, for example, nations in Latin America. In Brazil, for instance, the extended family frequently lives in a large compound similar to that found in Asian countries, and there is a clear distinction between family or in-group members and outsiders. Although different words are used to express the concepts in different nations, it is clear that the Western emphasis on clear-cut rules, written contracts, and a sharp division between personal and business relationships is anathema in many parts of the world. Thus, what Westerners consider unethical behavior, such as reneging on a written contract, is treated as ethical not only in Asian but also in other non-Western countries if dependency relationships and face are not upheld properly.

As briefly mentioned earlier, a good example occurred when the American Chamber of Thailand spent 2 years putting together a merger between a Thai entrepreneurial company and its American counterpart. The two presidents of these companies finally met face-to-face for dinner in Bangkok, but the American was accompanied by his lawyer, who was there to oversee the development of the written contract. This Thai businessman was so offended that he immediately left the table, and the merger never occurred. Similarly, a Mexican businessman will agree to deliver a shipment of goods to an American by a certain date, knowing that it is impossible for him to do so. This same Mexican is greatly offended when his American counterpart accuses him of lying; such commitments are seen by many Mexicans as a way of smoothing human relationships and making life bearable, a perspective that is quite similar to the Chinese concept of face. In fact, Mexican businessmen have joked openly among themselves about their American counterparts by comparing them to the bull that must be cleverly avoided through the adroit use of the bullfighter's cape, because the Americans are so insistent on obtaining hard-and-fast contracts and commitments.

We have used Hofstede's dimension of individualism-collectivism to structure our discussion in Chapter 2, and we can now turn our attention to power distance, that is, the degree to which members of a society automatically accept an unequal distribution of power and rewards in a society. People tend to accept unequal treatment much more in high power distance countries than in low power distance countries (Bond, Wan, Leong, & Giacalone, 1985). As a corollary, something which is considered unethical in a low power distance country may be quite acceptable in a high power distance country, such as having workers employed in an unsafe factory, or publicly insulting a subordinate.

Similarly, highly masculine and materialistic countries such as Japan make a sharp distinction between the roles and expectations of men and women, and highly qualified women are generally treated poorly and given inferior positions at work. Such treatment relates directly to the socialization process we described previously. Thus, when a recession occurs in Japan and other Asian countries, it is considered ethical to lay off the women first, even when they are more qualified and have longer service than the men. Given such practices, it is little wonder that many women in highly masculine countries have difficulty understanding the concept of female empowerment and there are no words in their languages to adequately express it. In the United States, although there are pockets of such behaviors, the overall trend is to treat the men and women in the same way.

Of course, these socialization practices relate directly to underlying cultural teachings. Confucianism, which is widely studied in Asia, explicitly subordinates women to men, and male children are particularly cherished because they are expected to perform the final rites of burial for their parents. Given such values, it is not surprising that parents in some Asian nations, after learning the sex of their future child through modern medical techniques, often are reported to abort female embryos. This practice could lead to major social problems in these nations, where it is expected that, within the next 20 years, there will be millions of males who cannot find wives.

Such socialization is reinforced by the types of reading to which children are exposed. In a path-breaking study, David McClelland (1961) showed that children's books vary widely across 40 countries. In countries that might be characterized as highly collective with high power distances, these books tend to emphasize that one should accept his lot in life, even if it be very humble, because the goal is salvation after death. Such reading materials, of course, strengthen the position of those in power and promote resistance to change. However, nations such as the United States that emphasize individualism and low power distance tend to infuse their young readers with a sense of achievement in this life through Horatio Alger stories or uplifting descriptions of individuals, such as President Lincoln's poor childhood but very successful

Item 4.1

David McClelland analyzed 1,300 children's stories in 40 countries, using a standard procedure for identifying the degree of achievement motivation in each of these stories. He then correlated achievement motivation in the children's stories from each country with the nation's state of economic growth and prosperity. There was a definite and positive relationship between achievement motivation and economic prosperity.

Later, McClelland also demonstrated that it was possible to socialize adults in such a way that they would increase their need for achievement. He selected 76 managers of small enterprises in India. During psychological training, the managers were taught to create high achievement fantasies, to examine work in terms of achievement, to internalize the characteristics of high achieving individuals, and to work together in achievement-oriented groups. Achievement motivation increased significantly after the training program had been completed. Furthermore, an experimental group of managers who had been trained was subsequently more active in an economic sense than members of a control group who did not undergo this training. Hence, we can say that parenting and socialization are critical for building values but it is possible, if difficult, to change values among adults.

SOURCE: McClelland (1961); McClelland and Winter (1969).

career. In the United States, it is often said that anyone can become president, and judging from the poor family backgrounds of some American presidents, the statement has some validity (see Item 4.1).

◥ EDUCATION

The United States is proud of its educational systems, particularly its college and university systems. This pride seems justified, as evidenced by the fact that in 1988-1989 there were 4.3 Asian college and university students studying in the United States for every Asian student studying in Europe. This lead has occurred, however, because education in such applied fields as engineering and business is considered superior in the United States. Education seems to be valued in the United States if it leads to short-term success; that is, there is a clear relationship between going to school and obtaining a job. This orientation is consistent with the cultural metaphor of American football and its emphasis on winning (Gannon & Associates, 1994).

The United States, which has a school year cycle of 180 days for grade school and high school students, compares poorly to other countries, including Japan (243 days), Italy (216 days), and Thailand (200 days). Also, American schools tend to emphasize sports and other extracurricular activities within the structure of the school, but countries such as Japan and Germany draw a sharp distinction between going to school and involvement in extracurricular activities, including sports, which occur in nonschool organizations. It is little wonder, then, that only the United States emphasizes the concept of the scholar-athlete. For such reasons, the cultural metaphor of American football seems very appropriate for describing American ethical behavior, because it stresses playing tough but within strict rules, seeing the world in black-and-white terms (winning or losing), and having a level playing field.

Other nations, however, stress different values, such as treating family members or insiders in one way and all others in a radically different way. Among the Japanese, for example, it is sometimes assumed that a business commitment made to a foreign businessmen holds only when the Japanese language is employed (DeMente, 1990). Such values are clearly related to the educational system.

In an important ethnographic study of three comparable preschools in Japan, China, and the United States, Tobin, Wu, and Davidson (1989) focused on what the parents expected their children to learn at school. These researchers provided the parents with a list of 11 items and asked them to rank these items; they analyzed both these rankings and the top three rankings in combination for all three countries. As might be expected, cooperation and how to be a member of a group were considered important in all three countries: 58% of the parents in China included it in the top three, and comparable figures for Japan and the United States were 67% and 68%, respectively. However, although 80% of the Japanese parents ranked sympathy, empathy, and concern for others in the top three, the comparable figures for China and the United States were 20% and 39%, respectively. Furthermore, 73% of the American respondents ranked self-reliance/self-confidence in the top three versus 44% in Japan and 29% in China. Similarly, 51% of the parents ranked affectionate, warm as the most important characteristic of a good preschool teacher in China, but the comparable figures in Japan and the United States were 42% and 18%, respectively. These results parallel the different approaches to language development that occur in these three countries (see Item 4.2).

This concern and empathy for other Japanese is brought to life in the preschool. Five- and 6-year-olds automatically clean up after lunch when the

Item 4.2

Communication is critical in society; some anthropologists have even argued that culture is communication. In Anglo-Saxon nations, one person speaks at a time and another person begins talking almost immediately after he or she is finished. In Asian countries, one person also speaks at a time but the pause after he or she has finished and another person begins to speak is much longer. Latin countries, on the other hand, are renowned for the fact that two or more individuals speak simultaneously at times.

In their study of preschools in China, Japan, and the United States, Tobin, Wu, and Davidson (1989) observed,

> Language in Japan, both in and out of preschools, is divided into formal and informal systems of discourse. Children in preschools are allowed to speak freely, loudly, even vulgarly to each other during much of the day. But this unrestrained use of language alternates with periods of polite, formal, teacher-directed group recitation of expressions of greeting, thanks, blessing, and farewell. Language in Japan—at least the kind of language teachers teach children—is viewed less as a tool for self-expression than as a medium for expressing group solidarity and shared social purpose. Americans, in contrast, view words as the key to promoting individuality, autonomy, problem solving, friendship, and cognitive development in children. In American preschools children are taught the rules and conventions of self-expression and free speech. (pp. 188-189)

teacher tells them that lunchtime is over. In the Japanese preschool, children are allowed to be expressive and noisy at times, but they are also expected to conform to rules that make life easier for their peers and teachers.

There is a downside to this emphasis on conformity, however, and many Japanese take seriously their famous proverb that the protruding nail will be hammered. If a student does not fit easily into the group, his peers bully, tease, and persecute him. Such documented instances of *ijime* or bullying are widespread; 155,000 such incidents occurred between April and October of 1985 (Tasker, 1987). In several instances, the bullied students have committed suicide.

In subsequent chapters, we describe several behaviors that members of different nations, particularly Japanese and Americans, view as ethical or unethical. There are wide differences and these behaviors are consistent with the descriptions of the socialization and educational processes that are emphasized in these nations. One pertinent example should be helpful at this point. In many Asian and non-Asian countries, education primarily revolves around the lecture; the professor is accorded great respect and status and the students rarely if ever ask questions. If, however, a student is so bold as to ask a question and the professor does not know the answer, he may give an incorrect answer, and the student will dutifully write it down. This process, which is in direct contrast to the American tradition of admitting professorial ignorance, is consistent with preserving face on all sides and emphasizing group values over those of the individual, in the sense that the class should not be disturbed by awkward questions. The process is also directly linked to situations where businessmen will promise to meet a commitment, knowing full well that they cannot do so (see above).

There is one final area that we need to examine, namely the degree to which the educational system reinforces the social class structure of a nation. The American system is relatively but certainly not completely open, and individuals from different social class backgrounds have the opportunity to attend the best schools if they possess the requisite ability, as measured through grades and performance on the Scholastic Aptitude Test. Moreover, the winnowing process, by means of which such opportunities are realized, occurs primarily after high school, because the quality of the college a student attends is determined at that time. The American system allows for a good amount of failure, however, and it is quite common for a student to switch majors, sometimes four or five times, before making a career choice. Thus, change is built into the American system, which is consistent with the values of self-reliance and achievement.

However, the educational systems of many nations tend to be much more reinforcing of the social class structure. We will use Germany as our example, because it separates children at an earlier age than other nations; however, many nations follow the German format.

In Germany, the children attend the *Grundschule* or elementary school from grades 1 through 4 or 6, depending upon the state. Frequently, one teacher is assigned to a class and remains with it until graduation from the *Grundschule*. The student is then assigned to one of three different types of school; in some German states, there is a standardized test for such placement; in others, the test is supplemented by the teacher's recommendation. This placement has a major influence on the individual's career, not only in Germany but also in many other European countries, such as Finland and Sweden.

The first type of school is the *Gymnasium*, which is designed for those who want to pursue a university education. If students are unsure of their aspirations, do not gain admittance to the *Gymnasium*, or both, they can attend the *Realschule* or real-world school, which combines education plus excellent vocational training. Students who cannot gain admission to these two types of schools have to attend the *Hauptschule*, which is quaintly translated as the chief school. It also combines education and vocational training, but the education is less rigorous and a few years shorter than that obtained in the *Realschule* and the vocational training much more cursory. As a result, many students who graduate from the *Hauptschule* have difficulty finding work.

Germany builds some corrective measures into its educational system, for example, allowing some students to transfer from the *Realschule* to the *Gymnasium* and giving the *Realschule* graduates the opportunity to attend college after some additional education. The system, however, tends to reinforce a rigid social class structure, because the major decision is usually in place by the end of the fourth or sixth grade. Competition is so fierce in the *Grundschule* that parents hire tutors for their students as early as the first grade. This pattern of hiring tutors at such an early age is also found in other European and non-European countries, including Japan. Needless to say, a student is at a great disadvantage if his or her parents are unable to afford a tutor.

There is a great debate over the relative merits of such a system when compared to the American approach. Although the United States has a population in which 20% of its citizens are substandard in reading and writing skills, almost all Germans are at least adequate in this area. Also, about 66% of the German workforce has completed the apprenticeship programs that are available in the *Realschule* and *Hauptschule*, and there is an easy transition between school and work, which is not true for many Americans. The American system, however, is much more flexible and responsive to changing needs and, in a time when the pace of social and technological change is accelerating, possibly better suited to the needs of the workplace.

From the perspective of business ethics, such an educational system may reinforce the concept that elites in a society should be treated differently from nonelites. As noted in Chapter 1, the United States does not emphasize such a difference, and it fined and imprisoned more businessmen than did all other developed countries in combination from approximately 1977 until 1992 (Vogel, 1992). Such treatment is in accordance with an emphasis on individual responsibility and low power distance. Since 1992, however, other countries such as Italy and France have had well publicized and wide-scale investigations into political and business scandals that have resulted in many fines and punishments. This abrupt change has been accompanied by the expansion of the European Community and the attempt to integrate the educational systems of European countries whenever possible. Thus, it may well be that there will be greater uniformity not only in educational systems but also in ethical standards and laws as this integration is strengthened (see Chapter 8).

▨ RELIGION

In this section, it is not our purpose to describe in detail the world's religions; others have completed this task most effectively. Rather, we want to show how specific religions influence ethical systems and behaviors.

There are many facets of religion, but of greatest concern for the study of ethics is its focus on values. Huston Smith (1958, 1991), whose classic book on the world's religions has sold more than 2 million copies, takes this approach when he describes each major world religion in terms of the following: The social and economic factors operating in a society that led to the evolution of a specific religion; its major ideas and leaders; and why it is still important in today's world. Just reading the daily newspaper confirms Smith's perspective, because wars between nations and subgroups within them, economic sanctions, and even modern genocide, as in the former Yugoslavia, are frequently the result of value conflicts expressed by different religious groups.

Emile Durkheim's *Elementary Forms of the Religious Life* (1915/1965) is generally considered to be the most important sociological study of religions, and he too focuses on values. Durkheim studied elementary or primitive religions around the world and he summarizes as follows:

> The general conclusion of the book . . . is that religion is something eminently social. Religious representations are collective representations which express collective realities; the rites are a manner of acting which take rise in the midst of the assembled groups and which are destined to excite, maintain or recreate certain mental states in these groups. So if the categories are of religious origin, they ought to participate in this nature common to all religious facts; they too should be social affairs and the product of collective thought. (p. 21)

Durkheim's reference to collective thought emphasizes that religion provides a forum for defining values or what is considered either ethical or unethical. Thus, it is imperative that we follow Huston Smith's lead and look at the social and economic factors leading to the creation of a specific religion, its major ideas and figures, and how it influences followers in the modern world. Although we cannot treat all religions in depth, we can sketch some of them.

Confucianism represents an excellent starting point. Confucius, who died in 479 B.C., lived at a time of great unrest and turmoil, and wars were frequent in China. Confucianism is not a religion as many people frame the concept, because it has no concept of a personal God and only an amorphous concept of heaven or a shadowy netherworld in which ancestors live and guide the living. As a result, the Chinese tend to be practical people and focus on this world rather than the afterlife; they are renowned as businessmen throughout the world. Confucius and his followers devoted a good amount of time and energy describing how people should conduct themselves in this life, starting with the concept of *Jen*, which is human heartedness or the simultaneous feeling of humanity toward others and respect for oneself. Of particular importance in Confucianism is *Li*, the way that things should be accomplished, and the five major relationships in the family are central to this concept. Appropriate conduct should occur between father and son, older and younger brother, husband and wife, older and younger friend, and ruler and subject. Most of Confucius's teachings describe in great detail how these relationships are to be carried out.

Given this religious orientation, it is little wonder that many Chinese are as interested in form as in substance, and this interest envelops ethical behavior in business. It is just as important, and sometimes even more important, to be polite and attentive to details of social etiquette than to whether a person has distorted the truth somewhat in order to save face for everybody. A person must live up to obligations, particularly family obligations. For example, a young professional Thai Chinese man's father died and owed his creditors a large amount of money. Such creditors are frequently related to one another, and everyone can borrow from a common pot of money for various activities such as attending college or starting a business. This professional could have forgotten the debt, because its was his father's and not his. In a country such as the United States, where personal bankruptcy has become a way to handle debt, such an action is countenanced and even encouraged in the legal system. Given the Chinese emphasis on personal relationships, however, it is not surprising that he devoted 3 years of his life to paying off the debt, thus saving face for the family and simultaneously guaranteeing that its members could borrow from the creditors in the future.

In Catholicism, there is a great emphasis on a personal God and the Ten Commandments as a vehicle for achieving salvation. As we saw in Chapter 1, this emphasis has resulted in the notion of a "just price," that is, not charging usurious rates of interest but just an amount that is sufficient to cover costs plus a small profit. An action is to be judged as ethical or unethical against the framework of the Ten Commandments. Thus, Catholicism tends to place much weight on being honest, even when doing so results in the loss of face.

Protestantism increases the burden of such obligations, as the individual is accountable directly to God and does not have the luxury of the Catholic sacrament of Confession, in which the individual can recount his business excesses or "sins" to a priest and, often, receive only minor penances to atone for them.

Islam, which Muhammad saw as the maturation of the religions of the Bible (Judaism and Catholicism) and therefore compatible with them, is noted for its envelopment of secular life, including business affairs and their attendant ethics. Five times a day, at specific times that are publicly announced so that everyone is aware of them, the individual submits himself to God or Allah through prayer. Moslem countries, with the exception of Turkey, are theocracies in which religious beliefs have a direct relationship with what is considered ethical behavior. Thus, the Koran, the Holy Book of Islam, is critically important when judging ethical business behavior. Many followers of this religion refuse to accept interest derived from savings accounts, because the Koran prohibits such profits. Oral promises are usually honored for the same reason. However, penalties for ethical violations can be severe, such as severing a hand.

Hinduism is distinctive in its emphasis on the cyclicality of life, that is, the past, present, and future are all variants of the same reality. Also, it assumes that humans and nonhumans go through several life forms, frequently numbering in the hundreds, before they achieve salvation or nirvana. Central to both Hinduism and Buddhism is the concept of karma, that is, a person's current position in life is determined by his or her past behavior; both of these religions also take the view that the world is like a dream and illusory; reality can only be realized through nirvana. If one does not behave ethically, he or she inevitably assumes a lower form of life. Buddhism was a reaction to the excessive preoccupation of Hinduism with the concept of many gods and giving tribute to them. To achieve salvation in Buddhism, it is necessary to follow an Eight-Fold Path, which is equivalent to the Ten Commandments. Different paths are specified in Hinduism, depending upon a person's stage of life and distinctive needs.

In business, these ideas are played out in interesting ways. Westerners tend to think in a linear fashion, and it is for this reason that they favor a hard-and-fast written business contract. Given the simultaneity of the past, present, and future in both Hinduism and Buddhism, however, contracts are frequently regarded as not fixed. Americans become particularly frustrated by this approach, because they frequently believe that they have achieved an agreement with a devout Hindu or Buddhist, only to hear him say, "Yes, but . . . " And even after the contract has been formally signed, Hindus and Buddhists may want to change its details or abrogate it completely.

Item 4.3

Max Weber is renowned for showing that religious beliefs are related to the development of capitalism. That is, doing well economically is a sign that an individual is doing God's work and helping others by providing employment to them, buying their goods and services, and so forth. Fons Trompenaars (1992) comments on this relationship as follows:

> There is considerable evidence that individualism and collectivism follow the Protestant-Ethic religious divide. Calvinists had contracts or covenants with God and with one another for which they were personally responsible. Each Puritan worshiper approached God as a separate being, seeking justification through words. Roman Catholics have always approached God as a community of the faithful. (p. 54).

SOURCE: Trompenaars (1993).

Some businessmen and even nations are much more influenced by religion than others (see Item 4.3). For example, although Catholics in America sometimes resist the dictates of the church in some areas, their counterparts in Poland tend to be more receptive of them. And the importance of a specific religion may vary greatly over time, even in one country. For example, although most Italians are Catholic, Italy now has the lowest birthrate in Europe, which suggests that its citizens are not following the Catholic church's restrictions on birth control. Also, although a religion may appear "dead" and not applicable to most people's lives in a nation—for example, only 2% of the British regularly attend church on Sunday—it represents the norms and values of a culture or society and helps to explain at least part of the reactions to different ethical dilemmas facing individuals with different religious backgrounds.

Perhaps the best way to demonstrate the enormous influence of religion on managerial and ethical behaviors is to compare and contrast two well-known concepts, the Protestant ethic and the Confucian ethic. Frequently, writers use these terms interchangeably but, in fact, these concepts are quite different from one another and are related to different behaviors.

Max Weber (1930) described some of the essential conditions of modern capitalism, including the evolution of a skilled middle class and the modern bureaucratic form of organization. One of his essential preconditions is the famous Protestant ethic, which he identified as a direct link between individual salvation and personal wealth. According to Protestant theologians such as John Calvin, only a few human beings are destined to achieve salvation or heaven, and the best indication of such destiny is the acquisition of individual wealth and using it wisely, as supposedly the individual directly contributes to the betterment of society in this way.

This viewpoint was most persuasively argued by Russell H. Conwell, the first president of Temple University and a minister of the Methodist church. Starting in 1861, he delivered his famous "Acres of Diamonds" speech, in which he boldly stated the following, which is clearly in conflict with Christ's notion that a rich man has as much chance of gaining heaven as a camel does of passing through the eye of a needle:

> I say you ought to be rich; you have no right to be poor. . . . I must say that you ought to spend some time getting rich. You and I know that there are some things more valuable than money; of course, we do. Ah, yes. . . . Well does the man know who has suffered that there are some things sweeter and holier and more sacred than gold. Nevertheless, the man of common sense also knows that there is not any one of those things that is not greatly enhanced by the use of money. Money is power; money has powers; and for a man to say, 'I do not want money,' is to say, 'I do not wish to do any good to my fellowmen.' It is absurd thus to talk. It is absurd to disconnect them. This is a wonderfully great life, and you ought to spend your time getting money, because of the power there is in money.
>
> Greatness consists not in holding some office; greatness really consists in doing some great deed with little means, in the accomplishment of vast purposes from the private ranks of life; this is true greatness. (quoted in Burr, 1917, pp. 414-415)

Andrew Carnegie was the living embodiment of the Protestant ethic. He rose from a modest background to become president of the Carnegie Steel Works and the richest person in America. Along the way he engaged in some activities that ethicians might well consider unethical, for example, hiring Pinkerton detectives and thugs to break a labor strike savagely; many of the workers died or were permanently injured in these encounters. Carnegie felt strongly, however, that a businessman should give away all or almost all of the money to charity during his lifetime and he followed his own beliefs strictly. Thus, the Protestant ethic focuses on the individual and his achievements.

Confucianism, as we have already seen, is grounded in a system of unequal relationships between father and son, older and younger brother, husband and wife, older and younger friend, and ruler and subject. The superior should behave ethically toward those subordinate to him, and vice versa. Confucius placed primary emphasis on the responsibilities within the family, as evidenced by the fact that three of the five relationships occur within it. Clearly, his ethic is social rather than individual in focus, thus leading to a differential treatment of those within the family or kinship group and those outside it. In fact, the 50 million expatriate Chinese who have settled in such countries as the United States, Singapore, Thailand, Taiwan, and Hong Kong base many of their business dealings on kinship or family relationships that preferably occur face-to-face. Businessmen in this group fly so frequently from one country to another, to strengthen these ties on a face-to-face basis, that they have been nicknamed "flyboys" (Kotkin, 1993).

Geert Hofstede (1980a) originally believed that the Protestant ethic, as it is encouraged in individualistic countries, was a major explanation if not the major explanation of economic development. In his study of the values of 53 nations, he found a very strong relationship between individualism and economic growth; the only developed country that fit into the most successful category in 1980 was Japan, and even this country ranked 22nd/23rd in individualism. However, the rapid economic development of the five Tigers of Asia led him to reassess his position (Hofstede & Bond, 1988). A group of Asian researchers calling themselves The Confucian Connection (1987) completed a study very similar to Hofstede's original study in 25 nations and found support for four of his five major dimensions; however, uncertainty avoidance was replaced by Confucian Dynamism or the Confucian Ethic, that is, a willingness to defer gratification in the short run to obtain long-term economic success. Furthermore, they distinguished between the so-called good and bad aspects of Confucianism, and it was only the good aspects of Confucianism making up the Confucian ethic that were related to economic growth in Asian nations. The good aspects included an emphasis on persistence and perseverance, ordering relationships by status and observing this order, thrift, and having a sense of shame for violating group norms. On the other hand, the bad aspects included an undue emphasis on protecting your face or dignity, respecting tradition, and reciprocation of greetings, favors, and gifts.

As this discussion suggests, the Protestant ethic and the Confucian ethic have been important for explaining behavior for centuries, but this linking of religion and behaviors is very different in individualized and collectivized nations. As a result, it should not surprise us that the resulting managerial and ethical behaviors are so different from one another. What is perceived as quite acceptable in the United States, for example, is frequently viewed as abhorrent in Asian nations, and vice versa (see also Item 4.3 for comparing Protestant and Catholic influences).

In sum, religions relate directly to what is considered ethical or appropriate behavior and, as we have already seen and will see much more in subsequent chapters, there are wide differences in what is considered proper or ethical. In this chapter, our concern was in showing why and how religions constitute a primary influence on what is considered ethical business behavior. Although we have only sketched the relationship between various religions and ethical business behaviors, the reader should be aware that his or her ideas on this subject are frequently different by a wide margin from those of others, even when they have known one another for years and have had extensive business relationships. Being aware of such differences may well help businesspeople avoid calamitous disagreements, especially when one of them accuses the other of lying or behaving dishonestly.

◩ DISCUSSION QUESTIONS

1. Historically, women have been treated as inferior to men in most societies. How do socialization practices and religion reinforce this viewpoint? Will it be possible to change this viewpoint when Confucianism is strong? Why or why not?

2. In the study of the three preschools in the United States, China, and Japan, there were some similarities and some differences between the Chinese and Japanese that were noted. Please describe the differences. What might account for these differences?

3. Some public school systems in the United States tend to separate the brighter students from the others through the use of so-called gifted and talented student programs. Do you feel that such programs are fundamentally different from the three types of schools found in Germany? Why or why not?

4. The Japanese educational system does not separate children by ability, as is common in both Europe and the United States. Still, placement in the prestigious colleges after high school is critical for success. What do Japanese parents do to ensure that their children will do well in the college placement test?

5. It is frequently said that Americans are primarily motivated by a sense of personal responsibility and guilt, and Asians by a sense of shame. How does socialization reinforce these motivational patterns?

6. What is *ijime*, and how is it related to socialization?

7. What is theocracy? What major religion tends to emphasize it today? Did other major religions ever emphasize it? How?

8. Discuss the historical origins of the Protestant ethic, the Confucian ethic, and the Catholic ethic. Describe the differential influences that each of these ethics possesses, and why.

5

Secondary Influences
on Managerial Behaviors
Laws, HRM Systems,
and Organizational Cultures

Bonuses and Customer Relations

A company supplying products to retail outlets had a large number of complaints one year from its customers, who were so angry that they threatened to take their business elsewhere. They said that the company's salespersons, or many of them, had loaded them up with a large amount of inventory that they could not sell and in fact had difficulty in storing. They had trusted these salespersons to look after their needs and had given them some discretion to do so. In investigating this matter, the company found that a number of these salespersons had quit at the beginning of the new year after they had received their high bonuses for exceeding their sales goals of the previous years.

Nash and Carroll (1974)

A Teamwork Culture

A large American food products company has a policy of very selectively hiring prospective entry-level managers and sales personnel. Sometimes, a dozen interviews are required over a period of several months and there is a long psychological assessment of the candidate, lasting an entire day, for those who pass the interviews. The company has indicated that all those who are employed by the company must not be too individualistic or achievement-oriented but team-oriented. This is because the company has stressed the importance of teams and teamwork as its primary focus in its operating systems. The company's culture has had this perspective ever since the nephew of its founder took control in 1932. This individual was the son of missionaries and had quite a different orientation toward managers than most of his contemporary managers. He, at that time, installed a very extensive team-oriented system at all levels of the company, which persists to this day and which has been copied by a large number of other firms.

Carroll (1990)

Why Did the Oldest Merchant Bank in Britain Collapse?

In February 1995, Barings, the oldest merchant bank in Britain, collapsed because of massive trading losses run up by Nicholas Leeson, a 28-year-old trader, whose bosses believed he was running a highly profitable operation in Singapore. Actually, a later investigation showed that Mr. Leeson's operations had lost money since the beginning. By the end of February 1995, those losses had escalated to $1.3 billion, causing the collapse of the firm. Causes of the problem have been attributed to a failure to supervise Mr. Leeson's operations properly, the huge bonus system that Mr. Leeson worked under, and his own personal characteristics.

(Burns, Dwyer, Foust, & Glasgale, 1995)

As we have indicated in Chapter 1, culture is to a large extent what a people think is right and what is appropriate behavior and action. The laws of a nation tend to reflect or embody these cultural expectations, because they define the rules, regulations, or thinking of a nation as to what behaviors are acceptable and unacceptable. As Friedman, in his review of the history of law in the United States, says, the law reflects the moral sense of the community (1993, p. 125). This would be especially so in the common law system used in the English-speaking nations, which, when it was created by King Henry II in the 12th century in England, initially simply codified the actual community or customary ways of dealing with certain types of behavior, problems, or disputes. Thus, the laws of a nation, by defining specifically what is legal and illegal, encompass to some extent what is thought to be ethical or unethical in a society. Of course, the law differs from mere customs or societal norms because it involves a formal legal process and the authority to impose punishments. One review of the historical definitions of the law indicated that it has four components. These are (a) norms, (b) which are regularly enforced by coercion, (c) by persons authorized by society, and (d) as stipulated by courts of law (Abadinsky, 1991). However, the overlap between what is lawful and what is ethical is far from complete, because typically the law is not sufficient to cover all of the behaviors considered unethical. The law as a practical matter requires a judicial system to enforce and administer it and there are limits to the size and domain of such a system. Obviously, the law must focus on the most common and the most harmful behaviors found in a society.

Laws do constrain behavior, perhaps not of everybody but of most people (more than 90%, according to some estimates; Abadinsky, 1991). Thus, when laws stipulate that certain behaviors are illegal, there does tend to be less of that behavior. Most people do seem to believe that most behaviors that are illegal are also unethical. Nevertheless, there are many individuals in a society who believe that it is ethical to violate particular laws in certain circumstances.

Perhaps the respect for certain laws found in a nation is to some degree influenced by the origin of the laws. For example, in Japan, there were many laws on the books that dealt with managerial issues such as discrimination against women and other groups when hiring individuals for certain positions. Such laws governing employment relationships were almost never enforced in Japan, most probably because these laws were copies of U.S. laws that were imposed on Japan by the U.S. occupational forces after World War II. They were often considered by the Japanese as inappropriate for their society and not representing the will of the people. Similarly, in totalitarian societies, imposed laws may not be accepted by a people and therefore may not have much to do with what individuals in that society believe is ethical or unethical.

Also, there is modeling behavior. If large numbers of people seem to hold certain laws in contempt by violating them on a regular basis, then adherence to such laws tends to be lower. Of course, the degree to which individuals are actually monitored to determine whether they are in violation of the law, and the severity of the punishment for such violations, are important determinants of the behavioral effects of laws. In addition, there are differences in attitudes toward the law and in terms of willingness to impose punishments for legal violations by race, ethnicity, and social class (Abadinsky, 1991). Thus, within the United States, various subcultures do appear to look at violations of the same law differently, with some groups being more lenient than others (Black, 1989).

▨ DIFFERENCES IN SYSTEMS OF LAWS AMONG NATIONS

The nations of the world all have their own laws, and an examination of the basis for such laws may provide us with valuable clues as to certain fundamental beliefs and values of a nation (Bohlman & Dundas, 1993; Hotchkiss, 1994; Ray, 1993). It is not only the specific types of behaviors or acts that are legal or illegal in various nations that illuminate a national culture and its basic values and beliefs but also the process of operationalizing the law in these nations. When the individual is pitted against the state, whose rights predominate? Are the laws very fundamental and somewhat vague or are they specified in great detail? These laws also guide what those in the nation such as managers think is ethical or unethical. In the intercultural study of managerial scenarios described in Chapter 3, individuals from countries where insider trading in the stock market was legal tended to rate the practice of insider trading as more ethical than respondents from nations such as the United States, where this practice is illegal. In fact, in describing the reasons for their ratings of ethicality, the business students from specific countries actually stated in their open-ended responses that this practice was legal or not illegal in their country as a justification for their ethicality ratings of this practice.

Even though individual countries have different systems of law, at a more fundamental level it might be said there are three basic types of law. The common law system, important in England and all former English colonial nations, emphasizes custom or the actual decisions made in legal disputes in the past. It involves collections of principles deduced from past decisions and it emphasizes precedent. One obvious characteristic of this type of law is that it provides a good deal of stability and predictability. Second, the civil law tradition, originating in the Roman law tradition and the French civil code of Napoleon passed in 1804, has had great influence on the laws of many countries around the world. All of the Scandinavian countries, for example, have had civil codes in place for several hundred years and Germany adopted a civil code in 1896. Communist countries developed systems of law derived from Communist ideology that has evolved into a civil code system. Under civil law, principles are first established and then applied to specific cases.

A third type of legal system is a religious system such as Islamic law, which began early in the 7th century. The prophet Muhammad preached the importance of a people's submitting to the will of God, and submission is the essential

Item 5.1

The International Court of Justice (ICJ) is an organ of the United Nations and is located at the Hague in the Netherlands. It decides on cases submitted to it by U.N. members and also on legal questions from authorized international organizations; it is composed of 15 judges. It can, however, only take jurisdiction over a case with the consent of the nations that are parties to the particular case in question. Recently, its workload seems to be increasing significantly.

SOURCE: Hotchkiss (1994, p. 74).

aspect of this system. Islamic law stems from divine revelation and does not change over time, because the law is stated in the Koran. This system of law has been closed to change since the 10th century; at that time, it was decided that further improvements in the law from scholarly analysis of divine law were not possible or likely. Furthermore, such law must often be defined by appropriate individuals as to its meaning in handling current or modern issues. Of course, some countries have mixed systems of law because of their historical association with other nations. For example, Japan's laws reflect the influence of Chinese law and Western civil law in addition to this nation's own historical customs and beliefs.

International law is that which affects relationships among nations or citizens of nations and is the result of international agreements (see Item 5.1). Such laws are not new and have existed even as long ago as 2500 B.C., when the codes of Hammurabi established remedies for breach of contract and damages for embezzlement. Reciprocity is a key issue in international law. Certainly, international law reflects perceived ethicality of practices just as domestic law does. When it comes to international trade, however, a nation may allow a certain practice to occur that it believes is unethical if carried out in its own country.

For example, let us take the issue of bribery. In Denmark, it is illegal to pay bribes; however, Danish firms are allowed to pay bribes abroad to obtain business (Bohlman & Dundas, 1993). These bribes are both legal and tax deductible and the form of the bribes, whether cash, sexual favors, or luxury goods, does not matter as long as the company reports them on its tax records. In Germany, foreign bribes are also allowed and are tax deductible for all resident companies. In the United States, however, the Foreign Corrupt Practices Act, passed in the 1970s, does not allow U.S. companies to pay bribes to officials in other nations, although certain types of small facilitating payments are allowed to expedite the flow of products. The exact difference between facilitating payments and bribes is not clearly defined in the law. An illustration of treating insiders and outsiders differently is found in Muslim countries, where charging interest to their own citizens is not allowed although foreigners can be so charged. Some of the laws in Muslim countries regarding interest and other uses of savings reflect a basic belief that hoarding money is unethical. Money should be used for the benefit of society.

In short, the laws within a country that managers must follow reflect what that nation believes is acceptable or unacceptable behavior and thus, they are an indicator, although an imperfect one, of that society's ethical beliefs. A brief overview of the laws of a few selected nations will provide examples of the fundamental role and perspectives underlying the legal systems of nations. Such nations differ not only in what behaviors are considered legal or illegal but also in the legal process that is followed in a society. An overall examination of the legal system of a nation also reveals cultural differences in such things as the relative rights of individuals versus the state, the discretion and latitude allowed individuals in authority positions (as judges, etc.), the degree to which certain behaviors in a society are proscribed in vague or in very specific terms, the relative importance in that society of certain offenses, and any inequalities or inconsistent treatment of the various subgroups making up that society.

Germany

Because Germany has a civil law tradition, the dominant source of law is from legislation (Hotchkiss, 1994). There is a German Civil Code of some 2,300 sections covering relationships among individuals and organizations. This includes contract law, agency relationships, property rights, and other matters of high concern and interest to the business community. In addition to business law, Germany, as compared to other countries, has very extensive labor laws. There is strong protection of unions, protections against unjust dismissals, social insurance programs, and even legislation that requires worker participation on the boards of directors of many corporations. Like other civil law nations, Germany may not have a relevant code or statute to cover a particular situation that the judicial system is called on to adjudicate. In these situations, customary practices are then examined or used, which is a common law philosophy. Only if there is no customary practice will the judges create laws derived from principles; however, in doing this, they are guided by other legislation, because there is a desire to avoid inconsistencies among the nation's laws. Even though in this civil law country there is not supposed to be reliance on precedents in judging cases, in reality German judges examine the decisions of previous judges on similar cases in arriving at a judgment (Hotchkiss, 1994). This is especially likely when the previous judge is prominent in the judicial community.

Some features of the German system probably contribute to a lower use of the judiciary in dealing with ethical disputes than is the case in the United States. First, in Germany, fees for legal work are specified by statute; the U.S. practice of contingent fees is not legal and in fact is considered unethical (Hotchkiss, 1994). In addition, the losing party to a litigation pays the fees.

Japan

Japanese law was affected very significantly by the values emerging in the nation during the Tokugawa era, which covered a period from approximately 1600 to 1868. One of the most important aspects of Japanese law, as established at that time, was that both the legal and the philosophical basis for society became the group as opposed to the individual. A feudal system was created in which there were various levels of groups (such as the daimyo or feudal lords, the samurai, and the commoners) who had not only certain obligations to each other but also certain rights and privileges. Also, occupational groups (warriors, farmers, artisans, merchants, etc.) were established, ranked, and became hereditary. In general, the goal of group or societal harmony was elevated and to obtain harmony, each individual was forced to accept his particular role in the group or in society. There were no individual rights established at all. What was just treatment depended entirely on the will of the members of the superior class. Disputing the judgments of higher-level classes was clearly not considered appropriate and was reserved for very serious transgressions only. Furthermore, different groups could be legally treated very differently. A Confucian perspective and legal code was adopted from China, which elevated the concept of the family as the essential ingredient in society, and ethics and the law were synonymous (Hotchkiss, 1994). After World War II, administrative law formulated by powerful government agencies such as the Ministry of Trade and Industry (MITI) became very important. At a time of severe economic difficulty and dislocation in Japan, this ministry was given great power to help distressed industries and promote favorable economic conditions for society.

At the present time, the Japanese are often considered by some Westerners to be engaging in unethical practices, because these practices are different from those of Western nations; also, the processes of the law itself and its orientation toward various parties in dispute often take quite a different perspective than in Western nations. Some Americans tend to react negatively to various Japanese practices under which litigation by individuals is discouraged: seemingly discriminatory treatment of various groups in society such as women and Koreans is common, little recourse from judgments and decisions made by higher authorities is possible, and the power of the government is used to advance the interests of particular companies or industries. However, the Japanese themselves, and also some Western observers, can see that these are perfectly ethical practices from the standpoint of the historical evolution of the legal system in Japan and the cultural philosophy that it represents.

People's Republic of China

China is another nation in which Western managers often have considerable ethical difficulties. Confucian attitudes toward the law and to the obligations of individuals in a society play a major role in explaining the system of Chinese law. Confucian ethical standards stress showing respect and honor for authority and hierarchy in the family and the nation itself. In addition, the Chinese created the idea of the bureaucracy, which would be in charge of the management of the society in the name of the emperor or official ruler of society. We see in this perspective the notion that individuals have few if any rights and the government and bureaucracy have almost unlimited rights.

With the Communist takeover of China in 1947, there was a breakdown in the nation's legal institutions because the law and lawyers were viewed as agents of the exploiting class in a capitalist system. A new legal system was attempted but, because of shifting political ideologies over the next 15 years or so, what was legal or ethical became a matter of considerable dispute, and extremely chaotic conditions prevailed, especially during the so-called cultural revolution from 1966 to 1976. More recently, however, starting with the death in 1976 of the Communist leader of China Mao Zedong (sometimes described as the newest Chinese emperor), an attempt has been made to modernize all aspects of Chinese society, and the importance of having the rule of law to facilitate this modernization has been recognized. In 1982, a new constitution was created that commits the government to operate within a system of law that, to at least some degree, has produced a greater amount of predictability in determining what behaviors and actions are legal and illegal. Nevertheless, it is still a Communist state, and the ethicality of various behaviors or decisions

Item 5.2

Not all disputes have to be settled in court. The Community Relations Services in Texas has worked hard to resolve tensions between immigrant Vietnamese fishermen operating on the Texas Gulf Coast and the American fishermen who have fished there for generations. Some of the disputes arise from cultural differences. For example, when operators of American shrimp boats would see another American boat at a good harvesting spot, they would pass it by, leaving the individual to reap the rewards of his labor. When Vietnamese shrimpers discovered a good spot, however, all the other fishermen in the area would be invited to share in the good fortune.

SOURCE: Hotchkiss (1994, p. 96).

of managers and officials is often judged from an ideological perspective. At the present time, litigation and the use of lawyers are still not favored, and the traditional approaches to interpersonal and intergroup conflict of negotiation, mediation, and arbitration are emphasized (also used in the United States, see Item 5.2). In addition, the decisions of the bureaucracy or ministries in charge of whole industries in China are given considerable weight in business disputes.

One problem that Western managers have in dealing with Chinese enterprises, which are under the control of various ministries in the highly centralized government, is finding somebody who has the authority to make agreements or contracts and enforce them. On the latter point, it is not unknown in China to invalidate contracts for public policy reasons. Chinese legal and ethical reasoning over the centuries suggests that this is perfectly ethical behavior, given the historical supremacy of the state over individual, group, and organizational interests.

The United States

The U.S. legal system embodies the philosophical basis on which the country was founded and, in contrast to much of the rest of the world, elevates the individual to a very high level in terms of rights. Protection of the individual without regard to that individual's group membership is a very important part of the American legal system, which reflects the cultural values of the nation.

The U.S. legal system, although initially relying heavily on the English system of law, has now incorporated various aspects of the French and German systems. It should not be forgotten that a good part of the United States was originally French before it was purchased by the third president of the United States, Thomas Jefferson, and a French legal system with French cultural thinking was already in place in this region. Unlike most other nations, in the United States the powers of the central government were limited from the beginning of the nation's history. There was a fear of the central government that has become part of the cultural tradition. At the beginning of the nation, most authority and power were reserved for the states and local communities. Of course, there were explicit guarantees of freedoms in the first 10 amendments to the Constitution, called the Bill of Rights. The judiciary system actually monitors government in the nation to ensure that the rights of individuals are not violated by any of the different levels of government or their subordinate agents. These inviolable rights include the right to be free of searches, protection against self-incrimination, free speech, freedom of religion, and so on.

Of great relevance to management is the right to own and operate property as one wishes. Property rights are protected under the Constitution. There are at times conflicts between property rights and individual rights that the judiciary system must resolve, and the U.S. courts in general have attempted to find constructive compromises. The rights of managers to operate a business in an efficient manner for the benefit of all of society, and the rights of individuals as protected by the Constitution and by laws passed by Congress, must be balanced in some way.

Variability in Laws Among Nations

These examples of legal differences do show wide variability in the laws of nations, which do lead to different conceptions of what is proper or ethical behavior. There are now some trends toward creating more consistent laws among nations to influence the conduct of business and management, given the realities of world trade as it exists today. Actually, as we have indicated, there have been trends toward trying to gain more uniformity in the commercial laws of nations for the past several hundred years in an effort to expedite trade among nations.

One striking and current example of how differences in laws mirror differences in cultural perceptions about an activity is the subject of intellectual property, which covers such subjects as copyrights, patents, trademarks, and trade secrets. The fundamental issue is the degree to which these should be protected in international or global trade. There tends to be large differences in the laws and perspectives on this issue between developed nations and those of underdeveloped or developing countries (Steidlmeier, 1993). The developed nations frequently argue that strong protections for intellectual properties must exist, for otherwise there will not be motivation to create them. Individuals and organizations must see a return for their considerable investment of time and resources in such properties. Developing nations, on the other hand, are primarily interested in the diffusion or use of technology or ideas for economic growth and thus support only weak protection of such properties. Certain industries are especially affected by this issue. For example, it has been claimed that on the average it costs a U.S. drug manufacturer about $100 million to develop a new product and bring it to market, but it can be easily copied or cloned. In some countries, especially Asian nations, intellectual discoveries have never been viewed as the private property of their discoverers or inventors. New ideas were traditionally considered to be public goods, and the rewards to inventors were to be esteem and respect but not material gain. Developing nations, such as South Korea, India, and China, have taken the position that intellectual property rights are a form of monopoly and therefore are bad. They also argue that any individual rights should be subordinate to social needs (Steidlmeier, 1993).

All of these arguments generally stem from differences in the individualism-collectivism cultural orientations of different nations (see Chapters 1, 2, and 3). Using political arguments as well, developing countries take the position that even the research and development activities of Western companies were made possible by the colonial exploitation of Third World countries and therefore such countries ought to be able to benefit from the use of such properties. Given this background, there is a reluctance to pass laws in various developing countries on the protection of intellectual rights and, even if such laws are passed, enforcement is often weak.

As indicated earlier, bribery is another topic where significant legal differences exist among nations and there are important differences in the toleration and acceptance of bribery as a business practice. The United States appears to be virtually the only advanced Western nation that has a Foreign Corrupt Practices Act (FCPA) that attempts to outlaw corporate bribery. It was passed by the U.S. Congress in the 1970s, after there were published reports of questionable payments by Lockheed Aircraft Company to public figures in Japan and the Netherlands that U.S. President Carter called "ethically repugnant" (Ball & McCulloch, 1993). In fact, in other Western nations, bribery appears to be supported by their governments because such payments are tax deductible, as we have indicated. English newspapers have also published accounts of the magnitude of this practice among British businesses in spite of the fact that the English government has said it wanted to cooperate with the

United States to stop this practice. About one third of all large U.S. businesses report they have lost overseas business because of these differences in the legality of using bribes to do business (Ball & McCulloch, 1993).

HUMAN RESOURCE MANAGEMENT SYSTEMS AS INFLUENCES ON MANAGERIAL BEHAVIOR AND PRACTICES

Human Resource Management (HRM) systems are part of the management function of organizing. They include all those practices used in creating the human organization, such as the hiring and training of employees, influencing employee behaviors through the organization's performance appraisal and compensation programs, and establishing rules about job behavior through disciplinary and collective bargaining systems. Many of these HRM systems also have the function of retaining such employees after they are hired, because such employees represent an organization's human capital and frequently its distinctive competence needed to carry out its corporate and business strategies.

The human resource systems of a company constitute an essential part of the organization's control system (Tosi, Rizzo, & Carroll, 1994). As such, the organization has a set of targeted behaviors that it needs and desires; through selection, training, and behavior-influencing programs, it attempts to ensure that they occur. The HRM practices of companies can affect ethical behaviors in a number of ways, as we indicated earlier. They not only communicate a society's and an organization's beliefs and values but also may provide direct incentives or pressures to override personal values.

In terms of representing societal values, first there is the employment law of the nation, which in large measure may reflect aspects of that nation's culture. All nations regulate the employment conditions for their citizens. These regulations may be laws or even such things as tax code regulations (see Items 5.3 and 5.4). The normative attitudes of a culture toward the treatment of employees are expressed in such employment laws. Obviously, nations that give employees many rights and protections under the law place less value on the authority of managers to dictate to them. Employment laws may not only reflect cultural factors but also simply the state of maturity of an economy. As a nation matures and prospers, more rights and privileges are given to employ-

Item 5.3

The U.S. federal government is one the largest purchasers of goods and materials in the entire world. It is not unusual for many of its suppliers to attempt to cheat and defraud it and, in fact, examples of such activities are reported very often in the business and general press. In 1986, in an attempt to reduce the amount of this fraud, the U.S. Congress adopted the Federal False Claims Act. This act establishes penalties for such fraud and attempts to protect those company employees (often called whistle-blowers) who inform the federal government of such fraudulent activities. Under this legislation, any employee who suffers discrimination or discharge because of such whistle-blowing activities may sue for double his or her pay plus attorney fees and costs. Fired employees must be reinstated with previous seniority rights.

SOURCE: Hotchkiss (1994, p. 42).

Item 5.4

The Internal Revenue Service has a new rule, which imposes a $1-million tax deduction limit on compensation paid to the CEO and the next four highest paid officers of publicly held corporations. This new rule does, however, exempt performance-based compensation such as stock options from the restriction. A survey of 350 large U.S. companies subject to the act indicates that 60% of them are already complying with the rule. Some companies have done this by deferring some portion of the compensation of these executives until they retire.

SOURCE: *HRMagazine* (Martinez, 1995a).

ees in that society; other groups, such as consumers and environmentalists, may also gain increased power. This scenario provides some support for a developmental theory of ethics, which holds that as a society starts to solve some of its most fundamental problems of insecurity and scarcity, increased concerns with justice and equity emerge. Out of this maelstrom come new norms or expectations of appropriate behavior for managers.

Furthermore, HRM practices mirror various other normative pressures in a society as to what is appropriate or inappropriate. For example, institutional theory tells us that existing practices in other organizations in a society have to be considered in planning and managing an HRM program because these become the norm in the minds of employees with respect to what should be (Martell & Carroll, 1995). Obviously, these institutional pressures or forces may reflect national culture as well. Certainly, the HRM practices of a nation like Taiwan or Korea can be significantly different from those of another country such as the United States because of cultural differences (Carroll, 1987). In fact, the extensive differences in the HRM systems of Japan and the United States have been well described and documented (Whitehill, 1991).

Of course, factors other than culture play a role in the design of HRM systems. The business strategies of the firm and its distinctive situation also are important in structuring HRM systems used for managers or executive human resource management (EHRM) systems (Carroll, Martell, & Gupta, 1990). Such factors then help to determine the nature of HRM systems that influence managers in carrying out their roles. One such factor is the difference between the HRM practices that govern managers themselves and those they must follow in managing their employees. The combination of some of these causal factors is then reflected in differences in HRM systems for lower-level employees and for managers in different countries, as some of the examples below confirm.

HRM Systems for Workers

In all or most countries, there is a clear distinction drawn between managers and employees in the area of HRM systems and practices. First, we focus specifically on HRM systems for the typical employees and later we shall discuss HRM systems for managers. In terms of legal requirements of HRM systems, these do differ from one country to another, although many such legal requirements are also common among countries.

HRM in Holland. Like most Western nations, Holland has many laws regulating the employment relationship. In Holland, the laws are quite strict and cover many areas. Firms must not discriminate and in fact must employ the disabled as a proportion of between 3% and 10% of the workforce. It is very difficult to fire employees once they pass the probationary period; working on Saturdays and Sundays is prohibited for most industries; and employees generally receive 5 weeks of vacation a year. Management is required to meet with employee-elected work councils and consult with them on any major decision affecting the workforce. Paid maternity leave is required. Currently, Dutch companies are attempting to shift responsibility for HRM from the staff departments to line managers (see Hoogendoorn, 1992).

HRM in Italy. The Italian economy is quite different from that in most European countries. The government intervention in industry is very high, and three large state-owned holding companies own large segments of industry in sectors such as food processing, banking, and airline travel. The labor relations system in Italy is highly regulated. There is a high degree of unionization, and trade union confederations negotiate with employer associations with respect to pay levels, holidays, hours, and working conditions. In Italy, a high proportion of managers, including even senior-level managers, belong to unions. Workers have significant job protection rights and termination indemnities. Outside of the state-owned companies and the large private firms such as Fiat, there is a large sector composed of small companies that are often family owned and often associated with other small firms in the form of cooperatives (see Caplan, 1992a).

HRM in Germany. In Germany, employers must gain the consent of worker-elected work councils before they can appoint or dismiss employees, set working hours, require overtime, or even change the prices of lunches in the company cafeteria. Germany seems to have the most highly regulated system of labor relations in the world. This has forced German managers to use management styles that are very informal, collegial, and participatory, in spite of stereotypes to the contrary. Most German workers are affiliated with industry-wide trade unions. It is very difficult to terminate employees and most promotions are filled internally. German companies are known for their enormous investments in training. The length of the workweek has recently been reduced by collective bargaining agreements in most firms and this has caused firms to use part-timers, flexible working hours, and overtime to more fully take advantage of the expensive new technologies employed by many German firms in recent years (see Arkin, 1992a).

HRM in Denmark. In Denmark, worker benefits are more extensive than in virtually all other European nations. Employees are the most highly paid in Europe, work a maximum of 37 hours a week, and have such benefits as paid parental leave. Working conditions and pay are negotiated by a national employers' association and the trade union confederation. Most of the human resource practices in Denmark are administered by line managers rather than specialized staff departments. Training and development are very extensive in Danish companies (see Arkin 1992b).

HRM in France. Like other European countries, France has a large body of laws and regulations regarding employment. Employees must receive overtime if they work for more than 39 hours, receive 30 days of vacation a year, have mandatory maternity leave and a minimum wage; there is also compulsory profit sharing for firms. Trade unions and work councils are the rule in French plants. As in other European countries, French HRM managers have been shifting operational HRM responsibilities to line managers and have adopted new roles for HRM managers as advisers to the line. HRM managers tend to be line managers, performing such responsibilities as part of a job rotation program (see Besse, 1992).

HRM in Ireland. HRM in Ireland over the years has emphasized a high degree of unionization among its workforce. This has created restrictive work practices that have led to some inefficiencies and to some employee alienation. Since the mid-1980s, however, with the large influx of foreign firms into Ireland consisting of about 1,000 U.S., Japanese, and European firms, the emphasis on unionization has declined steadily and strikes and other labor disputes are now at an all-time low. HRM policies and practices now emphasize employee efficiency, and the old emphasis on maximizing the number of jobs for citizens has changed Ireland in this nation's attempts to create a more competitive economy. Some of this new concern certainly arises out of the fact that Ireland is now part of the European Economic Community and feels it must adopt the standards and practices of other members of this group. The nation also feels it must become more business-oriented if it is to continue to attract foreign investment and raise the standard of living of its population (see Hannaway, 1992).

HRM in China. In a Communist country such as China, HRM practices have been tightly controlled by the central government for a number of years, although very recently there has been a loosening of such control. In the past, workers in China were assigned to companies by the government irrespective of the company's needs. The central government also decides on the rate of pay that Chinese workers receive by comparing descriptions of jobs to national sets of wage grades. Chinese managers typically must negotiate all decisions with trade union representatives in the plant and also with the office of internal security, which represents the ruling Communist party in the company. Because of the policy of assigning workers to plants, many Chinese companies are overstaffed. This can be expensive for them because Chinese companies must provide extensive training plus housing for the workforce in addition to health and medical care and many other benefits. Workers are normally retired at 60 years of age. In a typical Chinese company, superiors must periodically sit with subordinates and discuss their performance weaknesses. At the present time, many experiments with profit-based company bonus systems are being carried out (see Laaksonen, 1988).

In special zones of China, firms have been allowed more flexibility in recent years in managing their workforce. For example, power over enterprise affairs was taken away from Communist party officials and given to the top organizational levels. In turn, these top managers are allowed both to fire incompetent workers and to use an examination system to select new workers. In these newer experimental firms, there has been a shift from the use of ideological motivations to economic motivational methods; however, little power was shifted from top management down to workers or even to lower management levels in these Chinese companies (Laaksonen, 1988). It should be remembered that there are vast economic changes occurring in China today and HRM systems have been changing rapidly. Today, privately owned firms, joint ventures, and cooperatives are becoming increasingly important in China. These newer types of firms often use a variety of nontraditional types of HRM systems.

Individualism Versus Collectivism in HRM Practices

Ramamoorthy and Carroll (1996) and many others have examined the issue of how HRM systems of various nations seem to vary with differences in the cultural dimensions of individualism and collectivism in those societies. For example, wage systems in the United States, and to a somewhat lesser extent in Europe, tend to reward workers on the basis of equity, which means that individuals receive rewards in proportion to differences in effort and skill and individual performance. Many Asian nations base compensation to a larger degree on the basis of equality, which means that there are few if any differences in compensation among individuals on the same job. There is a far greater use of individual incentives and individual-oriented performance appraisal systems in Western cultures than in Asian cultures, which tend to be higher on collectivism. Also, there is much more concern with the principle of individual due process in U.S. and Western performance appraisal systems than in Asian countries. Higher due process means the right to disagree or confront one's superiors over performance evaluation issues, and the right to participate in the performance goal-setting process. Furthermore, the criteria for selection tend to be different in the United States and some Western nations than in

Asian nations, with individual characteristics receiving more weight in the United States, and cooperative or teamwork-oriented tendencies more weight in Asian selection systems. In attracting and motivating workers, more emphasis is placed on advancement in individualistic countries, and more weight is accorded job security in collectivist nations.

HRM Systems for Managers

There are times when the distinction between managers and workers is not always clear-cut. The first line supervisor, for example, is sometimes considered as management, sometimes as a lower-level employee, and sometimes as the so-called person in the middle. Above the level of first line supervisor, however, the managerial HRM systems may be quite different from what they are for workers. Three examples follow.

Great Britain. In Great Britain, less than one half of the 16- to 18-year-olds are still in the educational system, which is a lower percentage than that found in many European countries and the United States. This contributes to and also reflects to some degree a rigid class system of long standing. Managers in large companies are selected from better schools and universities, which obviously influences their self-concepts. Selection then is already partly done on the basis of the selection practices of British universities. As compared to practices in the United States and other developed countries, the manager's personality is a major consideration in selection and also later in performance appraisal. There is a notion that the manager should be a gentleman, with all that implies for behavior. Compensation for managers in Great Britain is much less than in both the United States and other European countries. Also, in the past, British managers received fewer bonuses and participated less in merit pay plans than their U.S. counterparts and relied more heavily on benefits and the increased earnings that would come with promotion. Managers were encouraged to stay with the same firm for life. In terms of training and development, there still is a feeling in Great Britain that managers are born and not made, thus placing a heavier reliance on selection, rather than training and rewards, in shaping behavior. Also, the reward systems that are used do not encourage innovation and individual achievement as much as is the case in the United States. In terms of unionization, some 40% of all British managers belong to unions, and this obviously influences their attitudes toward them (see Banai & Gayle, 1994).

Poland. In Poland, managers are held in lower regard than in many Western nations. This seems to be a reflection of the fact that when the nation had a Communist government, managers had little autonomy and were also political appointees. Managers in Poland tend to have lower levels of higher education than managers in other countries. There has been a tendency to allow labor unions, government ministries, professional associations, banks, and others to participate in the selection of managers. This may result in managers being selected who tend to be stronger on loyalty than aggressiveness and on the ability to get along with others. Management salaries tend to be quite low in Poland, and not much higher than those of skilled workers of the same age. There tends to be an egalitarian philosophy underlying compensation in the country. Although performance appraisal is used widely with managers, attitudes and skills are more important than performance goals but achievements are also frequently listed. In the past, all managers belonged to unions; however the majority of managers no longer are union members (see Kozinksi & Listwan, 1993).

South Korea. Managers in South Korea tend to be graduates of prestigious universities, as is the case in Japan. Individuals who make it into management in South Korea have survived a long and very competitive process. Also, they tend to stay for a lifetime with the company that selected them and are expected to be loyal and disciplined employees. There are many age-related ranks in South Korean companies and thus, progress is slow and through many different levels. In terms of performance evaluation and compensation systems, individualistic characteristics and behaviors are not encouraged. Rather, the emphasis is on inner organizational harmony and cooperation. There is a great emphasis on benefits and allowances and not any extensive use of bonuses or merit pay; however, good performers receive slightly higher salaries than poor performers. Subordinates are tied very closely to their supervisors, reflecting the high degree of dependency in personal relationships encouraged by the Korean culture. There is extensive company orientation training to instill company values. Although Korean managers can join unions, they generally do not (see Meek & Song, 1993).

In sum, HRM systems do vary from one country to another. Furthermore, there is a tendency to use home country HRM practices in plant locations in other countries even when such HRM practices create problems and strain relations with the local population both within such overseas subsidiaries and outside them. In addition, HRM systems for managers are different from those for ordinary lower levels of workers.

Item 5.5

Today, companies are faced with the need to prevent the increasing numbers of incidents of theft, violent acts against others, and various unethical behaviors on the part of their employees. Court decisions have been holding companies negligent for such activities by their employees. This requires companies to either carry out a wide array of investigations themselves or hire outside consultants specializing in certain subjects. These investigations can consist of extensive background checks of prospective employees, investigating thefts and other illegal activities carried out at the workplace, and looking into such matters as sexual harassment incidents. It is recommended that such investigations be carried out very carefully and supervised properly by an attorney, because many of them have significant legal implications.

SOURCE: *HRMagazine* (Vigneau, 1995).

The ethical implications of variations in HRM practices are fairly obvious. What types of people does the organization hire? If hiring is careless or if the organization does not set out to hire individuals who are trustworthy and reliable, than it could have extensive ethical problems (see Item 5.5). Some organizations have had problems because they carelessly hired dishonest people. Also, if the organization emphasizes hiring individuals who are very ambitious, very achievement-oriented, and very wealth-oriented, they may obtain high levels of performance but also most probably a greater incidence of unethical behavior. Of course, the content of the training given can be important. Are new organizational members taught to behave in ethical ways? Are employees taught by others to disregard ethical considerations and to actually behave unethically either directly or by example? What behaviors do the performance appraisal and compensation systems encourage; for example, results at all costs irrespective of the means used to achieve them? Extremely high compensation levels sometimes provide a very strong enticement to achieve results by unethical means. Naturally, punishments in the form of lack of promotion or even layoffs for those not performing at some targeted level might also create the conditions under which people behave unethically. Is the performance of employees ever actually discussed with them by supervisors? If there is little monitoring of behavior, there would be a greater tendency for ethical problems to occur.

The collective bargaining or employee governance systems of a company can also obviously affect how managers behave toward their employees. If the organization views its employees or their unions as enemies, there is a higher likelihood of distrust and mistreatment. On the same theme, there is a good deal of evidence that employees do judge their HRM systems as ethical or unethical. These assessments are made on the basis of the degree to which such HRM systems correspond to culturally determined norms of procedural justice (Taylor, Tracy, Renard, Harrison, & Carroll, 1995).

▨ ORGANIZATIONAL CULTURE AND MANAGERIAL ETHICAL BEHAVIORS

Within national cultures, there are also variations in organizational cultures but of course there is some relationship between the two. One example of variance in organizational cultures within a country was given in Chapter 1, where the differences in the organizational cultures of Sony and Mitsui in Japan were described. Mitsui is a company that is several hundred years old but Sony was created just after World War II, and their respective situations were quite different. Mitsui is far more bound by traditional Japanese thinking than is Sony. The culture of an organization reflects the patterned way of thinking, feeling, and reacting that exists in that organization. Thus, the organizational culture might be viewed as the modal organization personality (Hofstede, Nevijen, Ohayv, & Sanders, 1992). Organizational culture helps to create a certain homogeneity of behavior within an organization. It does this in a variety of ways, for example, by providing norms for what types of people and behavior are appropriate for the organization.

Much of organizational culture involves codes of unethical behavior, whether written out in a formal way or existing by informal understanding (Ott, 1989). Such culture is also manifested in a wide variety of formal company management approaches and in the extensive informal reinforcement activities that take place daily, such as the informal or formal mentoring programs of a company (see Item 5.6). Once established, the culture of a company tends to perpetuate itself and is not easy to change. Some of this inertia is due to the fact that the culture determines who will be preselected and hired, how they are to be socialized, and how deviates will be removed (Sathe, 1985).

Although organizational culture will reflect national culture to some degree, there is a great deal of variation within a national culture. Even in countries with a very strong national culture, such as Japan, there can be extensive differences between companies such as Sony and Matsushita. Of

Item 5.6

Mentoring is a type of informal program, found in many companies, that involves a senior manager's providing career assistance to a younger manager or protege. The mentor may play a number of roles, including that of providing the protege with career advice, providing emotional counseling, and acting as a champion of the protege to higher management. Some criticisms of the mentoring process, however, have been that some individuals who need mentoring do not receive it and that the different sexes may not be treated equally under this type of training. Also, some fear that any deviation from the purely voluntary aspects of this process will not work, because it is important that mentors and proteges are suited for each other. A program developed at the Bank of Montreal was designed to deal with some of these issues. It is a formal program consisting of 20 volunteer executives, each of whom is matched up with one male and one female protege.

SOURCE: *HRMagazine* (Martinez, 1995b).

course, virtually all organizational cultures within a nation will be at least somewhat congruent with national cultures; if they are not, then certain negative consequences such as low job satisfaction among organizational members is likely to be the result (Triandis, 1994). DeGeorge (1993) has described how organizational cultures can significantly influence the ethical behaviors of managers. He points out that sometimes there are ethical ideals in the organizational culture and at other times no such guides. Also, what is part of the organizational culture is important. Organizational cultures in which efficiency is overemphasized may detract from considerations such as ethical behavior.

Thus, the behavior of managers is influenced by both national culture and organizational culture. The relative importance of these two sources in influencing the behavior of managers is not precisely known, but one estimate by Hofstede (Hofstede et al., 1992) indicates that organizational culture might account for about 30% of the variation in the individual behavior of managers within a society. One basic difficulty that multinational companies face is that of preserving their organizational cultures across national borders (DeGeorge, 1993). Although there is generally some correspondence between a national culture and an organizational culture, in international operations this may not be the case.

There is a variety of ways to classify differences in organizational culture. A study by Hofstede et. al. (1992) on 10 firms located in Holland and Denmark identified some differences in organizational culture that would appear to be especially instrumental in explaining managerial ethical behaviors. The following critical organizational cultural differences were identified in this study:

1. A process versus a results orientation. In the process orientation, there is a primary concern with how something is done and an expectation that if things are done according to prescription, then the results will be satisfactory. The results orientation, on the other hand, focuses on the results obtained without much regard to how they were achieved.

2. A loose control versus a tight control orientation. Tight control firms are characterized by many formal practices and policies that act to restrict and control the behavior of organizational members. Loose control organizations obviously allow employees considerable latitude.

3. An employee orientation versus a job orientation. The difference is focused on the value and importance placed on people versus the work to be done. An organization with a high employee orientation emphasizes helping employees and fulfilling their needs.

4. Achievement versus avoidant orientation. In the achievement-oriented firms, there are very high expectations for performance and also policies and practices that facilitate them. In avoidant organizations, there tends to be a higher prevalence of safe and passive practices.

5. Open communication versus closed communication orientation. There is a much higher degree of information sharing in a firm emphasizing open communication between individuals, levels, and superiors and subordinates.

6. Customer orientation versus internal orientation. In firms with a customer orientation, there would obviously be a closeness to the customer and a strong desire to meet customer needs. The firms with an internal orientation tend to be less flexible in dealing with customers and more inclined to demand strict adherence to inviolable rules.

These differences are likely to affect the choice of management practices and thus have ethical implications. One would expect, for example, that firms with a results orientation as opposed to a process orientation would have more ethical problems. It can also be hypothesized that firms with loose controls would have more ethical problems. Organizational cultures with a higher respect for people should have fewer ethical problems in personnel matters than their counterparts. Also, firms with very high people orientations may create very strong firm loyalties, which may cause their members to put the organization's interests above those that might be best for outside groups such as customers. Achievement-oriented cultures probably have more ethical problems than avoidant cultures. Open communication cultures should have fewer ethical problems than closed communication cultures, for we would expect less suppression of such problems by organizational members. Finally, we might expect that highly customer-oriented firms may actually have more ethical problems than firms with an internal orientation. This is because such firms may be motivated to meet customer demands by unethical means, as compared to firms that see company rules as inviolable.

◎ PROFESSIONAL CULTURES AND CODES OF CONDUCT

We should not forget that organizations consist of different occupational groups and, at times, there is clash between the norms of the organization and the norms of professional groups within that organization. Such differences sometimes become involved in ethical issues, such as in the famous case of the *Challenger* space shuttle disaster, when an influential individual who was against allowing the vehicle to lift off on a given day was told to take off his engineer's hat and put on his manager's hat. Different professional groups have historically had their own codes of conduct; in societies where professional groups are strong and have a distinctive orientation and period of professional training, such codes may affect behavior significantly. To cite one group, military groups have often had codes of conduct over the past several centuries that proscribed certain behaviors (Fields, 1991). For example, as the result of a Catholic church council, called in 978 A.D. by religious authorities, warriors took the following oath, which specified certain behaviors as unethical and limited their actions in these areas:

> I will not force my way into a church in any manner since it is under God's protection; nor into the storerooms in the precinct of the church. I will not attack a monk or churchman if he be unarmed with earthly weapons, nor any of his

Item 5.7

Nynex, the New England Telephone Company, has had a series of cutbacks in employment over the past several years. Many of those eliminated from this company in earlier downsizings do not have jobs at this time, and more than 150 former employees have joined in a class action suit against the company. An interview with Pat, a current manager, about the latest proposed buyout offered by the company indicates that he does not feel that this is very different from terminating employees outright with severance pay. He describes the impact of the cutbacks on the self-esteem of the separated employees, and the fears that current employees have for their futures. They are pessimistic about their chances of obtaining new jobs. He feels that the years of loyalty, devotion, and commitment to the company shown by many employees in the past have not been reciprocated by the company and that such loyalty is now a thing of the past. Employees also see that the top managers in the company, many of whom have received golden parachutes or very profitable severance packages, are not experiencing the same pain as those at lower levels. He also feels that the Draconian downsizing measures of the past may not have been necessary, because other companies have improved their performance using more humane but effective programs.

SOURCE: *Business Week* ("The Victim," 1994).

company if he be without lance or buckler. I will not carry off his ox, cows, pig, sheep, goats, mare, or unbroken colt, nor the faggot he is carrying. I will not lay hands on any peasant, man or woman, sergeant or merchant; nor take away their money or constrain them to pay ransom. I will not mistreat them by extorting their possessions on the ground that their lord is making war.

Similarly, the Japanese samurai warriors had an elaborate code of behavior that they followed (Fields, 1991). More recently, there is a code of conduct for all U.S. military personnel that they must agree to abide by (Toner, 1995). It is especially relevant to their behavior when captured by enemy forces. Of course, medical doctors have taken the Hippocratic oath for thousands of years; however, this has not always proved to be a valuable guide in the actual practice of medicine, and extensive work in the field of medical ethics and on new codes has been carried out in recent years (Munson, 1995; Rest & Narvaez, 1994).

▧ CONCLUSIONS

In conclusion, the material in this chapter does indicate that nations do differ in terms of their laws and HRM systems or practices and also with respect to the cultures of their organizations. Although the laws of a nation do apply to all organizations in that society in the same way, and an international law may be created in the future, there are variations in HRM practices and in the culture of organizations within a nation (see Item 5.7). Given all of these facts, we would expect to find not only international differences as to which management practices and behaviors would be considered ethical or unethical but also quite a bit of variation within the nation as well, as we did find in reporting on the research about differences in the ethical values of managers by country (Chapter 3).

▧ DISCUSSION QUESTIONS

1. As a manager, which of the several fundamental systems of law, such as the common law, Napoleonic codes, and Islamic law, would you find it most convenient and effective to work under? Why?

2. Contrast some of the basic characteristics of HRM systems in Western countries with those in Asian countries and in Communist or former Communist nations. What accounts for these differences?

3. In which countries would you expect the greatest variations in organizational cultures? In which the least variability? Why?

4. What do you see as the interrelationships among the laws in a country, characteristics of a firm's HRM practices, and the culture of an organization?

6

Culture and Managerial
Ethical Behaviors
An In-Depth Look at Japan

Murder Chills Corporate Japan

*A Fuji Film manager, formerly in charge of the company's annual
stockholders' meeting, was stabbed by an unidentified person in his neck,
arms, and legs after he went outside to answer his doorbell. The
61-year-old manager later died in the hospital. A man with a samurai
sword was seen running from the area. The company had become a target
for sokaiya or gangsters who extort money from companies with a threat to
harass management at the annual stockholders' meetings. Recently, Fuji Film
had apparently stopped payments since the January 19 meeting of Fuji Film
had been disrupted by about 20 sokaiya who harangued the company's
president for more than 4 hours about the company's dividend policy and
other issues. Many companies evidently continue to pay sokaiya despite a
1982 law against it.*

Japan Times ("Sokaiya Link in Death," 1994)

The Recruit Cosmos Scandal

*This episode has exposed many aspects of corruption in Japan. It started
in mid-June 1988, when a city official in Kawasaki was forced to resign in
disgrace after he confessed to buying Recruit Cosmos shares on the basis of
inside information about the city's development plans. The newspaper*
Asahi Shimbun, *digging into details, uncovered a whole series of
payments made to a Who's Who of top Japanese officials, politicians, and
businessmen. Journalists eventually uncovered the names of 159 people
who had received Recruit Cosmos shares, including the secretaries or
relatives of almost all Japan's leading politicians, top ministry
bureaucrats, and chairmen of top Japanese businesses.*

Reading (1992, pp. 262-265)

The Bankrupt Japanese Business Tycoon

Although a Japanese real estate tycoon has $3.4 billion in debt against $1 billion in property, he is allowed to carry on as usual, because the banks and government refuse to take action against him and he can keep all of his buildings. One reason for this is that seizing properties costs more than letting them be. Not only that, but he so far has been allowed to dictate his own refinancing plan to his 50 creditors, which involves paying them only a sliver of interest on his loans. Finally, he and a group of similar tycoons are suing the government for $876 million in damages, claiming that the government's actions in raising interests rates drove them out of business. A government finance minister says that policy changes are a risk of doing business.

The Wall Street Journal (Sapsford, 1994)

In the past few years, Japan and Japanese companies have been the focus of considerable criticism from Western nations and companies for alleged unethical practices. Many nations have accused Japan of achieving its success through unethical methods and decisions carried out by officials of the Japanese government and by managers in Japanese companies, for example, stealing trade secrets, setting up barriers against the entry of foreign competitors into Japan, exercising discriminatory hiring practices, overworking and mistreating their own domestic employees as well as foreign employees, treating older employees unfairly, stealing product ideas from foreign companies, using predatory pricing, gaining business advantage through bribery, and numerous other types of behavior.

Similarly, the operations of Japanese subsidiary companies in the United States have also been subjected to considerable criticism. It is alleged that companies have been guilty of many unethical behaviors, which include violating provisions of the discrimination employment laws of the nation, conducting unfair antiunion campaigns, evading taxes, favoring Japanese over domestic suppliers, and treating domestic managers unfairly relative to Japanese managers (Carroll, 1992). Admittedly, these are just accusations, although some U.S. courts have ruled against Japanese companies in some cases.

In addition, the HRM practices of Japanese companies have been criticized as unethical in many respects (Carroll & Takeuchi, 1982). These criticisms focus on such issues as the inability of individuals to change jobs once hired, the lack of rewards and opportunities for those who exert more effort and achieve higher performance, discrimination against women for permanent jobs and promotions, the excessive conformity required, and difficulties in managing foreigners (March, 1992). Some see great problems for Japan in the future because of some of these and related problems (Reading, 1992).

This is not to say that Japanese companies and managers have been criticized only by foreigners. While on a Fulbright research professorship in Japan in 1992, Stephen Carroll carried out a computer search of English-language newspapers over a period of 3 years to identify changing issues in Japanese management. This survey identified many criticisms of Japanese management from inside Japan itself. For example, Akio Morita, the founder of Sony, gave a speech in the spring of 1992 to the national employers association that was widely reported in the newspapers. In this talk, Morita said that Japanese companies had to stop exploiting their own workforces so unfairly by imposing long hours and arbitrary treatment, because such practices represented unfair tactics in competing with Western firms who had superior working conditions for their employees. In addition, Mr. Morita cited predatory pricing, inadequate returns to stockholders, and insufficient concern for the high prices that Japanese consumers have to pay as being ethical issues for Japanese managers. Also, the newspaper survey indicated that there was a great deal of attention being given to the increasing number of cases of death from overwork (*karoshi*), to the issue of sex discrimination and sexual harassment in employment, to the failure of many companies to pay workers for their actual overtime, to the numerous publicized bribery cases of public officials by Japanese companies, and to a number of other problems such as the difficulties created for employees by the gift-giving obsession within companies. Finally, there was a good deal of mention of the problems that foreign workers have in Japan, such as their alleged unfair treatment in Japanese companies (Katzenstein, 1989).

On the other hand, there are many Western writers who have nothing but the strongest praise for Japan and consider this society to be a model for other nations in many respects (Abegglen, 1973; Abegglen & Stalk, 1985; Dore & Sako, 1989; Duke, 1986; Kahn, 1970; Reischauer, 1981, 1988; Vogel, 1979). These writers often have likened many of these criticisms of Japanese alleged unethical practices to so-called Japan bashing. Some Japanese writers have attributed criticisms of Japan by outsiders to U.S. racism, defensiveness because of Japan's economic success, or both. Thus, although there are critics of the Japanese system, there are also many in both Japan and the United States who believe that the Japanese are being unfairly evaluated by those who do not understand the Japanese culture and the realities of the roles that Japanese managers play in organizations, and how these affect the Japanese approach to management. This issue will be the subject of the rest of this chapter.

◫ JAPANESE CULTURAL CHARACTERISTICS

According to Hofstede's research (1980a, 1980b, 1991) on basic cultural values, Japan ranks #22/23 of 53 nations studied on the degree to which individuals have an individualistic orientation; #1 on masculinity or the degree to which individuals emphasize achievement, materialism, and a clear occupational differentiation between males and females; #7 on uncertainty avoidance or the degree to which individuals prefer to avoid risk and uncertainty in everyday life and work with long-term colleagues and friends; #3 on deferred gratification or a longtime horizon; and #33 on power distance or accepting an unequal distribution of power and prestige in organizations and society (see Chapter 3).

Edward T. Hall, a prominent cultural anthropologist, describes Japan as having a high context culture, in which communication is indirect rather than direct and where the meaning of a communication depends on knowing the situational clues shown by body language, seating position, and status differences (Hall, 1989). The communications in Japan thus tend not to be very open or candid as compared to many Western nations. In a high context culture, individuals can communicate a great deal with just a few words because everyone knows what to expect. Hall ranks societies as going from low to high context in the following way: the United States and Germany, France (in the middle), and Saudi Arabia and Japan at the other extreme.

Gannon (Gannon & Associates, 1994), in his creation of metaphors for 17 different countries, uses the Japanese garden for Japan. Here, the wet Japanese garden is described as representing what he believes are the four key aspects of Japanese culture, namely an emphasis on a harmony of elements (*wa*), *shikata* or the proper way of doing things, using *seishin* or spirit training as a basis for combining the activities of individuals into group activities, and finally, aesthetics. He believes that the search for harmony produced the feudal system in Japan in which the population is categorized into distinct classes, each with its own rights and obligations, and that this search also resulted in a rule-oriented society with severe penalties (such as death) for violations and an antipathy toward those who would destroy harmony. A rule-oriented society and the need for cooperation in group agriculture and other activities also increased the importance of following katas or prescribed procedures, and the expectation was that this approach would produce positive outcomes, just as Japanese total quality management systems do today. According to Gannon, to live comfortably within a rule-ordered society, each individual must have a great deal of self-control and a capacity for self-sacrifice. These are fostered by Japanese-style training, including a demanding educational system that is consistent across the nation, spiritual exercises as exemplified in Zen Buddhism, and an attention to physical discipline and sports such as karate and kendo. This training and education not only produce a group orientation in management decision making and operations but also spawn the powerful trade associations and the well-known *keiretsus* or networks of complementary business organizations, one of which may include 300 or more companies. In addition, such training and education create an identification with the nation as a whole and all of its elements, including government and business. Gannon uses the fourth primary cultural Japanese dimension of aesthetics to explain the Japanese acceptance of the idea of the inevitability of perpetual change in all things (concept of transience), an appreciation and reverence for simplicity, the desire to achieve a perfection in form, and an appreciation of the importance of silence and reflection. Gannon does point out, however, how the younger generation in Japan (the older Japanese use the term *new humans* in a negative way) has lost to some degree its appreciation for these older Japanese cultural values in favor of newer Western ideas of individuality, swift results, and immediate gratification.

Gannon and others who describe Japanese culture (Reischauer, 1988; Taylor, 1993; Varley, 1984; Whitehill, 1991) generally agree on the historical, economic, political, technological, and social factors contributing to the creation of the unique Japanese culture. Most point to the fact that the wet rice agricultural technology, adopted in Japan in historical times, requires a high degree of cooperation and group effort to build and maintain the irrigation system that this technology needs. This has helped create the collectivist mentality or group orientation of its people. Early contact with China, in the 7th century A.D., and the recognition by the Japanese of the superiority of the

Chinese culture led them to accept many Chinese ideas relating to philosophy and religion (Confucianism and Buddhism), political governance, literature and the arts, and even rice growing. The Japanese then adapted these ideas, institutions, and practices to create the Japanese system.

However, contact with a superior culture can create a concern about the future survivability of a nation. Later in Japanese history, the U.S. Navy, with its heavily armed "black ships," forced Japan to open up to the outside world again. The Japanese saw this confrontation with a technologically superior nation as a threat and they resolved to modernize as quickly as possible through the process of adopting foreign technologies and systems but at the same time adapting them to fit the Japanese culture. Thus, a pattern was established of being open to outside ideas but modifying them as needed to fit their own circumstances.

Another key feature of Japanese history was the violent internal strife in Japan that lasted for so many years, well into the last century. This strife probably contributed to the willingness of the Japanese to show deference to higher authority and to be very concerned with doing things in the appropriate manner. The fact that a samurai warrior had the right to cut off an ear or even the head of an individual of a lower class, if he did not perform according to his satisfaction, is likely to have had profound effects on the willingness to comply and the need to learn the acceptable modes of behaviors. Furthermore, the exalted position of the many priests or monks in Japanese society, given to them by ancient rulers, had much to do with an appreciation of certain aesthetic ideas that have been carried down to recent times.

Taylor (1993) and others (Abegglen & Stalk, 1985; Cole, 1989; Japan Productivity Center, 1984) have focused on the characteristics of the Japanese culture most salient to managers in performing their jobs. Groupism is one of these and Taylor points out that the Japanese manager sees the company itself as being just as obligated to its employees as to its stockholders; hence, one of the Japanese managers' roles involves mediating between these sometimes competing interests. The orientation toward harmony motivates Japanese managers to do all they can to minimize interpersonal and intergroup conflict in the organization. According to Taylor, this perspective requires them to get to know the needs and concerns of all so these can be incorporated into decisions. This of course requires devoting a great deal of time to personal contact with others and gathering information. The emphasis on hierarchy in the Japanese culture is translated into a system of orderly progression from one level to another. Taylor believes this means that Japanese managers are not threatened by subordinates, who can never overtake them, and therefore managers can stand to be told by subordinates what to do and even to be corrected by them. She also believes that the *amae* or emphasis on mutual dependency in Japanese firms allows or requires managers to become very much involved in the personal lives of subordinates to a far greater degree than would be acceptable in many other nations. Furthermore, Taylor points to the importance of *on* and *giri* in the Japanese culture, terms which refer to the idea of being in debt to others and having obligations to others for past favors received. These mutual obligations promote strong interpersonal ties among organizational members and also contribute to the heavy paternalism found in Japanese firms. Finally, the concept of *gambare* in Japan requires of all organizational members the acceptance of the need for very high effort and the need to endure difficult transfers, rigorous training, and other stressful situations.

▧ THE TRANSMISSION OF CULTURE TO JAPANESE MANAGERS

As indicated in Chapter 1, culture is transmitted to managers through parenting, the educational system, a nation's laws, and the HRM programs of companies. Other obvious forms of cultural transmission would be through its arts and literature. There has been considerable research on all of these aspects of Japanese society that is far too extensive to describe in one chapter, so only some selected points about these channels of cultural transmission will be made.

Parenting and the Educational Process

With respect to parenting, there seems to be evidence that parents and especially the mother inculcate in the young Japanese child a concern for the evaluations of others very early in life. A child who misbehaves, instead of being physically punished by the mother, is more likely to be told that he or she will be an object of shame to others, that others will ridicule him or her for behaving in that way, and so on. This approach has the effect of indoctrinating in the child the overwhelming saliency of the evaluation by the group, the horror of incurring negative reactions, and the importance of conformity to group norms. Japanese parents are also likely to emphasize the importance of hard work, scholastic success, and achievement and how these can bring honor, parental pride, and love and affection. Even the Japanese fairy tales parents read to their children encourage the behaviors that the culture values. One collection of such stories indicates that they stress the moral standards important to Japan, especially respect and obedience to parents and authority figures, courage, and keeping one's word (Smith, 1992).

Japanese schools have been lauded by several U.S. observers who are acutely aware of the performance problems now current in U.S. schools (Downs, 1994; Duke, 1986; White, 1987). Japanese schools, however, are quite different from U.S. schools and some have indicated that their approach may be inappropriate in the United States. In Japanese schools, the children are encouraged to have a collectivist rather than an individualistic orientation; they wear the same uniform as all the other students; the clothes of boys and girls are very much differentiated; and girls and boys learn that they must always speak in the language appropriate for their gender. The Japanese students also learn the pain of being an outsider to the group, either through their own experiences or vicariously through the experiences of other children who have been subjected to bullying behaviors imposed against those who are different, which teaches them the value of conformity (see Box 6.1). The school system uses a rather rigid and inflexible approach to learning, which is imposed on all students irrespective of any differences in talents, and this encourages conformity. Individual creativity is not fostered under this educational system. Of course, the students are held to a high standard of performance and thus, positive work habits are encouraged, as are mental discipline and the ability to overcome difficulties.

Japanese HRM Practices for Managers

The experiences that Japanese managers have as employees are also very likely to influence their thinking about what is right and appropriate in ethical choice situations. As indicated in Chapter 1, practices common in any society, whether management practices or any other type, tend to be considered correct by most of that society's members. Such practices gain credibility and thus serve as a norm or standard. Also, a common set of experiences gives individuals a similar mindset because they have not had an opportunity to examine the alternatives. In Japan, it is likely that there is far less diversity in practices than in Western nations, which tends to promote similar ways of thinking and judging. Obviously, any HRM system, by selecting certain types of people,

Box 6.1 Bullying in Japan

A study by the Japan Youth Research Institute examined bullying behaviors among students in Japan. Although this study said that only 74% of the Japanese teachers noticed bullying, as compared with 85% of the American teachers, the form of bullying in Japan was different from that in the United States. In the United States, it was usually two groups quarreling; but in Japan, it was typically a large group tormenting one or two individuals. Furthermore, although 40% of the U.S. students said they would intervene to stop the bullying, only 20% of the Japanese students would do so, and some 30% would pretend to not notice it was going on.

SOURCE: Woronoff (1990).

socializing or training them to think in a certain way, and influencing their behavior on the job through a system of rewards and punishments, does tend to create a particular inclination to perform and behave on the job in a certain and perhaps quite predictable manner.

Selection of Managers

In large companies in Japan, virtually all managers at the middle level and above are male (approximately 98%), are hired for lifetime jobs, and are not members of any minority group (such as Korean-Japanese). In addition, they have not had experience in any other company because they were recruited right out of college. Also, they were very selectively recruited, probably from the best colleges in the nation. These managers are likely to possess a considerable amount of lifetime success by their country's standards and to consider themselves a very elite group. In addition, hiring in Japanese firms is often heavily influenced by recommendations from key university professors or from the student's family members who are known and respected by company managers. Of course, because of this system, Japanese managers are likely to have a very thorough knowledge of the operating realities and customs of their companies as well as a strong stake in their survival (Carroll, 1987).

Socialization and Training of Japanese Managers

All Japanese managerial recruits start work on the same day, April 1. The first training is likely to be a socialization program that may last several weeks, in which the recruits learn a great deal about the history of the company and its products and facilities, are taught expected behaviors of company members, learn any company songs and creeds, are exposed to the top managers of the company including the president, and are imbued with the company spirit. There are sometimes military-like physical activities and exercises, perhaps conducted in a remote area in a forest, and often a type of military boot camp training where recruits are sometimes subjected to a great deal of psychological abuse, similar to what happens at fraternity hazings in America. All of these activities have the intended function of developing strong ties among the entering class of recruits and of engendering strong positive feelings of allegiance to the company itself. This period may be followed by a stint on a factory floor itself to learn first-hand about the production of the company's products. There then might be a rotation through various units of the company to develop generalist attitudes and also to identify the areas of most mutual interest for future placement. Box 6.2 describes briefly the socialization program of one Japanese company.

Compensation of Managers

Japanese managers are generally rewarded for their place in the hierarchy rather than for performing a specific job. Salary rises with seniority, thus rewarding loyalty and stability. Small merit increases are given for especially fine performance but pay differences among those with similar seniority tend to be small. The Japanese manager receives a substantial portion of his pay in the form of a bonus often paid twice a year, and this may amount to five or six times the basic monthly salary. During very difficult times, this bonus may be adjusted downward, although there is a reluctance to do this, because families tend to count on it (Taylor, 1993). This bonus may reinforce the manager's expectations that the company's fortunes are related to his own well-being.

Japanese managers receive many benefits, including medical care, pensions, housing allowances that include low-interest loans to buy housing, and various family allowances. With respect to housing, if the manager is single, as is typically the case when starting employment, he lives in a dormitory with other single managers in a military-type existence where many rules must be followed. While in this type of living arrangement, the young managers may participate in many recreational activities together. This has the effect of creating both strong interpersonal ties among younger managers and an internal sense of discipline and rule conformity.

Box 6.2 The Orientation Program at Japan Ink and Chemicals Co.

The Japan Ink orientation program started off on April 1, which is freshmen day in Japan for new employees. All the various levels of employees were seated in the same room, in assigned seats but grouped together. The various groups were dressed quite differently. The new college graduates had on new suits, but the new factory workers, who were high school graduates, usually were in jeans. The young women who were to be the office workers dressed in a variety of outfits, from informal to professional suits. Each group kept to itself and communicated only among its own members.

All the groups received the same overall training the first week. Lectures were given on the company's history, its many products, its plants around the world, and other facts about the firm. In addition, the benefits provided employees were discussed along with all employee rights. Etiquette was stressed, with information provided on how to speak to others correctly (the various levels of politeness found in the Japanese language), how to speak to customers, how to bow appropriately, and so on. A good deal of attention was spent on the company's total quality management (TQM) program and the many quality circles in the company. The groups were taught the importance of good nutrition, of getting enough sleep, of obtaining the proper amount of exercise, and similar information. Attempts were made to excite the orientees about the company. Each day, they were pressured to give a more enthusiastic collective "hello" than the day before. The management trainees appeared to be much more interested and excited about the orientation than the lower employees. The young women seemed especially bored with the proceedings.

After the first week, the college graduates went into a much more extensive monthlong orientation program, but the lower-level employees were finished. This monthlong program focused much more on the future careers of these individuals. Visits were made to various plants, functional divisions, and to the company's art museum and other facilities.

SOURCE: Tosi, Rizzo, and Carroll (1994).

Managerial Performance Appraisal in Japan

Performance appraisals are conducted two or three times a year, on standardized forms, and this information is deposited in the HRM unit for use in deciding optimum future job placements for the manager (Taylor, 1993). Thus, there is very little direct feedback to the manager partly because of the Japanese aversion to candor in conversations and also because of their intense dislike of interpersonal conflict. However, in the frequent socialization activities that often take place in the evening in work units, managers may at that time receive indirect feedback on performance, strengths, weaknesses, and the like. Nevertheless, the

TABLE 6.1 Content of a Performance Appraisal Form for Japanese Managers

Work Attitudes
    Obedience: Follows rules?
    Cooperation: Makes suggestions? Works toward self-improvement?
    Responsibility: Reliable?
Comments:

Performance
  Goal achievement:
    achieved 50% above goal
    achieved 20% above goal
    achieved goal
    achieved less than goal
    achieved 20% under goal or less

SOURCE: Taylor (1993, pp. 257-286).

Japanese managers know that their performance is being evaluated through the formal system and they are also aware of the factors that are being appraised. This knowledge certainly influences their behavior to some degree. A sample of some of the items on an appraisal form for Japanese managers is presented in Table 6.1.

Labor Relations

Japanese managers often have first-hand experience in dealing with unions because they actually join the enterprise or company unions that are common in Japan (Taylor, 1993). Actually, managerial recruits are not managers in the sense of a person having subordinates. These union experiences have the effect of making such younger managers aware of the needs and thinking of their blue-collar employees as well as creating a certain amount of psychological affinity with them. Such experiences also tend to contribute to favorable union-management relations in Japan. In addition, these experiences in the union probably give Japanese managers a perception that these types of union-management relationships are the only ones that are appropriate in a company.

Paternalism and Autocratic Management

Japanese companies tend to be quite paternalistic in their HRM practices compared to most other nations. For example, younger single managers and

Box 6.3   Almost a *Karoshi* Victim

I first noticed the symptoms after about a year of working very long days with no time off. I am an engineer by training and worked in the product design section of my company. On a typical day, I got up at 6:00 a.m. to go to work and returned home on the last subway train from central Tokyo around midnight. Sundays, I took a bulging briefcase home. I found I could not stay awake on the subway and often missed my stop. This was a problem [because] the subway trains were then not operating and I often had a very difficult time in finding a cab. Sometimes, I had to call my wife to get the car and pick me up. It was especially a problem on cold winter nights. Sometimes, I hung a sign around my neck, telling others to wake me up before my subway stop, but most of the time this did not work. I found that increasingly in the mornings I could not wake up, no matter what my wife did, and I was late for work. I would then receive a great deal of humiliation when this happened from those at work. Later, I found I had a physical problem—my legs or just one of them became paralyzed. I could not move them at all for a long time. Also, I developed very intense headaches and stomach problems. I became very frightened at these health difficulties and asked the company for days off or for a vacation. My bosses said that my work was very important to the company at the time and I should just suck it up and get on with it. Increasingly, they seemed to view me as a whiner and somebody who was disloyal. They had no sympathy for my plight. Then, I fainted a few times. I still could not get any sympathy from my bosses and they refused my request to transfer out to another work unit. By this time, my wife was extremely alarmed. I decided to quit, although my wife was strongly against this even though she was worried about my health. She said that I would never get another job, and my children and herself would suffer because of this. I knew that it was unlikely that I would ever get another job with a Japanese company but I thought that perhaps I could get a job with a foreign firm. I did quit but could not find a job but finally started to do consulting work, which is what I do now. Although I do not make as much money, I finish my work at 6:00 p.m. every evening and my life is much happier than it was. I feel that I saved my life by taking the action that I did.

SOURCE: Interview by Stephen Carroll with a Japanese engineer in Tokyo (March 1992).

single lower-level employees usually live in a highly regimented dormitory. Many benefits are provided and paid on an as-needed basis, such as housing and daily travel allowances. Hours tend to be quite long, and often employees are discouraged from taking all of their vacation time, which has become a matter of some controversy in Japan today (see Box 6.3).

Japanese Laws and the Legal System

What the legal system in a nation indicates is legal or illegal provides strong guides to managers with respect to what their society considers ethical and unethical; however, as indicated in Chapter 1, there is not a perfect correspondence between what is considered illegal and what is considered unethical.

In general, Japanese law was affected significantly by the values emerging in the nation during the Tokugawa era, which covered a period from approximately 1600 to 1868 (Hotchkiss, 1993). One of the most important aspects of Japanese law established at that time was that both the legal and the philosophical basis for society was the group as opposed to the individual, which is exactly opposite to the United States (see Chapter 1). A feudal system was created in which various levels of groups (daimyo or lords, samurai who pledged allegiance to them, commoners, etc.) had certain obligations to each other in addition to various rights and privileges. Also, various occupational groups (warriors, farmers, artisans, merchants) were established and ranked on a hereditary basis. In general, the group goal of societal harmony was elevated to a very high position, and to obtain this goal individuals had to accept their assigned roles in society. There were few if any individual rights. Disputing the judgments of the higher classes was not considered appropriate and was reserved for very serious transgressions only. Naturally, different groups could be treated very differently. There was acceptance of the Confucian perspective and legal code from China, which identified the family as the essential ingredient in society, and there was an attempt to make ethics and the law synonymous (Hotchkiss, 1993).

In terms of type of law, Japan is a civil law country rather than a common law country (see Chapter 5). This means that the law lacks the precision found in the United States, which is a common law country. As Huddleston (1990) puts it, in Japan, statutes are supposed to cover the legal universe, and judges mold laws to fill in the blanks; in the common law countries, judge-made law is basic, with statutes filling in the blanks. Civil law, because it is designed to cover every conceivable situation, must be rather vague. Of course, the Japanese culture and language put a high premium on vagueness as well. As Huddleston points out, Japan is a society of status rather than contract. The Japanese do not need detailed contracts to tell them what to do with other Japanese. Perhaps because Japanese law is so different from Western law, the Japanese have severely restricted the ability of Western lawyers to practice or operate in Japan (Young, 1988).

Furthermore, there are many regulatory rules in Japan that are also very often vague but which the government enforces. Article 22 of the Japanese Constitution permits restrictions of business activities for promoting the general welfare (Matsushita, 1993). As discussed previously, some regulatory or administrative laws were imposed on the Japanese by the U.S. occupational forces after World War II, and in fact, many statutes and regulations in Japan are copies of similar U.S. rules. Most probably, such imposed rules were never accepted to the same degree as were those derived from Japanese values. Regulatory laws are administered in Japan by the government bureaucracy, which, unlike the situation in the United States, is generally accorded very high respect by Japanese society. This gives these bureaucrats considerable power.

Literature

All cultures transmit cultural values to some degree through their literature. Japanese novels over many centuries certainly have characters and situations that exemplify and personify Japanese values of loyalty, courage, obedience, respect for authority, and so on (Kato, 1979; Rimer, 1988). When Japanese novelists visit other countries and observe other values, their writings are frequently influenced. Soseki, the great Japanese novelist, was sent by the Japanese government to England just after the turn of the 20th century (Gessel, 1993). His later novels often reflect a high degree of tension, both among and within his characters, between individualistic needs and the need to maintain a position or a role within a social hierarchy such as that of protege or mentor. Soseki, like many novelists, also lectured extensively in Japan and wrote essays on such topics as the meaning of individualism. He indicated that individualism, which he seemed to favor over a group orientation, required a high degree of internalized moral values in a society. He said that collectivist societies like Japan can rely more on coercive social pressures derived from the many rules that exist. He did openly wonder if it was possible for Japan to ever become a more individualistic nation, given this lack of internalized moral sense.

Although some Japanese managers do read extensively both classical and modern Japanese literature of high quality, many do not. Many managers, however, read the Japanese business novels, which are probably unique to Japan and are also read by students and the wives of managers who are interested in the operations of business enterprises. These novels frequently focus on some management issue in Japan and often explore the ethical dimensions of this issue in some depth. They focus on such things as the need to replace an old-fashioned manager with one with new ideas, the loneliness and difficulties experienced by managers sent far from home, and the consequences of following certain management actions in times of economic change. Such novels may explore at length a current ethical issue, such as in the novel titled *Kinjo the Corporate Bouncer,* which describes some of the mutual help between the gangster element in Japan and the business community (Prindle, 1989). This particular novel describes at length how a legendary corporate bouncer does his job for the company and the consequences of this work for the firm's executives.

◪ CASE STUDIES: CULTURE AND ETHICS

Table 6.2 presents eight different ethical situations that have occurred in Japan in the past few years. Each of these represents a somewhat different type of problem, and some of them also depict situations that may not seem to be unethical in another culture. Each of these will now be evaluated in terms of specific features of the Japanese cultural tradition and certain situational realities facing Japanese managers.

In *Case A,* apparently a Japanese trading company had in effect turned over to a member of the industrial *keiretsu* group with which it was associated the product that supposedly it was helping an American firm to market. The product was copied by this Japanese firm, and the U.S. firm was then excluded from the Japanese market. Gundling (1991), who described this case and considers it a common experience for U.S. firms in Japan, attributes the situation to the fact that the U.S. company involved was small, unimportant, and not socially connected in any type of trusting relationship with a Japanese firm. Given the fact that Japanese culture in general is very status conscious (with respect to companies and to people) and that this firm would be viewed as a complete outsider, there could be no place for it in the Japanese economy. Undoubtedly, the small U.S. firm viewed its relationship with the trading company as a type of agency relationship that is found in the United States and is based on an obligation established by payment, but this is not sufficient grounds for a trusting relationship in Japan.

In *Case B,* an American firm has run into what it sees as an unfair advantage for its Japanese competitors in Japan, who are able to skirt government regulations that the Americans cannot skirt. Gundling (1991) points out that this case merely reflects the fact that in Japan the laws and regulations are actually in so-called gray areas, where there are all sorts of exceptions and possible ways to get around certain regulations. The American firm, and especially its lawyers, do not understand that the Japanese legal system is quite different from their own and, therefore, they operate as if they were in America. Actually, this is a great disadvantage to them. What seems to be favoritism to

TABLE 6.2 Eight Ethical Managerial Cases in Japan

Case A. A small manufacturer of high-tech innovative products hired a U.S. import/export firm to market one of its measuring devices in Japan. A Japanese trading company took it on, but sales were slow and later, in the third year, the marketing agreement was terminated. The small U.S. manufacturer then found out that a Japanese manufacturer was selling a product just like its own in Japan (Gundling, 1991).

Case B. An American firm in Japan has great difficulty in dealing with the many complex regulations present in that country for the company's product line. Although the same regulations apply to the U.S. company's Japanese competitors in Japan, by going to the right government agency and official and doing the right thing, the Japanese competitors have been far more successful in skirting the regulations than the U.S. firm (Gundling, 1991).

Case C. A Japanese trading company executive complained bitterly about the poor ethics of an American employee. He had been with the Japanese company for 3 years and was beginning to win the trust and respect of his Japanese colleagues. He had even been invited to attend a series of important strategy meetings at the U.S. headquarters of his company. However, shortly after attending these meetings, he quit and joined a competing firm (Gundling, 1991).

Case D. A leading-edge U.S. computer firm announced in the United States that a new product would be available to its Japanese customers in October 1988. This availability date was later postponed by 4 months and then postponed again several times. The employees at the Japanese subsidiary were furious about this and humiliated at having to inform their customers about these delays. Later, a key sales manager was so ashamed of his company's behavior that he left the company (Gundling, 1991).

Case E. A well-known Japanese company in the United States was sued by 13 of its female clerical employees for sex discrimination. The suit was settled out of court (Gundling, 1991).

Case F. A U.S.-based subsidiary of a major Japanese company was sued in a U.S. court for laying off approximately 83 of its 94 U.S. managers while retaining all 7 of its Japanese managers. The charge was ethnic discrimination, which is illegal under U.S. equal employment opportunity laws (Carroll, 1992).

Case G. A well-known Japanese company in the United States was sued by some of its American higher-level managers for failure to live up to assurances that said managers would have significant management authority in their jobs (Gundling, 1991).

Case H. Three well-known Japanese companies paid gangsters (*yakuza*) to act as company bodyguards to protect the firm's executives, during the required annual stockholders' meeting, from having to deal with embarrassing questions about their operations during the previous year. In addition, these individuals were hired to pay off other gangsters, who threatened to disrupt the meeting, and to discourage legitimate stockholders from asking questions that would delay a quick ending to the meeting (Wordnoff, 1992).

local Japanese competitors may simply be a lack of understanding of the differences in the way these two societies operate.

That U.S. firms can learn to negotiate such regulations and the complex government bureaucracy is shown in the case of Jackson Huddleston, a general manager of a division of American Express in Japan. Mr. Huddleston (1990) describes how he was successful in attaining several objectives of his company through the government bureaucracy. He points out that a fundamental difference in a common law country, such as the United States, and a civil law country like Japan is that in the latter the laws must be vague to cover all the various circumstances that might arise. In a common law country like the United States, these situations can be handled by judges establishing case precedents. Of course, in Japan, it is the government's responsibility (regulatory agency) to interpret how a particular law applies, so there is a great deal of discretion left to various Japanese government officials in terms of the administration of the laws of the nation. Because such officials are human, it is not surprising that they may well be somewhat favorably biased, at the beginning of a particular case, toward somebody with whom they are well acquainted. Thus, what seems to be blatant favoritism or unethical behavior on the part of Japanese officials is behavior that must be recognized as reflecting a system entirely different from that of another nation, even though superficially laws and regulations may appear to be the same.

Case C involves behavior that appears to be very unethical to Japanese managers but is perfectly acceptable to American managers. In this situation, an American manager quits the employment of a Japanese firm to accept employment with a competitor. The primary issue from a Japanese perspective is loyalty (Gundling, 1991). In the Japanese culture, there is a long feudal tradition in which master and servant are bound together by lifetime ties of mutual obligation. The superior is to protect the subordinate in return for the subordinate's unswerving loyalty to and support of the superior. This issue has very high salience among the Japanese, who often view such an action as taking a job with a competitor as an act of betrayal of a trust and a dishonorable violation of a human bond. In the U.S. culture in which individual rights are given precedence over group obligations, leaving one job for another that pays more is perfectly acceptable and in fact may be viewed as commendable, because now such an individual can provide better financial support for his family.

One of the charges made against Japanese firms in the United States is that such firms are acting unethically toward their U.S. managers by not allowing them to assume the highest managerial roles in the company. Japanese U.S.-based subsidiaries have even been sued in U.S. courts for this restriction

(Carroll, 1992). We can see, however, from Case C how Japanese managers may view it as a very risky practice to put U.S. managers in very high-level positions in the subsidiary where they are privy to all kinds of proprietary technological data and secret competitive strategy information, with respect to not only the subsidiary but also the parent Japanese company. There will probably never be complete trust between an organization and its managers so long as these managers may leave at any time to join a competitor. Thus, what might be viewed as unethical behavior from a U.S. manager's perspective could be seen as quite ethical from a Japanese perspective.

Case D also involves a difference between Japanese and U.S. perceptions of what is ethical or unethical behaviors. An American company made a statement that a product line would be available by a certain date, then not only failed to make that deadline but also failed to meet several subsequent promised dates. This created enormous problems for the company's reputation in Japan and its Japanese managers and sales staff were very ashamed and humiliated. In fact, a key sales manager quit the company because of this problem. As Gundling (1991) points out, keeping commitments is extremely important in Japan and a reputation for reliability is also very important in that country. There are probably a number of reasons for this orientation. One is that the Japanese score quite high on uncertainty avoidance, which means that they do not like risk. They wish to have predictability, so they do not like to do business with companies or individuals who are not predictable because of their unreliability. Also, a failure to achieve promised commitments by a company is taken as a personal humiliation more in Japan than in the United States, because the self-identification of the Japanese tends to be collectivist rather than individualistic, as we have previously indicated. This means that when the referenced collective entity fails, the managers also fail, which brings more humiliation and shame to them than would occur in a similar circumstance in a U.S. company.

These situations also illustrate the apparent functionality of other common Japanese behaviors. Here, we can refer to both the tendency for Japanese vagueness in making commitments in the first place and a tendency to apologize so very profusely and frequently for failure to attain commitments. An avoidance of making specific deadline commitments is a way of minimizing the perception that one is unreliable if such promises cannot be met. Also, given the fact that promises or commitments must sometimes be broken due to various circumstances, very profuse apologies demonstrate the seriousness that one makes of such matters, which can communicate to others that these are atypical rather than typical behaviors. This approach obviously can help to foster the close and trusting relationships critical in Japanese society.

Case E. In this not uncommon case, Japanese companies have been sued by U.S. employees for violating the discrimination laws of the nation. Most Japanese companies have been subject to such discrimination suits (Carroll, 1992) and this issue has even been investigated by the U.S. Congress. Of course, many thousands of U.S. firms have been similarly sued over such issues. Obviously, there are aspects of the training and experiences of Japanese managers that can create special problems in this area. As we indicated previously, the Japanese culture tends to emphasize a very strong sex or gender social differentiation. Men and women are viewed as belonging to very distinctive groups, which of course is true, but the Japanese seem to have a tendency to overlook individual variability within groups to a much greater extent than is the case in the United States The U.S. courts have in fact made the assumption of individual variability within male and female groups as an integral part of their court decisions. For example, the courts have said that maleness is not an acceptable bona fide occupational qualification for jobs requiring strength, because many females are stronger than many males. This awareness of large individual differences within groups does not seem to be widely recognized in Asian societies. Of course, most jobs in Japan have been traditionally sex-segregated (in addition to various types of ethnic segregation) and still today there is little mixing of genders within an occupational classification (Carroll, 1992). The human resource management practices of most Japanese companies support this sex segregation and, as practices are widespread, they become internalized as normal or appropriate. Also, the laws on such discrimination have not been enforced in the past in Japan, thus leading Japanese managers to view them as not important (Hanami, 1991). All of these facts probably make it quite difficult for Japanese managers in the United States to truly understand the justification for U.S. equal employment opportunity laws and the seriousness with which they are taken by U.S. citizens.

Case F is an interesting one because it involves a rather unusual situation, that is, a Japanese company laying off employees, although in this case they are American managers. It is unusual in the sense that Japanese companies in fact are very reluctant to lay off employees and do view this as more unethical than do U.S. managers. In addition, layoffs in Japanese companies in Japan are much rarer than they are in the United States (Whitehill, 1991) and also are rarer in U.S.-based Japanese subsidiaries than in their U.S. competitors (Carroll & Takeuchi, 1982). The reluctance of Japanese managers to lay off employees can be accounted for by the various cultural factors described previously, by Japanese HRM practices, and even perhaps by Japanese law. First is the historical Japanese feudal tradition of paternalism toward employees and anticipated loyalty in return. In addition, the Japanese tend to view themselves as roles within a larger social context, which establishes in the minds of Japanese managers somewhat of a closer emotional relationship with subordinate employees than is the case for the more individualistic U.S. managers. Furthermore, the employees themselves wish much more to work in companies that do provide high employment security than do job seekers in Western nations. Of course, Japanese HRM practices have also given considerable legitimacy to the notion of lifelong employment and the avoidance of layoffs. Furthermore, the Japanese courts have increasingly forced Japanese companies to adjust to economic downturns in a variety of ways before considering layoffs. These other alternatives include avoiding overtime, stopping recruitment, eliminating the use of temporary workers, and using transfers, retraining for other jobs, and efforts to identify other areas of business activity (Hanami, 1991 p. 36).

In the case involving the U.S. managers, however, Japanese cultural factors would not be operating to the same extent. First, Japanese companies in the United States do not provide the same implied employment guarantees to the U.S. managers that they offer managers back in Japan. This is primarily because of the refusal of the U.S. workers to commit themselves to a permanent employment relationship with the Japanese companies, as reciprocity would demand (Carroll & Takeuchi, 1982). Japanese managers say that they would prefer being able to count on the loyalty of their U.S. managers to stay continuously employed with them over their careers, but that the U.S. managers prefer to maintain high career mobility. This means that the Japanese and the U.S. managers are hired under different sets of expectations and the Japanese companies do not feel the sense of obligation (*giri*) to them that they do for their domestic employees. Of course, the traditional Japanese view of foreigners as always being outsiders may also play a role in these different perceptions of obligatory responsibilities.

Case G is a so-called bamboo ceiling case, much discussed in regard to the operation of Japanese subsidiary companies in America (Carroll, 1992; Woronoff, 1990). Here, the charge is that Japanese companies exclude foreigners from the effective management of their overseas companies, unlike the practice of most other nations that tend to use locals in managing such subsidiaries. Gundling reports that in the United States, some 85% of the CEOs and 68% of the executives in the Japanese subsidiaries are from Japan, although in Japan the comparable figures for American CEOs is 20%. Some commentators also charge that although such U.S.-based Japanese subsidiaries often do have some U.S. executives with high-ranking titles, the company is really being managed behind the scenes by Japanese staff members who stay at work very late to receive detailed instructions from Tokyo (Carroll, 1992).

Some aspects of the Japanese cultural inheritance as well as certain Japanese HRM practices can help to explain this behavior. Gundling mentions that promotions in Japanese companies often involve a long waiting period and that Americans, who are accustomed to a faster promotion pace, do not understand this orientation or perhaps are too impatient for this type of career development process. Furthermore, it is frequently true that Americans do not truly understand the Japanese authority system, which does not really involve the allocation of much authority to specific individuals (Carroll, 1992). In addition, this case involves a cultural clash, as Gundling shows in his analysis of the manner in which disputes like this should be settled. In Japan, the idea of going to court and suing the company would generally not occur to managers. A superior way of resolving some dispute like this would be to have a meeting about this problem, perhaps during a night of drinking at various bars and nightclubs, where a friendly atmosphere and a type of recreational bonding can take place between those who have the misunderstanding. The Japanese believe that if this were done, there would be no need for court suits like this one. One factor that may help explain the large difference between the percentage of Japanese executives used by U.S. firms in Japan and the small percentage of U.S. executives employed by Japanese companies is language skills. Very few U.S. executives speak and write Japanese although many Japanese executives do understand English quite well. Certainly, in communicating with a Japanese company in Japan, one needs to be able to use the Japanese language.

In *Case H*, we see a rather strange aspect of Japanese corporate life, namely dealing with the problem of disruptions at stockholders' meetings. In Japan, gangsters who are members of the *yakuza* or organized crime syndicate are often involved with these activities either as meeting disrupters or meeting pacifiers. Anyone can attend a stockholders' meeting by buying a single share of a company's stock. It would appear from these cases that the Japanese executives do not like to receive embarrassing questions from anyone and do prefer that the stockholders' meetings be managed so that the communication flow is from the company to the stockholders and not the other way around. It also appears that these managers would like to provide a minimum of information at these meetings. Apparently, it is these needs that some of the *yakuza* are taking advantage of.

With respect to this issue, a number of cultural factors may be explanatory. First, to some outsiders, dealing with the *yakuza* at all may seem strange, but it has been said that in Japan there is a recognition that there are many elements of Japanese society and all must be expected to have some means of making a livelihood. Thus, even shunned groups in Japanese society do appear to be given, in effect, certain realms of the economy so that they may support themselves. This, to some degree, reflects viewing Japan as an organic whole, all parts of which are interrelated in certain ways. With respect to the meetings themselves, it seems likely that the Japanese aversion to disturbance and conflict and unpredictability could motivate Japanese executives to try to ensure that none of these things happen, and that huge payments to prevent them are well worth the price. In addition, it must be remembered that stockholders are not accorded the high rank among executives that they receive in the United States. From the Japanese perspective, the stockholders are just one stakeholder group and no more important than are the company's own employees. Also, although there is some emphasis in Japan on minimizing status differences, the notion that those lower in social power and ranking could be impolite and could humiliate those of higher ranking would not be accepted. Thus, this rather strange behavior fits with Japanese culture.

OTHER CURRENT ETHICAL ISSUES IN JAPAN

There are many other ethical issues currently of importance in Japan, and these include the general treatment of foreign firms in Japan, acting unethically toward dependent employees, and the differential treatment of insider groups and outsiders.

The General Treatment of Foreign Firms in Japan

As we indicated at the beginning of the chapter, a frequent assertion made by many Western political and business leaders is that Japan does not play fair in the way that the economy actually is organized and managed. It has been alleged that the Japanese government and Japanese companies often treat foreign business firms much more severely than Japanese firms are treated. The unfairness of this lies in the fact that in other countries, the Japanese firms may be treated the same as a domestic business. In one analysis, the Japanese were compared against the criteria of fair competitors, as outlined in a popular and widely accepted model of international competitiveness, and declared to be unfair (Brouthers & Werner, 1990).

One view of the way the Japanese economy works and the logic behind it is provided by the American Chamber of Commerce in Japan (1973). The view of the executives putting together this publication, designed to train American managers, is that of Japan's being a business society, which, although it is capitalistic, is not really competitive in the Western sense of this term, because there are limits to competition that are agreed to by different societal components. Various industrial groups or *keiretsus* have emerged that do compete against each other within the rules established by government bureaucracies. Each group has a right to exist and play a role in the society even if this requires that some efficiency and economic benefits to society are sacrificed. This is all viewed as necessary in a nation that is resource poor and aims at ensuring the economic well-being of almost all of its citizens. Foreign firms are viewed as quite disruptive to such a business society, which is organized and managed to produce a harmonious equilibrium where all can survive. It is also thought by some Japanese that foreign firms, if allowed to operate unchecked, may in fact prove to have certain competitive advantages over domestic firms, which are forced to respect the government's wishes to operate in a way that benefits the national good. Of course, pressures from foreign governments and the threat of retaliatory actions against Japan have forced the country to allow foreign firms some economic rights in Japan. This limited degree of openness, however, is still viewed by many as a threat to the achievement of several deep-rooted cultural objectives and values, including those of harmony and a stable society with its various elements in balance with one another.

Still, the Japanese do realize the benefits of learning from other nations, as we have seen. Conflicting needs do create some cultural dilemmas—in this case, internal harmony and the minimization of internal turbulence against the need to grow and adapt to a changing world. Obviously, this requires many compromises and adjustments.

Acting Unethically to Dependent Employees

Carroll and Takeuchi (1982) have pointed out that there are many myths held in the West about the management of Japanese workers. One of these is

Box 6.4 My Assignment in Kuwait

Now that the Gulf war is over, I am really worried about being sent back to Kuwait by my company. Before the Gulf war, my construction company had a project there and I spent 3 years living in a tent. I did not even have a vehicle or any means to get into a town. I just went from the tent to the work site and back again. Also, no alcohol was allowed. I really missed my family back in Japan. Well, if they tell me to go, of course I will have to. I have no alternative.

SOURCE: Interview by Stephen Carroll with construction engineer in Tokyo (Spring 1992).

that Japanese managers are much more humane in their treatment of subordinates than are Western managers. Another is that Japanese workers have much higher job satisfaction than Western workers, although the data show it is much lower (Kashima & Callan, 1994). Of course, there have always been Japanese managers who as individuals have been as autocratic and mean-spirited as any management situation in the West.

As indicated earlier in the chapter, Akio Morita, the founder of Sony, declared that Japanese firms were guilty of exploiting their workers to an unfair degree, which in turn gave them an unfair advantage in competing against U.S. and European firms. Japanese employees work more hours than employees in almost any other developed nation: more than 500 hours more than European workers and more than 200 hours more than U.S. workers (Carroll, 1992). Furthermore, many of these hours are donated, in the sense that Japanese companies have not paid these employees for overtime despite the fact that Japanese labor laws require them to do so. Also, Japanese workers are often pressured to work during vacation days. This heavy pressure on employees, coupled with little time off, can result in the condition known as *karoshi,* or death from overwork syndrome (see Box 6.3), which has been documented in Japan and has increasingly been the subject of court suits against companies there (National Defense Counsel for Victims of Karoshi, 1990). Another prominent problem in Japan currently receiving a lot of attention is that of the unwanted job assignment and the required solitary job transfer of permanent employees without their families (see Box 6.4).

Why do Japanese managers treat their employees in this way, and why is such treatment so widely accepted, even by the employees themselves? Given the realities of the lifetime employment system and the virtual impossibility of finding another permanent job, most employees must accept whatever the company asks of them. These are the realities of the Japanese human resource management system. There has always been a price for security and that is usually some loss of freedom, which is the case here. Furthermore, employees in Japan, as elsewhere, are concerned about performance appraisals, which, as we have seen, may even mention obedience as a factor (see Table 6.1) and are increasingly related to promotions in Japanese companies. In addition, the absence of strong unions in Japan removes a source of countervailing power that often exists in Western manufacturing firms. Typically, unionization of a company is associated with requirements that a company follow various due process procedures and agree in advance to protect certain employee rights against arbitrary treatment by management. We have also seen that there has been a lifetime of conditioning to accept higher authority and do as one is told. If not, the whole social system might be turned against an individual, which would be quite threatening to any collectivist-oriented Japanese. For example, take the case of Gary Katzenstein (1989), a U.S. MBA employed at Sony: When he took some holidays to which he felt he was legally entitled, he was ridiculed by his fellow workers, ostracized eventually, and subjected to many other kinds of negative social pressures until he made a public apology.

From the Japanese manager's point of view, one accepts a rather open-ended commitment to do all that is necessary in the interests of the company when one accepts a permanent position with the firm. Moreover, the prosperity of the company is viewed as a necessity for the survival of all individuals in the company. In addition, managers believe in the often mentioned Japanese cultural values of sacrifice for the good of the whole—a collectivist ideal—and giving a project all of your possible effort without restriction. Finally, the Japanese managers believe that their formal authority represents experience and judgment that should be respected by subordinates. Thus, Japanese managers do not view heavy work demands as inhumane or unethical at all.

The Differential Treatment of Inside Groups and Outsiders

The Japanese have often been strongly criticized for not really accepting outsiders and for also providing differential treatment for various insider groups. For example, Katzenstein (1989), the U.S. computer specialist who took a job with Sony, felt that the company's refusal to recognize his two advanced degrees and his advanced knowledge over his peers, as well as his desire to be free of dormitory restrictions and to have the right to associate with female workers, was unfair and unethical. Also, many Western observers in Japan, especially feminists, have been very critical of the reluctance of the

Box 6.5 Dormitory Life for Japanese Women

A study was made of the life of female office workers in a large Japanese company. The dormitory in many ways seems like a prison in terms of its rules and security arrangements. For example, to enter the dormitory, one must first pass a cast-iron fence with spikes and barbed wire on the top. Next, one must pass through a cast-iron door that is locked between the hours of 9:30 p.m. and 6:00 a.m. Then, there are two glass doors before reaching the reception area, which is under the observation of the dormitory supervisor who lives there in an apartment with his family. Records are kept of those who enter and leave the dormitory and where all dormitory residents are at a particular time. There are many rules to follow, and written permission must be obtained from the dormitory supervisor to stay away overnight, as when visiting one's parents. The rules are published in a 40-page booklet, issued to all dormitory residents, titled "Happy Dormitory Life." Punishments are received for violating rules. For example, those who come home 10 minutes late after the 9:30 p.m. curfew could receive a punishment of washing the bathrooms at 6:00 a.m. for 1 week. None of the residents smokes or drinks in the dormitory.

SOURCE: Lo (1990).

Japanese to change the lower status and opportunities of women (Carroll, 1992; Lo, 1990).

As we have seen, Japan has always differentiated various groups within its society, in the name of the achievement of social stability and the minimization of internal turbulence. Certainly, looking at the extreme social turbulence and conflict in other nations has given many Japanese the feeling that their system of group relations is the most effective one. In a historical sense, as an isolated nation, Japan has always feared outsiders to some extent and the old Japanese folk saying, "Regard all strangers as enemies," still holds true to some extent. Also, there has always been occupational specialization by groups within nations, and in Japan this seems natural. In addition, Japanese groups are expected to accept their roles and not complain of differences in treatment. Furthermore, there appears to be little complaint in Japan of such differentiated treatment, although some discontent is rising. Thus, even among those who by Western standards would seem to be oppressed, such as Japanese women (see Box 6.5), there is often a great deal of acceptance of such differentiation (see Reischauer, 1981). Some say that one reason for this acceptance is that most Japanese women do not actually see themselves being in the underdog position that many Western women do and even see advantages for themselves in this differentiated society (Reischauer, 1988). Among such perceived advantages are the ability to enjoy family life, to be free of the tremendous work pressures exerted on men, and to be in control of one's time and also the family's financial resources. A recent study of female graduating seniors at a private Tokyo university indicated that very few had any interest at all in a management or a professional career even if this were readily available to them, as it is at least in foreign firms in Japan (Araka et al., 1992).

▧ CONCLUSIONS

In looking at the characteristics of Japanese culture and how aspects of that culture have been transmitted to managers through parenting, the educational system, and the managerial HRM systems of companies, we can gain an understanding of why such managers behave as they do. We see, for example, why Japanese managers tend to view non-Japanese managers with suspicion. Outsiders are to be treated very much differently from insiders. Outsiders to Japanese managers may also include minority ethnic peoples in Japan or even, in many cases, women. In general, outsiders are to be ignored, and often not to be trusted, and sometimes considered to be an enemy.

We can also see from the perspective of Japanese cultural characteristics that the Japanese in general feel a greater sense of unity with the state and all Japanese people and institutions within that state than do the citizens of other nations. The nation as a whole is looked on as a giant family. Plausibly the most important value that we find in any group conceptualized as a family is that of mutual help and assistance. These factors, along with the cultural imperative to cooperate and to avoid conflict and disagreement, operate to produce not only closer relationships between business managers and government officials than we find in other countries but also closer relationships among home country firms than in virtually all other countries. It's not surprising that a Japanese trading company would prefer to work with an in-country firm than with a foreign company.

What outsiders see as discrimination, the Japanese see as the normal nature of things. In Japanese history, groups have been differentiated, each with its own specialized roles and responsibilities, with little mobility among them. There is a tradition of inherited jobs. Reserving certain jobs for only members of a particular group is very much a part of the traditional Japanese culture.

The borrowing of technological ideas from other cultures by Japan has been viewed as something related to national survival. Japan has had enemies throughout its history, making it wary of other nations. It has never really had a strong ally on whom it could rely in an armed conflict. It has had to depend on itself in these situations. This again leads to cooperation and a feeling of untrustworthiness of outside peoples.

The very long hours and heavy pressures put on domestic employees in Japanese companies certainly reflect the basic cultural belief that effort is everything and that *gambare* is something you should have. These attitudes were certainly functional for life in a very poor country with few resources.

Sometimes, the Japanese are accused by Americans of failing to fulfill promised terms in contractual arrangements. This has been called unethical behavior. However, in the Japanese culture there is a different perspective on agreements among people. The Japanese are believers in the context of a situation. If the context changes, than the situation is different and has to be handled differently. Western culture views things as immutable once they are written down.

Such differences in fundamental perspectives can lead to conclusions that one is acting unethically when one is simply seeing things from the perspective of a different culture. We can see from this analysis that culture does appear to significantly affect managerial behavior. Such behavior is often viewed differently in terms of ethicality, depending on the cultural perspective of the viewer.

◩ DISCUSSION QUESTIONS

1. Under what conditions would you accept the regimented dormitory life at work that is described in Box 6.5? Why?

2. Analyze the eight critical incidents or short cases presented in Table 6.2 from the perspectives of American culture and your American subculture, such as Irish American, if appropriate. How would the values, attitudes, and behaviors differ from those described?

3. Under what conditions would you accept all aspects of the orientation program at Japan Ink and Chemical Co.? Are there any features of this program that you would absolutely refuse to accept? Why?

4. Do you feel that managers tend to treat employees in Japan unethically? Why or why not?

5. Would you ever accept a job situation in which you knew that there was a good possibility of becoming a *karoshi* victim? Why or why not?

6. Analyze the performance appraisal form in Table 6.1. How does it differ from standard American performance appraisal forms?

7. According to Hofstede's research, Japan ranks #22/23 out of 53 nations on individualism. This suggests that the Japanese are far more individualistic in orientation than other nationalities. How can this finding be reconciled with the Japanese emphasis on harmony and conformity?

7

Culture and Managerial Ethical Behaviors

An In-Depth Look at the United States

The Medicaid Case

A drugstore chain was accused of double billing and using fraudulent billings for Medicaid patients. It was found guilty after several of its executives admitted to employing these practices. The fine of $50,000 was only a fraction, however, of the earnings from the fraudulent behavior. The company agreed to make restitution of $500,000 to the State of Ohio Public Welfare Department. Two executives were fined $2,000 each.

Blumberg (1987, pp. 244-247)

Government Bond Case

The U.S. Treasury bond market is a massive activity, with more than $100 billion in U.S. government bonds traded daily. The economic stability of the nation, and to some extent the rest of the world, rests on perceptions that order, fairness, and efficiency exist in the buying and selling of such bonds. To ensure that these goals are met, the U.S. Treasury has established rules to guarantee competitiveness in this market. In the second half of 1991, Salomon Brothers, a Wall Street firm, was accused of intentionally violating these rules so as to achieve domination of this market by itself and to enhance its own profits. The firm's managing director of government bond trading manipulated bids by falsifying buyer names so that the firm could obtain a high volume of bonds at low prices, which in turn could have escalated bids to absurd levels. Also, it was revealed that the firm's chairman, vice chairman, president, and internal and outside counsel failed to disclose their knowledge of trading violations to the Treasury. It was reported that the chairman and others were angry and resentful that their actions were being penalized by government agencies such as the Department of Justice *and the SEC. According to some firm employees, the motivations of the chief government bond trader reflected primarily an ego factor rather than a desire for high profits.*

Aram (1993, pp. 7-9)

The Dalkon Shield Case

A. H. Robins Company bought the rights to a birth control device, the Dalkon shield, from its inventors in 1970. It was able to rush the product to market quickly in 1971, because at the time medical devices like the shield were not regulated by the Food and Drug Administration and did not have to be tested for any harmful effects on users. By 1972, an estimated 1 million shields had been placed in women around the world, 3 million in the United States. The company widely advertised the product as trouble free in spite of many reports to the contrary from physicians. In 1973, some studies attributed hospitalization for complicated pregnancies and some deaths to use of the shield. In 1974, the company stopped marketing the device; by March 1975, more than 186 court suits had been filed against the company; and by 1980, more than 4,300 suits were pending against the company. All this time, the company and its managers had engaged in what many felt were unethical behaviors. The product had been assigned for marketing to its Chap Stick Division, which had no competence with medical products. The company failed to test the product and relied upon the biased research of its inventors; it also covered up all adverse reports and misled customers, physicians, and everybody else about the dangers in this product. Furthermore, the company concentrated entirely on defending itself in a strictly legal way and showed no concern for the plight of those injured by its product. In February of 1984, a judge dealing with a combined suit against the company, brought by seven women seriously injured by the device, rebuked three company executives standing before him in the courtroom:

> *And when the time came for these women to make their claims against your company, you attacked their characters. You inquired into their sexual practices and into the identity of their sex partners. You ruined families and reputations and careers in order to intimidate those who would raise their voices against you. You introduced issues that had no relationship to the fact that you had planted in the bodies of these women instruments of death, of mutilation, of disease. . . . Another of your callous legal tactics is to force women of little means to withstand the onslaughts of your well-financed team of attorneys. You target your*

*worse tactics at the meek and the poor. . . . You have taken the bottom
line as your guiding beacon and the low road as your route.*

Hartley (1991, pp. 349-350)

Recently, the ethical behavior of U.S. managers has come under intense scrutiny. The media and the general public in the United States have become increasingly concerned about the ethics of American managers. Some of this concern reflects very well publicized cases of the ethical behavior of companies, as shown in the introductory cases. In the middle of the 1980s, the *New York Times* said that the news from business "has been reading like a drawn-out Hollywood script of corruption. A corporate crime wave appears to be exploding across the nation" (Williams, 1985, p. 4). Morgan (1988), a recent immigrant from France who has very positive opinions about the United States, nevertheless states:

> Businessmen, who once thought of themselves as the stewards of economic and social order, are now seen as polluters and plunderers. . . . Adam Smith's invisible hand went arthritic, and all these great ideas, like private ownership of capital, profit, free enterprise, efficiency, and technology, ended up ruining the environment, impoverishing the human spirit, fostering worldwide corruption, and contributing to international instability. (pp. 273-274)

Morgan also states that fraud has been an integral part of this country's history and, in fact, the American virtues of ingenuity, hard work, and know-how have been applied in this country to illegal gain for many years. A national survey of the country conducted by the Gallup Polling Company, in 1993, indicates that only 20% of the respondents rated business executives high on honesty and ethics, down from 23% just a few years ago (see Item 7.1).

It is not only businessmen whose ethical behavior is increasingly being called into question. Our newspapers regularly bombard their readers with stories about citizens who cheat on their welfare benefits, workers who cheat on their unemployment benefits, school teachers who abuse students and overuse their sick leave provisions, government officials of all types who are guilty of accepting bribes and favors, students who cheat on examinations, and even professors and scholars

Item 7.1

A Gallup poll in the United States indicated that in 1993, only 20% of the respondents rated business executives as high or very high in honesty and ethics. This was down by 3% since 1985. The business executives were rated higher in honesty and ethics than were members of Congress and stockbrokers but lower than journalists, newspaper reporters, and TV commentators.

SOURCE: *The Washington Post* (May 21, 1994, p. F1).

who are sometimes found guilty of plagiarism, stealing the work of students without giving them credit, and even falsifying research data.

On the other hand, it can be argued that ethical behavior in all aspects of American life has improved significantly over the years. After all, a look at American history, and especially industrial practices, hardly gives one an indication that the past was necessarily more ethical than the present. Monopolies, cartels, violent labor disputes, dangerous foods and drugs sold to the public, shoddy goods produced and sold to consumers and the government, the complete lack of private benefits for ordinary workers, and no social safety net at all constituted the state of affairs. The subject of business ethics was certainly not discussed at the time; there were no codes of ethics; there was little professionalization of management; and there were very few if any regulations of business in any age. As Benjamin Franklin once said, throughout human history the golden age is never at the present time.

◳ AMERICAN CULTURAL CHARACTERISTICS

Outside Observers of the American Culture

Arguably, outsiders are the ones who are best suited for observing a culture accurately. They have a certain emotional detachment that insiders do not have and also possess a basis of comparison, which is necessary in any type of evaluative process. To an outsider, certain cultural aspects may be noticed as "figure," but to insiders, they are "ground" and not especially salient. Certainly, Julius Caesar, in his commentaries, made very insightful observations about the culture of the Gauls, and Lafcadio Hearn did the same for the Japanese.

In *Democracy in America,* published in 1840, the French writer Alexis de Tocqueville (1840/1945) wrote extensively about the American character as he found it at that time. Many believe that his comments about the national American character are still valid in spite of the many years that have passed. Of course, Tocqueville was primarily interested in the political system of the United States and especially in the concepts of democracy and equality, because America represented such a different perspective from what existed in both Europe and the rest of the world at that time. In spite of his heavy emphasis on the concept of equality, including its origins and its consequences not only for political institutions but also for everyday behavior, he pointed out that there are many cultural factors other than equality that account for the behavior of Americans.

For example, Tocqueville emphasized the critical importance of individualism and especially the tendency to depend on oneself for moral guidance rather than on group standards. According to Tocqueville, Americans tend to reject philosophical and religious theories and in fact frequently do not even expose themselves to them. He felt that the system of democracy itself forces human beings to look to themselves for their moral standards. In spite of the heavy emphasis on individualism in America, it was softened by the many voluntary associations of Americans, which he felt were much more extensive than in any other nation. Of course, membership in such organizations does not mean that persons allow their lives to be controlled by these groups. They can serve merely as a vehicle for advancing one's self-interests. He argued, however, that, ultimately, unbridled individualism without a social commitment to others might eventually undermine democracy in America.

Tocqueville was struck also by what he saw as the American passion for accumulating wealth or riches, which he felt far exceeded that found in Europe. He thought that this was partly because the social distinctions in America tend to be based on wealth rather than on other factors, such as family background, which are more important in other nations. Thus, a democratic country gives rise to higher ambition, because opportunities for social mobility are higher than in more traditional societies. According to Tocqueville, this strong desire for wealth in turn creates work habits and behaviors that are conducive to this activity, including hostility to interferences with the accumulating of wealth. Such barriers to wealth include not only government rules and regulations but also moral laxity that impedes domestic life and orderly habits. Logically, such sexual mores are influenced by the fact that higher equality means more attention to love as a basis for marriage than basing marriages on property

Item 7.2

A difference in opinion about the morality of a firm's using bankruptcy as a defense against economic problems is indicated in two discussions of this issue in *The Wall Street Journal*. A Japanese CEO points out that, unlike what seems to be the prevailing sentiment in the United States, bankruptcy in Japan is seen as a social "sin" and that a Japanese company going into bankruptcy has no future. This Japanese CEO indicates he was very surprised to find that U.S. companies that have gone bankrupt can still operate.

SOURCE: *The Wall Street Journal* (Hamaji, 1994).

considerations. In addition, Tocqueville says that their admiration of wealth accumulation also makes Americans much more tolerant of the risk-taking behaviors, and their inevitable consequences of bankruptcy, than is found in other nations (see Item 7.2).

Tocqueville identified other American characteristics such as the suspicion, and even great antagonism, toward government, especially the national government. These are not surprising attitudes, given the origin of the nation and the fact that its population in many cases fled oppressive governments in other countries or was forcibly sent to the colonies by other governments as punishments for crimes. Finally, Tocqueville felt that the modern nation exemplified by the United States would eventually lead to a society where differences in material well-being will be diminished and, as a result, many positive social effects, such as lower social turbulence, will occur.

Another Frenchman, Jean Baudrillard, visited America recently and has commented on America today in contrast to Tocqueville's report written some 150 years earlier (Baudrillard, 1988). Like Tocqueville he was struck by the extreme self-absorption of Americans—hooked into their own brains and not those of others. To him, Americans seem totally preoccupied with themselves—their careers, their psychological needs, and even their bodies. He seems to find Americans shallow, without deep spiritual moral reserves; he also feels the country as a whole is primitive in the sense that it has no past of significance that provides lessons for modern life. Also, he believes that Tocqueville, in his laudatory treatment of America, overlooked the lack of equality for many groups, such as Native Americans and African Americans. However, Baudrillard still believes that Americans are not much different in a basic sense from the way their ancestors were when Tocqueville arrived many years ago. They still tend to be utopian and pragmatic and very different in their outlook and perspectives from Europeans, because philosophies and thought patterns did not easily travel to America from the Continent. He also does find in America an enormous amount of conformity to rules and customs that its people agree upon, and he is quite taken with the naturalness and candor of Americans and their lack of prejudice and pretentiousness. According to Baudrillard, America is democratic but not egalitarian. Thus, it is important that everyone starts out equal but not that they end the race at the same place. He sees some hostility to the new emphasis on giving a great deal of attention to the needs of the formerly disadvantaged. With respect to the future, he also describes trends in America that may be leading to a deemphasis on rewards for individual achievement. Moreover, he speculates that there is an emerging emphasis on the importance of maintaining traditional values and the need for unity among the various groups making up the nation.

A third profile of America was completed by still another Frenchman, who recently changed his name to Ted Morgan from le comte de Gramont. He is from a French aristocratic family and has become a U.S. citizen. In general, he is positive about his new country. His book (Morgan, 1988), like those of his two French predecessors, examines the American character and comes to conclusions similar to theirs. More specifically, he lists 10 American traits that he feels explain many of their behaviors, some of which were mentioned by Tocqueville.

Puritanism is the first and it includes trying to live a virtuous life, a certain amount of hypocrisy because ideals cannot be attained, and looking to oneself for spiritual guidance. The second trait is altruism. Among other evidence, he points to the large amount of money given to charity in the United States. Third, Americans exhibit an anti-intellectualism or a lack of reverence for theories, great ideas, or very intelligent people. Fourth, he sees provincialism or a lack interest in the rest of the world as an American trait. Fifth, there is the success cult or a preoccupation with achievement on the part of everybody. Sixth, there is exploitation, which refers to using up resources and the environment and resenting attempts to stop this behavior. Seventh is an emphasis on a belief in the possibility of perfectibility in life and its many roles. Morgan termed the eighth trait as fraud and moral accounting. He believes widespread fraud and cheating of others have been common in the nation since its beginning, partly due to a lack of controls and partly to a certain amount of American ingenuity in promoting illegal gain for themselves. The ninth trait is good sportsmanship, as when most political losers accept their losses well. It is part of an American concern for fairness and for accepting defeat if the game was played according to the rules. Finally, we have the characteristic of individualism, which he profiles as an emphasis on self-reliance. However, like Tocqueville, he is struck by the frequency by which such individualists commonly join voluntary organizations. Still, he does not see this as a contradiction. Rather, voluntary organizations represent a means by which individuals defend themselves against perceived enemies and enhance their individual egos.

Another recent European, the Dutch psychologist Geert Hofstede (1991), carried out research on individuals in one company in 53 countries, as indicated earlier. This study demonstrated that, relative to other countries, the United States was the highest country on the individualism dimension. The United States also was moderately low on power distance, medium on uncertainty avoidance, and moderately high on masculinity. Thus, Hofstede's study provides more evidence that Americans value individual initiative and achievement, are not much concerned with the needs of society as a whole, believe in the right of the individual to make his or her own decisions, and tend to be more motivated by individual rather than group work assignments. In addition, they tend to be more assertive, materialistic, and action-oriented than other peoples; are less accepting of authority; and can handle ambiguous situations fairly well. The United States clustered with the other Anglo-Saxon nations on these dimensions. Still, using Hofstede's data alone might give a misperception of the realities of differences among nations. As compared to Australians, for example, Americans tend to be higher on an emphasis on material achievement, lower on humanistic values, and higher on success orientation, competition, and risk taking (Deresky, 1994). Nevertheless, Americans are closer to Australians than they are to most other nationalities around the world.

Other foreign writers have explored other aspects of American cultural attitudes and their causes. For example, Evans (1976) has summarized the views of many European writers such as Charles Dickens, Evelyn Waugh, Franz Kafka, Graham Greene, Simone de Beauvoir, Vladimir Nabokov, and several others who have described the American nation and character in essays and other writings. As in the case of previous observers, several characteristics of Americans have intrigued them but other characteristics have repelled them. Evans (1976) also points out that many such writers have commented upon the antiauthoritarian bias both in American institutions and among individual Americans. Some of these writers have even theorized that this bias has evolved because America was created out of the rejection of paternal authority in the early settlers' homelands. In addition, other writers such as Dickens have argued that dissent from religious authority in other countries was also often a characteristic of immigrants. All of these observers, however, have not necessarily looked favorably at this antiauthority orientation. Dickens held, for example, that freedom from tyranny produces the right to tyrannize others. This theme of too much liberty that in turn gives way to excessive license to hurt others has also been mentioned by other European writers (Evans, 1976) and they frequently cite the unethical treatment of minorities in the United States as an example. European writers also identify excessive wastefulness and extravagance as American characteristics, not only in terms of wasting environmental resources such as land, water, fish, and the like but also in tendencies to build too high, decorate too lavishly, travel too fast, and so on. This wastefulness and extravagance are sometimes attributed not only to the abundance of natural and other resources found in the nation in its early years (the psychology of affluence) but also to what is viewed as an excess of energy, or perhaps the lack of a sense of moderation in the culture itself. Thus, some European intellectuals are fascinated by the American desire to be the best, the fastest, the biggest, and so on. Some European writers have said that this desire to be the best in a visible way reflects an American suspicion of the nature of intrinsic worth or unquantifiable quality (Evans, 1976). They are oriented toward success, but that success must be obvious in visible terms such as money or quantity or size. There has been speculation by some Europeans on what underlies this perspective. One conjecture is that Americans are really seeking goodness and virtue and this must be demonstrated in a quantifiable way.

Some Recent U.S. Observers

In his metaphorical look at 17 nations, Gannon (Gannon & Associates, 1994) chooses American football as his metaphor for the United States. He points out that even though this is a team sport, there are many awards (named after individuals) that are given to players for individual achievement. In addition to national awards (e.g., the Heisman trophy and the Lombardi award), virtually every team at each level of football also bestows individual awards at the end of the season. The game seems to reflect enduring American values of equality of opportunity, independence, initiative, self-reliance, and aggressiveness in addition to a high degree of competitiveness. There is little pity for losing teams. Players, although given a very specific assigned role on a team, are expected to be creative and to act appropriately for the situation. The teams are made up of players with very diverse socioeconomic, racial, and ethnic backgrounds. They also tend to have various support organizations such as bands and cheerleaders. Football is a highly organized activity with large complex organizations, consisting of many specialists such as trainers, equipment managers, public relations and marketing personnel in addition to many specialized coaches and the various players themselves. Like business firms, they employ a great deal of specialized equipment and advanced technologies to pursue team objectives. Gannon points out that the huddle before a play, which is used by both the defensive and offensive teams, reflects a type of structured decision making that has been very characteristic of American life since the beginning of its history. Of course, football teams, like many other American organizations, are constantly changing their members. On teams, it is performance that counts and loyalty is not necessarily rewarded.

In their book *American Cultural Patterns*, Stewart and Bennett (1991) point out that the United States is a gesellschaft society, which relies on formal and contractual ties. It is not a gemeinschaft society, which relies on established customs and traditions, although early in its history it was. They also show that America really includes a number of subcultures or variations in culture that must be recognized and they feel that these internal cultural variations have been insufficiently stressed in analyses of American cultural characteristics. Perhaps one of the most interesting and distinctive approaches these authors take in analyzing Americans is in focusing on typical U.S. thinking or reasoning patterns in contrast to those of people in other cultures. In the American model of perception and thinking, there is a heavy emphasis on personal agency or an individual's responsibilities for his or her situations, because these depend on individual decision making and judgment. This belief in human agency causes Americans to try to warn people in advance at certain choice points. This is not done in other cultures. They point out that Americans are not abstract thinkers, like many Europeans, but tend to be very empirical. They think inductively and in operational terms and they want evidence for assertions that are made. Another aspect of American thinking that Stewart and Bennett highlight is the ability to think in terms of the probabilities of events and they indicate that this ability is by no means universal in other cultures.

Of course, we are more interested in the ethical behaviors of American managers and not of Americans in general. Peterson and George-Falvy (1993) have written more specifically about managers in the United States and their characteristics. They state that a professional managerial class primarily arose in the United States after World War II and in private rather than in public companies. Unlike that of many other nations, managerial professional training is quite extensive in the United States. Most managers have received undergraduate or graduate training in business schools in the United States. Those who have not received such education often take specialized training courses, taught by business school professors in companies or in university executive development programs. Peterson and George-Falvy describe how such programs socialize managers to accept certain fundamental principles, including the values of individualism, the rights of private property, the primary role of the market in economic activity, the right to accumulate individual wealth and profits, and the desirability of freedom from government control. Although individual managers differ in their attitudes about these matters, they tend to agree more than they disagree on these and other values. Also, the authors review research that has focused on American managerial values, which tends to show that American managers have a high regard for achievement and success, hard work, efficiency and pragmatism, optimism, puritanism, scientific thinking, impersonality in interpersonal work relationships, equality of opportunity in getting ahead, and in the acceptance of competition as a fact of life.

Newman (1970), a leading scholar of American management, has also written about the values of American managers that affect their ethical behaviors. He points out that American managers believe in a "master of destiny" concept; that is, what happens is the result of self-determination and the individual's efforts and choices. They are not as prone to attribute circumstances to "fate" and to "bad luck" as are those in other cultures. Furthermore, he suggests that U.S. managers tend to a *pragmatic realism,* which means that they are not too idealistic in their thinking and that what works is accepted as right or correct. American managers also know, and expect, that things will go wrong and that nobody is necessarily to blame. Thus, they tend not to be Monday-morning quarterbacks. Newman also emphasizes that American managers are firm believers in commitments and living up to promises and implied contractual terms. This orientation extends to a belief in the importance of loyalty to the firm. All of these characteristics suggest that American managers place a high value on predictability and dependability. Also, perhaps because of this, they have a preference and a belief in an objective analysis of situations as opposed to the use of intuitive feelings. Finally, Newman points to the widespread acceptance among American managers of the notion of improvement and change, and a bias against maintaining the status quo, which is unlike managerial thinking in some other cultures.

Item 7.3

Notes from a Japanese negotiator:

1. Americans are difficult for the Japanese to understand. One reason for this is that they are different from each other. Those from small towns are different from those from cities. They differ also because of religious differences and regional differences.
2. Americans in negotiating like to feel they have won something and then like to gloat about it.
3. Americans like to take one problem at a time. They fail to see how all of these problems are linked together.
4. The Americans are very ethnocentric but they are not aware of this. They also think their success comes from knowing the truth.

SOURCE: Felicita (1994).

Subcultures Within the United States

Even though we can describe a modal personality (Hofstede, 1980a, 1980b) for a society that represents a national culture's typical characteristics, all societies are made up of subcultures. This is especially so in the United States, which is a nation of immigrants, and where, according to Baudrillard (1988), a "terrifying diversity" exists. In addition to ethnic and racial subcultures, a Japanese observer has pointed to regional and urban-rural subcultural differences among Americans (see Item 7.3). Because of such subcultures, there is great variability in the behavior of individuals, which is true of not only managers but also other occupational groups. However, subgroup membership is only one of many factors that tend to influence an individual's beliefs, perceptions, and behaviors. Members of ethnic subgroups within a nation often face a dilemma of conforming to either subgroup norms and values or those of the larger majority.

Bowers (1944) in his *Foreign Influences in American Life,* includes a number of essays that deal with the subject of assimilation of immigrants into the American culture. These essays indicate that only in some ways and at some times did the melting pot concept and programs for creating assimilation work. There has always been some separation of ethnic and racial groups in the United States. This may be less today than formerly, when U.S. cities were divided into ethnic neighborhoods, and woe to the teenager who had to travel through or attend school in another group's neighborhood. Bowers indicates that immigrants typically feel "culturally marginal" and second- and third-generation immigrants have conflicting feelings about their status. In certain instances, conflicts between the present nation (United States) and their ancestral homeland had an enormous impact on such individuals, forcing them to choose one reference culture over another. In the case of German Americans, it was World War I (Luebke, 1978); and for Japanese Americans, it was World War II (Daniels, 1978). In both of these cases, highly accommodationist stances occurred and the influence of the subculture itself greatly diminished. In the case of Native Americans, extreme factionalism and tribal differences among the Indian nations have made it almost impossible for a unified Indian subculture to emerge (Berkhofer, 1978). For African Americans, on the other hand, the subgroup cultural unity has often been quite strong, probably because of the high degree of discriminatory treatment and bias shown this group over time by the majority population (Huggins, 1978). For example, the higher degree of helping behavior found among African Americans than in the general population, and perhaps even tendencies to form gangs, may reflect this fact (e.g., see Liebow, 1967). On the other hand, after centuries of living in the United States, African Americans probably have little in common with people from Africa (Baldwin, 1955). Other ethnic cultures, such as the Irish Americans, Jewish Americans, and Eastern-European Americans, have perhaps had only moderate influences on the behavior and thinking of their members, given the lower levels of discrimination experienced and also because it was possible for them to ultimately pass successfully into the majority culture (Higham, 1978).

Some of the influence of a subculture on its members probably depends in large part on the degree to which a person from a subculture is immersed in that group versus living primarily in the majority group. For example, Japanese Americans, Italian Americans, or Irish Americans who live in ethnic neighborhoods in the United States are probably far more affected by their subcultures than their counterparts living within the majority culture (Higham, 1978). There is evidence that the number of American contacts and degree of English spoken in the home are related to the cultural assimilation of immigrants from non-English speaking countries (Kagan & Cohen, 1990). We should remember, however, that it does seem to be a fact that there is not nearly so much diversity in the ranks of management at the top of organizations as there is at lower levels, which would suggest that the ethical behaviors of managers would tend toward some uniformity. The research in fact indicates that American managers are quite similar in many ways, including their ethical propensities and actual behavior.

▨ THE TRANSMISSION OF CULTURE TO AMERICAN MANAGERS

The managerial class in the United States probably began after the Civil War (1870s), when rapid industrialization shifted from self-employment to working for industrial organizations. Overall, however, there was not a significant proportion of the labor force in management positions until after World War II (late 1940s and 1950s), when American companies expanded greatly in size, which led to the creation of many line and staff management positions. Currently, the category of executive, administrative, and managerial workers now includes about 10% of the entire labor force (Peterson & George-Falvy, 1993).

Managers in the United States have considerable legitimacy and autonomy, primarily because of their rights under the concept of private property that derived originally from the English legal system (Bendix, 1956). They also have considerable status as compared to individuals in other fields. This is much more true of private company managers than of managers in the public and nonprofit sectors. The high salaries of managers in the United States, when contrasted to those in other careers, probably contribute to this perception. Unfortunately, such prominent status and high earnings of U.S. managers may be associated with a very strong sense of superiority and arrogance. After all, why would a manager earning millions of dollars a year be motivated to accept ideas and suggestions from somebody earning far less? Would not such managers feel that their high earnings reflect their superiority in terms of knowledge, skills, and abilities?

U.S. Educational System

The socialization of managers begins in childhood in the public school system (for most managers), continues through college and organizational training programs, and is shaped by the organization's human resource management practices. The educational process in the United States primarily emphasizes individual performance and, often, competitive performance against one's peers. There is not the emphasis on cooperation and sharing that one finds in the Japanese educational system, for example. American students are taught about the superiority of Americans as a people and America as a nation of destiny, compared to most others in the world. This seems to have generally produced a marked ethnocentrism. It has been said that this gives Americans a certain arrogance toward other peoples and their ideas, something that was noted by the French observer Tocqueville in his travels around America more than 150 years ago, and more recently by other foreign observers, as noted previously.

American Literature as a Socialization Influence

As indicated earlier, the literature of a nation often captures its cultural characteristics quite well, because it often involves an analysis of some type of cultural ideal as compared to cultural realities. Of course, much of the more popular literature of a nation may focus primarily on the ideal and not on the reality. Literature also affects behavior because it is often incorporated into the memory. Its influence may be direct to the reader or indirect from readers to others, in the form of behaviors or training. American literature, especially popular literature, historically has often supported the cultural values of individualism, upward mobility, the classless society, and the desirability of high individual achievement. Much of this literature was mandatory for many years in the U.S. public and private educational systems. Literary characters can exemplify or illustrate culturally important traits, such as the feudal loyalty often idealized in Japanese literature (e.g., mass suicides in honor of a departed lord). In addition, such characters can serve as role models or positive/negative examples for managers or for those critical of managerial behavior who wish to regulate it.

In the early days of America, certain writings were probably quite influential in establishing a distinctive American ideal, which became part of the culture. Benjamin Franklin (1732/1936) developed many ideas in his *Poor Richard's Almanac,* which might be called distinctively American, as contrasted to a European view. Certainly, his maxims and normative suggestions for the importance of self-control, self-effort, self-reference, and hard work are examples of these. One of the most influential early literary American figures was Ralph Waldo Emerson, a clergyman and then an author who wrote and toured the nation, giving lectures that were quite normative in their focus (Rohler, 1995). He was a very famous and influential person at the time who established the public lecture as not only a very popular source of entertainment but also the primary method for public education in the United States. Emerson's influence on the thinking of Americans appeared to be quite significant, perhaps not only through his direct lectures and writings but also through his considerable influence on the literary community, such as the family of Louisa May Alcott and other writers living in the Boston area. Upper- and middle-class families would read his famous essays on various topics (1841, 1844) to each other in the evening. In some of his writings and lectures, he advocated a distinctively American view and philosophy and a rejection of European cultural views. In his famous and widely read essay *On Self Reliance,* he stressed the importance of nonconformity and letting your own ideas be your guide irrespective of what others think. In this essay, he also preached the importance of achievement through one's efforts without the crutch of inheritance or other outside support. Of course, other early writers such as Hawthorne, in *The Scarlet Letter,* attacked the unfairness of the community and the group and their distorted thinking in their treatment of individuals. Later, great American writers such as Henry James extolled the virtues of the free American woman, as compared to those who were members of a more stifling European aristocracy (James, 1984).

In terms of providing role models, Bendix (1956) has discussed the popular literature of America in the past century, which emphasized the concept of the Horatio Alger stories. These were stories of poor individuals who rose to fame and fortune through high individual effort and performance. He pointed out that this literature was critical in the development of cultural ideas, especially among the middle and upper classes. Certainly, the popular culture literature of the U.S. West, and the conquest of the frontier through individual effort, were common themes in American literature and still are, for that matter. The individualistic and self-directed cowboy as the central hero in the Western novel (and Western movies) became the embodiment of prized American values and a defender of a national code of honor. In many stories and movies, the theme was the moral individual in conflict with corrupt groups and communities, winning in the end at least partly through not only greater moral character but also through adherence to American cultural ideals.

Although the specific genre of the business novel does not exist in the United States as it does in Japan, some literature specifically focuses on the issues of careers and the workplace itself. For example, some of Eugene O'Neill's plays, such as *Long Day's Journey Into Night* and *The Iceman Cometh* (O'Neill, 1950, 1957), do deal to some extent with American perspectives on success and failure, the importance of rising to the top, and how the top is often identified in a material way.

Some of Arthur Miller's plays focus more directly on the workplace (Miller, 1957). His *Death of a Salesman* highlights not only the success syndrome in American life but also the attendant widespread sense of failure and disappointment when hoped-for achievements of oneself or one's offspring are not realized; this play describes specific ethical issues in management. The firing of the primary character, after many years of faithful service to the company, reflects a common ethical criticism of the U.S. business system. Miller's play *All My Sons* describes the unethical behavior of a businessman who puts his firm's and his family's interests above those of society as a whole, and represents an early attempt to identify a stakeholder concept in managing a business; that is, managers have responsibilities to those beyond their immediate family. Another Miller play, *A Memory of Two Mondays,* illustrates both the often transitory nature of employment relationships in U.S. companies and the psychological consequences of an inability to establish satisfying personal relationships on the job because of this. Of course, these more literary treatments of the American culture were not positive about American ideals and values and represented the view of critical intellectuals in the society. In addition, only a small, more highly educated segment of the population was exposed to them, although this group is often influential in many ways.

In a more positive view of business and American values, popular magazines of the 1930s and 1940s such as the *Saturday Evening Post* often had many short stories describing the ingenuity and resourcefulness of the individual business figure. The novelist Ayn Rand (1943, 1957) in more recent years has written novels such as *The Fountainhead* and *Atlas Shrugged,* which have sold in the millions and have extolled the virtues of the heroic individual fighting an oppressive group or collectivist system. A few more popular or mass cult business novels over the years, such as *Disclosure* (Crichton, 1994), have also championed the individual manager fighting an oppressive organization and ultimately succeeding.

Over the years, certain books have strongly attacked the ethicality of the business system itself in very persuasive ways. These would include Ida Tarbell's *The History of the Standard Oil Company* (1904), Upton Sinclair's *The Jungle* (1906), Theodore Dreiser's *The Financier* (1912), and Sinclair Lewis's *Babbitt* (1922). These books were often used in college courses and were probably chosen by professors sympathetic to the ideas expressed; they were perhaps useful in identifying bad or unethical examples of managerial behaviors, or at least that was their intention. Certainly, these books ultimately did influence American political thinking about the issue of business ethics and social responsibility, and some did have a role in changing the regulatory environment of American business.

As indicated previously in Chapter 5, the behavior of managers in any nation is significantly affected by the nature of the organizational human resource management practices to which they are subjected. These practices determine the types of individuals selected and promoted, and the job behaviors taught, evaluated, and rewarded. Such practices represent specific activities designed to socialize American managers as to what companies demand and expect. Again, such systems may also serve to override individual values or propensities for certain actions stemming from individual values or beliefs.

Recruitment and Selection of U.S. Managers

Although, in the distant past, many U.S. managers worked their way up to and through the managerial ranks from the position of ordinary worker, virtually all managers today are college educated (Peterson & George-Falvy, 1993). In the United States, this does not mean that all the college graduates are likely to be similar in their personal characteristics (social class, etc.), because of the wide diversity in colleges and universities in the United States as compared to other countries. However, a significant proportion of U.S. managers do have business or engineering degrees, both of which tend to emphasize pragmatic and technological/scientific values in the educational process. This tends to produce some uniformity. Also, in the United States, as compared to those in other countries, there is far more diversity among managers with respect to demographic characteristics. For example, in 1987, roughly 38% of managers at all levels were women and 10% were minorities (Peterson & George-Falvy, 1993). There are a number of documented studies indicating some significant differences in general in the ethical values and behaviors of Caucasian men versus women and minorities. Thus, this diversity in hiring is likely to create some diversity in reactions to different ethical situations. On the other hand, even though such gender and minority differences in attitudes do exist, those individuals attracted to management careers do seem to have similar personalities and outlooks irrespective of differences in sex, ethnicity, or race (Powell, 1993).

There has been a great deal of research both on what traits American companies tend to look for in managerial applicants and on what characteristics seem to be related to success and failure as a manager. This research pinpoints characteristics of managers in the United States who are able to survive and keep their jobs (Yukl, 1989). Traits such as decisiveness, persistence, social dominance, emotional stability/stress tolerance, self-confidence, dependability, and assertiveness have often been identified as important to managerial success. Furthermore, skills such as interpersonal competence, decision making, leadership, and planning/organizing have also been found to relate to management effectiveness and upward mobility. In terms of basic values and personality, such factors as a high degree of competitiveness, a strong desire to excel and achieve, a propensity for exercising authority or power, a desire for higher organizational status, and a respect for authority figures have been associated with both satisfaction with the management role and advancement in management (Miner, 1965). The individualistic nature of people attracted to management positions means that managers tend to have an unfettered, exclusive, and impatient conception of themselves, which may cause them to neglect the social aspects of their jobs or the negative consequences of individual managerial decisions (Aram, 1993).

Czander (1993) has recently completed a fascinating and quite different analysis of the characteristics of many managers who are successful in rising to the top in large organizations. He applies clinical psychological and psychoanalytical theories to the issue of occupational choice and, specifically, to the job of the top managers in companies. Czander points out that some individuals choose an occupation such as management because of a high need for exhibitionistic striving. He also discusses at some length the high frequency of the narcissistic personality among top managers by indicating that individuals with this characteristic have an advantage in rising to the top of bureaucratic organizations. Furthermore, he profiles the dysfunctions created by leaders with this type of personality, such as insensitivity to others and how this in turn can create a reluctance to accept information or suggestions from others. As he puts it,

> The narcissistic character disorder is generally marked by a pervasive pattern of grandiosity either in fantasy or in behavior. Narcissists demonstrate a lack of empathy in their relations with others and are usually bent on using others to advance their own needs (exploitative). They have a strong desire to be noticed and singled out as being special, often without appropriate achievements. They have a powerful sense of entitlement. They have a need for constant attention and admiration, and tend to be exceedingly jealous of others and often downgrade the achievements of others. (Czander, 1993, p. 77)

In addition, he indicates that such leaders have a constant need to confirm themselves in their job activities. This then creates behaviors at the top that are primarily self-oriented instead of organization-oriented. Czander also emphasizes that many of the behaviors of top managers may arise from their fear of having certain inadequacies exposed, and that they often engage in essentially self-defensive behaviors, as contrasted to functional managerial role behaviors.

Some scholars have emphasized the diversity of individuals in management positions and roles as contrasted with attempts to identify a modal type of person. They have described how different managers will respond to various events and situations in radically different ways. These different types of individuals may vary in their susceptibility to organizational influences. For example, Tosi and Carroll (1976) describe three types of involvement with the employing firm. One type is the organizationalist, who is highly committed to the place of work. This individual is very concerned about the organization's success because that is associated with his or her own success. This person probably has a background that orients him or her positively to authority figures, such as having a dominant father. Another type of accommodation for managers is the externally oriented person. Such individuals tend to work only for the pay they receive and seek most of their satisfactions outside the organization. Finally, there are the professionals, who are oriented toward a profession and a career, perhaps in several organizations rather than in just one organization. Often, professionals are primarily concerned with recognition by external colleagues. Michael Maccoby (1976) uses different labels to describe similar types of persons. He describes the *company men* (conformists), the *craftsmen* (professionals, etc.), the *jungle fighters* (entrepreneurs), and the *gamesmen* (success- and power-oriented effective managers). All of these descriptions suggest that although there is clearly a common culture among American managers, great diversity also exists.

Performance Appraisal

There is clear evidence that the most common method for appraising managers in the United States is by use of the *management by objectives* procedure (Carroll & Schneier, 1982; Carroll & Tosi, 1973). Some 86% of all large American firms use management by objectives systems, which generally involve having each manager work under a set of objectives set jointly with his or her superior at the beginning of an evaluation period, often the fiscal year used in the company. This is because such targeted objectives require the use of budgeted resources that must be established in advance. Obviously, the objectives established for a managerial position target the outputs that particular managers will be held responsible for. These objectives, then, are the primary determinant of that manager's work behaviors for that period of time. Under the management by objectives approach, as actually used in most U.S. companies, the objectives established tend to be individual rather than group goals. Furthermore, they almost always tend to be

TABLE 7.1   Degree to Which Results of Performance Appraisal Are Discussed With
911 Japanese Managers and 450 U.S. Managers

	Japan	United States
To a considerable extent	30%	38%
To a very great extent	9%	49%

SOURCE: Baba, Hanoka, Hara, and Baba (1984).

performance-based and usually stress the attainment of quantitative performances. Thus, the system of performance appraisal used for most U.S. managers
tends to strongly orient such managers toward the attainment of quantitative
performances, with the means of reaching such targets often left to the discretion
of the managers involved. Most recently, the system of management by objectives
has been attacked by the famous quality guru Edward Deming in his principles of
quality management (Ross, 1986). Deming believes that forcing employees to work
under a system of objectives leads to errors and mistakes and in general to
low-quality work, which in the long run leads to poorer performance. Deming
takes this position in spite of the research that shows the management by objectives
system is actually associated rather significantly with higher performance if it is
backed by higher management (Rodgers & Hunter, 1991). However, it is possible
that primarily short-term performance is being measured in such studies. Obviously, performance appraisal systems are much more likely to affect managerial
behaviors in countries where they are used extensively and seriously than in
cultures where they are used perfunctorily, if at all. Table 7.1, for example, shows
that performance appraisals are likely to be more important to U.S. managers than
to Japanese managers, because they are much more likely to have such appraisals
discussed with them.

Compensation

As indicated earlier, reward systems will obviously influence the behavior
of managers to a very significant degree. This is especially likely to happen when
such managers have strong materialistic orientations, as is the case for U.S.
managers. A study of the reward systems of 14 large U.S. companies (Kerr &
Slocum, 1987) identified two fundamental types of reward systems used for
managers, namely, a hierarchy system and a performance-based system. Both
systems paid a certain percentage of the manager's salary in terms of a bonus,

but the proportion of compensation based on bonus was typically 20% to 30% in the hierarchy system and 40% to no limit in the performance-based systems. The performance-based systems tended to use primarily quantitative measures of performance. The authors did not state the proportion of firms using each system; however, other surveys of executive compensation indicate that most managers work under bonus systems (Nash & Carroll, 1975).

Training

Managers are given a significant amount of training and company orientation in U.S. companies; however, exactly what is covered in such programs in terms of subject matter has not been documented. It is not known to what extent managers are taught rules of ethical behavior in most U.S. companies. Still, we do know that U.S. managers are increasingly being exposed to ethical issues in training programs, and programs dealing with diversity and sexual harassment that involve aspects of ethical training are becoming almost universal in U.S. companies (Korman, 1994). As company codes of ethics become more common, we can expect even more training time devoted to this subject.

There are also some descriptions of specific company programs in which ethical behaviors are discussed. For example, Armstrong World Industries has had a long history of concern with the ethical behavior of its employees and this concern is communicated in both formal training and informal training activities (Aguilar, 1994). Part of the concern with ethics stems from a conscious strategic decision to guide the company, as shown by its motto adopted in the 1860s: "Let the buyer have faith," to contrast it with the "Let the buyer beware" philosophy. This company has developed a set of principles for behavior that is taught to every manager and these are supported by a system of evaluation against these principles. Informal training involves stories told to newcomers about such things as the company's deciding it was making too much profit on some of its products in the 1940s and sending back refund checks of more than a half million dollars (Aguilar, 1994). The Hewlett-Packard training program, called "Working at HP," teaches newcomers the company's values and its policies and practices in a similar way (Aguilar, 1994), and The McCormick Spice Company's orientation program operates in a similar fashion (Carroll, 1990). Attention must also be directed to the importance of mentoring and the modeling of behavior as major influences on managerial behavior (Carroll, Olian, & Giannantonio, 1987). Managers do learn what is both appropriate and not appropriate by observing and listening to actual higher-level managers in their firms. This type of social learning can be much more important in terms of guiding behavior than participation in various types of formal training programs.

Labor Relations

There has been a long history of labor-management conflict in the United States. Employers in general have bitterly opposed unions in this country. The widespread recognition of unions, in the 1940s, came about only because of legal requirements imposed on companies by the Wagner Act of 1935. Whenever given the chance, managers typically attempt to rid themselves of their unions, to mitigate their power if they are already unionized, and to avoid unionization if unions do not presently represent their employees. Unionization can be avoided in many cases through various types of union avoidance activities, which are legal under the Taft-Hartley Act of 1947, and various court decisions, such as strong antiunion communication programs, paying compensation and benefits equal to those earned by unionized companies, and the judicious choice of locating and relocating plants. Of course, there are also many cooperative union-management relationships in existence, such as the well-publicized Xerox and ACTWU relationship. Still, surveys over the years have indicated that such cooperative relationships are the exception rather than the rule (Foulkes & Livernash, 1989). Management generally believes strongly in what it calls management prerogatives, namely that management interests are the supreme claims and this is what is required if a business is to be viable and to survive (Freeman & Gilbert, 1988). Selekman (1949) has classified union-management relationships into four types. These are (a) conflict, (b) containment-aggression, (c) accommodation, and (d) cooperation. Although there are many cooperative relationships, there has been a great deal of opposition to unions on the part of management in recent years and, over the past several years, more than 600 bargaining units have been decertified (Anthony, Perrewe, & Kacmar, 1993)

▨ CASE STUDIES: CULTURE AND ETHICS

Table 7.2 describes a number of ethical incidents published in books on managerial ethics or in the *Journal of Business Ethics*. Following the format in

TABLE 7.2   Some Current Ethical Cases in U.S. Companies

Case A. A company producing several nonprescription medical products obtained the opportunity to buy a medical device to be used in birth control. It was rushed to the market without systematic investigation of its potentially harmful effects. In addition, its effectiveness was oversold in advertising for the same reason. It later turned out to be harmful to many women (Hartley, 1991).

Case B. A stockbroker working for a Wall Street firm used an investment of $447,667 from a client to make $6.1 million in trading over 21 months. His commissions on these trades amounted to $140,000. The client's investment declined to $112,000 during this period (Cherington & Cherington, 1992).

Case C. An American bank was found to have made more than $3 billion in loans to Iraq. Under the law of the nation at that time, such loans were illegal. A large number of bank employees was found to have participated in the cover-up, keeping such loans from the government and from their own stockholders (Cherington & Cherington, 1992).

Case D. Several senior managers of a shipping company in Louisiana pleaded guilty to charges that they dumped chemical waste, oil, and even engine parts into the Mississippi River on a regular basis. All of the dumping was done at night. Their attorney indicated that they were doing business in the same way that everybody else on the Mississippi does. He said the government was making scapegoats of his clients and that major chemical companies were dumping anything they wanted into the Mississippi (Lee, 1995).

Case E. An American oil company and its CEO agreed to pay a very high price to an official of a Middle East government for a company that he owned. The same oil company was then given a crude oil contract for 1 year with a discount price of $3 per barrel. The company claimed the discount was because of technical services it had provided to the country's government (Shaw, 1988).

Case F. An American company is the leading manufacturer of automobile batteries. In 1985, because of a documented finding that exposure to lead might lead to birth defects, the company excluded women who were either pregnant or capable of bearing children from all jobs involving exposure to lead. Present female employees on such jobs were transferred to lower-level and lower-paid jobs (Sprotzer & Goldberg, 1992).

Case G. In 1969, a major U.S. chemical company agreed to build a pesticide manufacturing plant in India. On December 3, 1984, the plant had an accident in which a toxic gas cloud was released, killing about 3,000 nearby villagers and injuring perhaps up to 300,000 more people. The company, probably under the guidance of its insurance carrier, has fought all attempts by the Indian government to sue the company in U.S. courts. Four years after the accident, due to various legal defenses of the company, none of the victims of the tragedy has been compensated, although it is expected they eventually will be. In the meantime, the victims have suffered terrible economic hardships (Trotter, Day, & Love, 1989).

(continued)

TABLE 7.2 Continued

Case H. Three plant managers at a Chevrolet truck plant in Michigan secretly installed a control box that enabled them to override the speed of the assembly line. They were able to speed up production in this way and achieve their production targets, which they felt were impossible to meet without such a speedup. Unfortunately for the managers, a group of workers discovered the scheme, and the three managers were suspended and later transferred to other plants (Carroll, 1981).

Case I. On January 28, 1986, the space shuttle *Challenger* exploded, killing all seven astronauts plus a New Hampshire schoolteacher who was aboard, some 73 seconds into its flight. It was revealed later that there was a problem due to seal failure in one of the solid rocket booster joints. Also, there was evidence that one of the company's engineers had warned the company of this weakness one year earlier but no action was taken by management. The same engineer had recommended against the flight on this particular day because of the low temperatures, which increased the probability of a failure. The company initially supported its engineer's recommendations to delay the flight but, after strong objections by two NASA managers, four of the rocket-manufacturing company's managers recommended the flight be made, and the company engineers were left out of the decision-making process entirely. After telling what had happened, during a later government investigation, the engineer who had warned against the launch was disciplined by the company and eventually left the company's employment (Boisjoly, Curtis, & Mellican, 1989).

Chapter 6, we want to see if any of the U.S. cultural characteristics we have identified in this chapter might help explain the behavior of the managers involved in these cases.

Case A. This is a well-known American case that is quite representative of a large number of product safety cases in the United States over the years. In many of these cases, management seemed to be relatively unconcerned about possible safety or health problems associated with their new or redesigned products and often rushed the product to market, frequently with disastrous results. Of course, in the United States as in many other countries, products may be marketed to the general public that are not actually dangerous to most people but might be dangerous to some, are unreliable in the sense of breaking down quickly, or are ineffective in the sense of not living up to their promises (see Item 7.4).

A number of U.S. cultural characteristics probably come together in a case like this to contribute to the problem. We have the characteristics of managers

Item 7.4

A U.S. division of an international drug company justified its efforts to obtain a relaxation of restrictions on the export of one of its drugs, which has been associated with some incidence of blindness and paralysis from its use. The company argued that such drugs should be exported if a culture-specific, cost-benefit analysis should point to this recommendation. For example, for the drug in question, the government of India has requested that it be produced, because it is a treatment for dysentery, which can be life threatening.

SOURCE: Donaldson (1989, pp. 110-112).

themselves. Individuals are selected for management positions partly on the basis of their general optimism, high self-confidence, and orientation toward action. All of these factors can contribute to bringing products to market quickly, with insufficient testing or identification of safety problems. Also, we have seen that Americans in general and especially managers have a highly individualistic rather than a collectivist tendency, which causes them to think primarily of themselves and their personal objectives and to spend little time in thinking about the needs and problems of their customers. The tendency of many managers for self-absorption or narcissism, discussed earlier, could be related to this perspective. Of course, current emphases on the total quality management approach attempt to combat such tendencies with, however, only limited success (Reger, Gustafson, DeMarie, & Mullane, 1992). Furthermore, the very negative opinions often held by Americans, and especially managers, about government contribute to a desire to escape government regulations in these areas as much as possible. In this particular case, there was no regulation of medical devices at the time, partly due to lobbying efforts by business groups to exempt themselves from such regulation.

Case B. There are many hundreds if not thousands of cases like this, which have been described in the press over the years. Bankers, lawyers, even psychologists, as well as stockbrokers have often been found guilty in court cases and in hearings conducted by professional associations for abuse of the client-professional relationship. Case B represents another situation in which the interests of the consumer or client are given far less weight than the interests of the producer or seller of services. Here, a client's wealth is exploited by a stockbroker for his own benefit. Of course, one major factor is simply the compensation or reward system in place. The stockbroker's earnings, in this case, are directly affected by the amount of trading taking place in the client's account. One can imagine a situation in which the stockbroker would earn compensation only if the value of investment increased; this might produce a quite different scenario from the one described. Again, we have the situation where self-interest is given more weight than the interests of others, which is likely to be the case in more highly individualistic societies. Of course, professionalizing an occupation and enforcing codes of conduct, as is done to some extent in such fields as medicine and psychology, can help reduce these types of exploitative relationships.

Case C. In Case C, we have a conspiracy among higher-level employees to cover up and to evade certain laws of the nation. This is an example of the so-called company man syndrome described earlier, which, in turn, is an accommodation to an organization. It probably is most common in organizations in which individual managers work for the same organization throughout their careers, leading to a situation where the company's fortunes are intertwined with their own; they also develop strong emotional ties to their colleagues. In turn, these factors encourage a desire to protect colleagues and the organization. Of course, some of the behavior of the managers in this case can reflect the often negative view among American managers of the government's attempt to regulate them. This view is in contrast to that found in other countries such as Japan (see Chapter 6).

Case D. This is also a case illustrative of many thousands of others involving acts of environmental destruction or degradation by U.S. companies and their managers. The fundamental economic problem of the commons area (Mississippi River) is that it belongs to everyone but it also belongs to nobody and is therefore exploited for individual advantage. In a nation in which private property is not only highly esteemed, valued, and sought but also protected by the Constitution of the United States, it is difficult for many individualistically oriented individuals to identify with protecting the commons. This is especially the case when it is in the individual's interest not to do so. Also, in the United States, there is a high societal value placed on fairness or a level playing field. If competition is to be used to manage the economy, then it should be perceived to be fair. In this particular case, the shipping company sees itself as a victim because it was penalized for doing what its competitors are doing. From the shipping company's point of view, it is being singled out and treated unfairly. In addition, there is the factor of no respect for government and its rules and regulations, which induces many managers to believe that violating government rules and regulations is not unethical, because they were established by incompetent people. Also, individuals may believe that such government regulation is outside the mainstream of cultural norms and values. Finally, there is the extravagance factor in the American culture, which contributes to a spirit of wastefulness. Again, this was partly the result of a situation of abundance in the nation when it was first settled. It is a philosophy of "there's plenty more where that came from."

Case E. This case, which involves international bribery, is not an uncommon one. The famous Lockheed Aircraft Company scandal case, in which this company admitted to bribing foreign officials in many countries (including the prime minister of Japan) to get business, is well known. What aspects of the American managerial culture does this activity reflect? First, most American managers feel that such bribery or payments are a normal cost of doing business, and they should not be punished for doing that. Here, again, is the deep cultural notion that competition is only fair if there is a level playing field. Many U.S. managers do not believe it is fair for their foreign competitors to be allowed to have an advantage over them. Also, the fact that many Americans often believe that the people in other countries are less noble and trustworthy than they are may also play a role in this acceptance of bribery in other nations. Furthermore, the pragmatic nature of American managers, as identified in research (England, 1967) and described in Chapter 2, probably leads to an essentially amoral attitude and to the notion that any means is acceptable to a desirable or worthy end (A. B. Carroll, 1987).

Case F. This case reflects a not uncommon situation in which court decisions and accusations may lead to both an ethical and a legal dilemma. In this situation, the dilemma arises because, in an attempt to ward off a future problem in the form of a court suit, the company may be guilty of illegal discrimination. Perhaps the unethical behavior in this situation is in not offering the displaced women the opportunity to maintain their current earnings. There will be a natural resistance on the part of any workers to being placed in a job that is less desirable in terms of income, status, or work interest. American managers generally do not feel that workers have rights to a job that are earned over time, in spite of the fact that many court decisions have affirmed such a right (Gutman, 1993). There is a tendency among U.S. managers to believe in their superiority and competence to exercise unquestioned authority and to downgrade the importance of the arguments of others. In fact, the needs of individuals have never been as important a determinant of practices and policies in America as in most other advanced countries. Part of this pattern may be due to the American belief that individuals are masters of their own destiny and, therefore, one's circumstances are one's own doing or are self-determined. Also, American managers by and large hold to the doctrine of shareholder rights but not stakeholder rights, and employees fall into this latter category.

Case G. This is a very famous case in which an American company has been widely criticized in the press of a number of countries for unethical behavior, although sometimes it has also been defended. It is a case in which a number of factors came together to create the problem, making it difficult to state the exact cause of the problem and therefore to assign blame. From the company's point of view, it was not its fault, except perhaps partially, and therefore, it is not ashamed of its behavior in attempting to minimize its liabilities and costs. As indicated previously, the United States is not a shame culture, as so many other countries are. Partly because of this, Americans do not have the high sense of guilt that is found in other nations when unfortunate accidents occur. American managers have also a strong belief in self-determination of one's situations. In this case, the fact that the Indian villagers moved their houses to the plant after it was built would be viewed as a strong mitigating factor in the culpability of the company. Finally, the company is likely to view the actions of the Indian government, which is somewhat socialistic in its orientation, as unfair, arbitrary, unreasonable, and without merit. The situation, then, has probably deteriorated to the status of a war between the company and the Indian government, with the needs of the workforce largely forgotten in this conflict. The fact that the workers are from another country or culture may also have affected managerial attitudes in this situation, and the managers may feel that these Indian citizens and the government are somewhat ungrateful for what the company has done for their nation.

Case H. This rather simple case may reflect a number of causal factors. One is simply the managerial performance appraisal and compensation systems that hold managers accountable for unrealistic goals; if these goals are not met, the managers may have to suffer a severe financial penalty. Many unethical problems in industry can be attributed to characteristics of the performance appraisal and reward systems (see Item 7.5). In addition, in the United States,

Item 7.5

The organizational culture of a well-known Wall Street investment firm was extensively described by a member of the firm's 1985 training class, who was employed for the next $2\frac{1}{2}$ years. In this firm, which recruited from only elite business schools, those who did the bond trading were the most highly rewarded in terms of both financial rewards and higher status. Women recruits were not assigned to trading, the higher prestige activity, but to selling only. This made it very difficult for the women to gain organizational power and access to the higher positions and earnings in the company. The everyday behavior of individuals in the company was characterized by gutter language, sexist jokes and analogies, and various other macho behaviors. Seduction attempts were common. A good deal of humiliation of peers and superiors, through the form of ridicule, was also common in the company. This was especially directed at those who did not make as much money for the company. The large power differences among groups and individuals were denoted clearly by the clothes, salaries, offices, furnishings, and other means. Very little cooperation among the investment professionals was present. To some observers, the groups most mistreated were customers and women.

SOURCE: *Business Ethics Quarterly* (Collins, 1992).

labor relations tend to be more commonly adversarial than cooperative, and the relationship can become one of war between the two parties, with the use of spying, trick tactics, and various types of political maneuvers on the part of management and labor.

Case I. This well-known case has been discussed in a number of textbooks. Many of the comments made about the case focus on it as an illustration of groupthink processes, in which a group suppresses dissent and disagreement to arrive at a consensual decision. These groupthink decisions often tend to be risky, because critical comments are discouraged and the disadvantages of certain courses of action are therefore not identified. To be sure, these elements did seem to be present in this situation, as they may well be in many top management decisions. Often, such decisions turn out badly because of failure to identify the negatives in the situation. A number of cultural factors may operate in managerial contexts like this to make these groupthink problems more likely. First, the managers themselves, because they are managers, tend to be optimistic and more action-oriented than other occupational groups. Thus, they are somewhat adverse to pessimistic worries and to the options of delays or procrastination. Also, managers as a group may tend to be somewhat arrogant and not really susceptible to influence from those they consider inferior to themselves in authority and competence. In this situation, it was the engineers who were suppressed by the managers. Frequently, managers have negative stereotypes of engineers, whom they often view as excessively cautious and unaware of operating realities and organizational pressures (Carroll & Tosi, 1976). In this particular case, the managers of NASA were certainly very much aware of the great publicity surrounding this event and they would have felt considerable pressure to ensure that the flight took off as scheduled.

One of the several ethical problems in this case was the punishment received by the dissenting engineer, Boisjoly. Perhaps this is not surprising, given the strong value that many managers tend to place on organizational loyalty and their perception that this engineer showed a lack of this attribute in his later testimony to a congressional investigatory panel. Also, the managers may not have had much sympathy for the importance of professional values and ethics that many engineers incorporated during their academic and other professional socialization experiences (Tosi & Carroll, 1976). Other characteristics of U.S. managers mentioned previously, such as a short-term orientation, persistence, and a lack of patience, may have also contributed to the problem. One major contributing factor was taking the decision away from technical personnel and making it a managerial decision by forcing those present to assume their management roles rather than their engineering roles in this situation.

▧ OTHER CURRENT ETHICAL ISSUES IN AMERICA

There are other contemporary ethical issues that American managers need to address, and these include sexual harassment, the glass ceiling, CEO compensation, downsizing, and American operations in foreign countries. In this section we treat these issues.

Sexual Harassment by Managers

Sexual harassment or unwelcome sexual attention directed at one organizational member by another is increasingly in the news (see Items 7.5 and 7.6). Such behavior is considered by most as not only illegal but also unethical. As an ethical issue for managers, it is found more commonly in the United States

Item 7.6

A female trading room secretary at a California brokerage firm worked for a man who called her a "hooker," "bitch," and "streetwalker" at various times. He also once left condoms on her desk and sometimes brandished a riding crop in front of her. The case went to an industry arbitration panel allowed under the law and it ruled against the secretary, largely on the basis that the boss's behavior was the norm in the industry.

SOURCE: *The Wall Street Journal* (Jacobs, 1994).

than in other cultures, because the proportion of female managers tends to be higher in the United States than in most other nations. In addition, there appears to be more legislation on this issue in the United States than in other nations. In a legal sense, there are two types of sexual harassment—quid pro quo and hostile environment (Gutman, 1993). In the former, there is a request for sexual behaviors along with promises of reward or threats of punishments for compliance or noncompliance. The hostile environment type usually refers to the creation of an unpleasant and unwelcome environment related to sex that interferes with work performance in some way. Studies indicate that men and women differ significantly with respect to their perceptions of the frequency of sexual harassment, what constitutes sexual harassment, and the attributions of the causes of such incidents (Powell, 1993). Most harassment is directed at women by men (probably around 90%, but about 10% of the cases involve the harassment of men). The harassers of women are likely to be older married men, and those of men to be younger single women (Powell, 1993). A number of theories have been developed to explain the reasons for the occurrence of such harassment and to predict when it is most likely to occur. Some of these are related to the cultural characteristics mentioned in this book.

In terms of explaining why harassment occurs, the biological model points simply to the physiological sex drives as the most important causes of this behavior. The political model states that the culture is basically patriarchal in nature; men tend to have the power, and this gives men in general the perception that they have the right to exploit women. The organizational model points to the hierarchy as the source of the problem, with individuals in higher positions tending to take advantage of their organizational power to further their dominance over those below them. However, the sexual spillover model says that individuals cannot differentiate between appropriate off-the-job behavior and on-the-job behavior with respect to gender and sex relationships, and this is what causes the problem. In a related fashion, the sex ratio models attribute the problem to the fact that being in a minority or token status in a group differentiates a person and creates expectations in others that special rules apply to him or her.

Some feel that these models can be tested, to some degree, by comparing them to certain facts about the incidence of sexual harassment. The fact that single, divorced, and separated women are more likely to be targets of sexual harassment than married women provides some support for the biological model. In one government study, it was found that most sexual harassers were primarily at the same level as the victim instead of being a superior (Powell, 1993). This refutes to some degree the organizational model. Attitude surveys provide some support for the sexual spillover model (Powell, 1993). There is also some evidence, based on the recipient of sexual harassment, that the sex ratio model does have some validity. There is, however, some controversy about the validity of the political model. Obviously, these alternative models provide some guidance for the tactics that are most likely to be successful in diminishing this problem.

With respect to cultural factors, American managers appear to be moderately masculine only and thus, as compared to other countries, not excessively prone to gender stereotypes. However, such stereotypes exist widely throughout the world. Many U.S. managers have high power needs, which could contribute to sexual harassment. Of course, there are not as many cultural rules restricting relationships between men and women in the United States as in many other nations. This also might be a factor that could lead to higher harassment frequencies than in more gender-restrictive nations. Furthermore, there is a higher percentage of females in traditional masculine occupations in the United States than in other nations and yet, in many of these occupations, the percentage of females is still low enough for such employees to be considered differently and to attract a significant amount of unwelcome attention from some of the males present. Naturally, we must be cognizant that probably only a small proportion of males do engage in such harassment activities. This is not to say that most females at work have not been harassed, because many in fact have (Powell, 1993).

Glass Ceiling Issues

A great deal has been written about the failure of American companies to promote women and various racial and ethnic groups into the top management

Item 7.7

A significant amount of criticism has been levied recently at the Calvin Klein company for its advertisements featuring nude females and males, which are often placed in public on the sides of buses and on billboards surrounding transportation waiting stations. One set of ads, featuring a nude young woman in poses suggestive of sexual victimization, has been especially criticized for sexualizing children. In addition, some critics have said that the ads also appear to glorify anorexia, which is a major medical problem among present-day young women.

SOURCE: *U.S. News & World Report* (Leo, 1994).

positions in companies (see Item 7.5). This has been called the glass ceiling problem to refer to the ambiguous and subtle barriers to such promotions. At the present time, women seem to constitute only 3% of the senior executives and less than 1% of the highest-paid officers and directors (Adler & Izraeli, 1995). The situation for racial and ethnic minorities is even worse (Fernandez, 1991). In many other nations, the problem is also very common and even more so than in the United States (Adler & Izraeli, 1995).

A number of reasons have been advanced for this lack of upward progress for women. First is that of gender stereotypes, which have been documented over the years. These imply that the characteristics of women are different from those of men and are not congruent with the role demands present in various jobs (Adler & Izraeli, 1995). Attributions as to the cause of such gender differences are to innate biological differences or to differences in early socialization patterns (Adler & Izraeli, 1995). Another theory focuses on the act of tokenism itself, in which just a few women are promoted to very visible positions. Although in theory this approach might create positive role models for other women managers and also demonstrate female competence in that role, it actually draws high degrees of attention to such individuals and intensifies perceptions of gender differences (Kanter, 1977). Cultural or societal expectations that women will act subserviently to men are carried over into the organization itself and create the feeling that women should not be exercising power over men (Adler & Izraeli, 1995). Such societal expectations may be the result of exposure to various influences, such as advertisements, movies, and TV shows, and to popular literature and other influences (see Item 7.7). Finally, the power perspective indicates that men who have power and have strong desires for top positions will simply use it to limit change in this area (Adler & Izraeli, 1995).

Item 7.8

Michael D. Eisner, who is the chairman of Walt Disney Co., made $203,010,590 in earnings in 1993. This was in spite of the fact that Walt Disney's net income fell by 63% that year. However, the value of the company's stock has risen considerably (1,400%) during Eisner's tenure. In an editorial on the issue, the editors of *Business Week* said that any success that a business has must also be credited to many other employees who are learning better teamwork skills, developing improved technological skills, and working a lot longer and harder than before. And yet, *Business Week* pointed out that "compensation has not increased very much—if at all—for the minions."

SOURCE: *Business Week* ("That Eye-Popping Executive Pay," 1994).

Several of these theories are certainly compatible with cultural factors in both the United States and other countries. Male managers do tend to be power-oriented and are very much concerned with gaining a maximum of upward mobility in business and other organizations for themselves. Managers already at the top are likely to have gender-based stereotypes, especially if they are older and attended business schools at a time when the number of female students was very small and sometimes even zero.

CEO Compensation

Another issue that is receiving a great deal of attention today in the popular press is that of the extremely high salaries of top executives, especially CEOs (see Item 7.8). When President Bush visited Japan in 1992 with several top automobile company executives, the Japanese press focused a good deal of attention on the fact that these CEOs were getting much higher salaries than their Japanese counterparts even though their company performance was much lower. This topic has also been discussed extensively on American TV and radio and in the general and business press.

Defenders of high CEO salaries say they are not excessive, because the stockholders are grateful for the high stock appreciation they have received during the CEO's tenure (Anders, 1991). But the business press has presented many examples of very high salaries given to CEOs in spite of the fact that the performance of their businesses has been poor or has actually declined during the tenure of the individuals involved. This situation has caused stockholders to become angry in several cases and they have pressured the boards of directors to do something about this problem (Greenwald & Thigpen, 1991; Salwen, 1992). Critics of CEO salaries say they are only high because the chief executives of companies control their boards of directors through rewards or threats and influence them in this way to give them very high salaries (Crystal, 1991). The critics also point to the widespread feelings of inequity that occur among lower-level employees, and even lower managers, when their salaries do not keep up with the standard of living or are nonexistent due to layoffs or salary cuts. In addition, it has been argued that such very high CEO salaries create both significant social turbulence in the nation and inflationary pressures.

In all probability, the very high salaries obtained by CEOs are sought for a number of reasons. We indicated earlier that Americans in general, and especially executives, are seekers of achievement and are oriented toward visible and quantitative indications of achievement; and money itself is the best example of such a success symbol in America. Of course, Americans do seem to exalt wealth to a very high degree and thus it is a path to many other goals and consequences, such as status and very respectful, if not fawning, treatment by others. Individuals who are already oriented toward power might be especially stimulated by this viewpoint. We also indicated earlier that several European writers have been struck by the extreme extravagance and excessive displays of wealth of the upper-income classes in America (Evans, 1976). There is little tendency toward the understatement that one might notice in similar social classes in Europe. It is as if such individuals are somehow afraid others might not notice how important they are. Perhaps also, the extreme egotistical orientation of such managers has them believing that they are very superior beings and worth all the salary they are receiving, as our previous discussion of narcissism implies. This narcissistic orientation purportedly causes individuals to put themselves at the center of things and leads them to being rather insensitive to the needs of others.

Downsizing Programs

In recent years, millions of employees, including many middle-level managers, have lost their jobs due to corporate downsizing or so-called rightsizing programs of companies (Anthony et al., 1993; see also Item 7.9). These reductions in the workforce have been accompanied by many social problems, including suicide, marital distress and divorce, displaced aggression, alcohol and substance abuse, and others. Furthermore, they have tended to create considerable stress, anxiety, fear, and resentment in the survivors of these

Item 7.9

Owners of KB Cinemas in Washington, D.C., closed their theater chain and left about 90 employees in the dark. Several employees said they had not received any warning that the company intended to do this and, in fact, had showed up for work on the afternoon of January 8, 1994, and were informed that the theaters were closing. Three days later, they were officially told by a corporate manager that they no longer had jobs and would not get paid for their last 3 weeks of work. Several employees, many of whom are minorities, said they should have been told beforehand so they could have had more time to find other work. The firm's former competitors condemned the way the employees were treated. "The . . . owners have conducted themselves in an immoral fashion," according to one local theater owner, who went on to say, "A lot of businesses go out of business but they treat their employees in an honorable fashion."

SOURCE: *Washington Post Business* ("When the House Lights Go Up," 1994).

programs. There is strong documentation that trust in higher management and loyalty to companies have been decreasing significantly in the past several years. This is at least partly due to these downsizing programs.

Although downsizing is not illegal, and advance notice is not required in certain states, there have been many ethical issues raised as to the necessity of downsizing and to the manner in which it is carried out. Some research shows that downsizing is typically not followed by higher organizational performance (Anthony et al., 1993). Some believe that, in fact, many downsizing efforts decrease company performance, leading to a vicious cycle of downsizing efforts (Anthony et al.; Cameron, 1994; Korman, 1994). One major effect of downsizing is that many individuals are let go who are really too old to find other jobs very easily. This also may be a time when the expenses of the affected family are at their highest point due to college and other costs. Furthermore, a number of downsizing efforts have been created by so-called greenmail tactics, where companies have been forced to borrow huge sums of money to buy back stock from corporate raiders at a premium. Clearly, how the downsizing efforts are carried out is very critical. If individuals are given fair early retirement provisions or sufficient severance pay or useful retraining, the impact on individual employees may not be so severe. Companies vary widely in how this is handled.

It seems that downsizing and layoffs are becoming much easier for companies to make. A recent survey indicates that the number of layoff notices given to employees at Christmastime has risen to new heights in the United

States. That used to be the one time of year when such layoffs were avoided. One reason for the increase in layoffs is probably that the practice is now considered normal and perhaps even proof of "good management." American managers certainly try to conform to prevailing standards of managerial styles or effectiveness. Again, the short-run orientation of American managers must play a role in this, because downsizing often pays off in an immediate benefit such as a quick rise in stock prices; the long-run detrimental effects may not occur until the managers have left the company. Of course, the fact that huge bonuses can be earned under present managerial incentive systems, if the price of the stock rises, may also be an important factor in the behavior of top managers. Also, the inability of many managers to develop a sense of empathy with others, because of the narcissistic tendencies, may also contribute to this outcome. American managers may also strongly believe in the employment-at-will doctrine, which says that the organization does not have any responsibilities to employ individuals who are not contributing sufficient value to more than equal their costs. American managers tend to elevate economic considerations higher than managers in most other countries, so this type of perspective is quite common.

U.S. Operations in Foreign Nations

U.S. operations in overseas locations have long been a subject of considerable controversy with respect to various ethical aspects of such operations (Ball & McCulloch, 1993; Hill, 1994). Moving plants overseas to diminish domestic labor costs has long been one such controversy. It becomes even more controversial when the company then uses much lower standards of behavior in the foreign country than it would in the domestic country (see Item 7.10). The operation of U.S. firms in foreign countries obviously can also affect the attitudes of the people in other nations toward the United States itself. U.S. managers often have a low regard for other peoples and may treat foreign workers much worse than domestic workers, because they do not identify with them in any emotional way and do not feel guilty about such treatment. Also, as we have seen, U.S. managers tend to be very pragmatic and goal-oriented in their managerial style and perhaps rather amoral in their ethical style. This means that many simply take the most expedient route to reaching certain goals.

Item 7.10

An American company was hired to build a highway across the Andes mountains in Peru. The resident engineer, an American, learned that Peruvian safety standards were significantly below those in the United States in general. He also learned that the company was not taking special precautions to prevent landslides from occurring where the highway was being built across unstable rock formations, and protested such building practices to both Peruvian government officials and his U.S. managers, with no success in changing the building practices. Thirty-one workers were killed by landslides while building the road. The American engineer was fired for his trouble.

SOURCE: Donaldson (1989, p. 47).

◻ PUBLIC AND NONPROFIT MANAGEMENT

Although the examples given in this chapter are of unethical behavior in American business firms primarily, we should not assume automatically that these types of problems are found only in private industry. Managers and others in many other types of organizations have also been found guilty of unethical or questionable behavior. For example, in recent years, there have been many charges of highly questionable behaviors among the organizations classified as charities in the United States. One well-known example was the United Way of America scandal of 1992. Its national president was alleged to have spent almost $100,000 over a 3-year period on limousine services for himself. He charged many trips to the organization for visits to his much younger girlfriend and gambled in Las Vegas while earning almost $400,000 a year (Bennett & DiLorenzo, 1994). Similarly, a look at the three biggest charities—the American Lung Association, The American Cancer Association, and the American Heart Association—indicates very questionable uses of the money they collect. A large proportion of this money was purportedly paid to maintain salaries, expensive buildings, and offices, and it was allocated to other purposes rather than being used effectively for the purpose for which people give money to such charities, namely, helping the needy and sponsoring research (Bennett & DiLorenzo, 1994). In fact, the major medical charities have been accused of actually sending messages to citizens that are misleading and perhaps actually harmful to their health in order to enhance their own power and to increase their own wealth (Bennett & DiLorenzo, 1994). Similarly,

Morgan (1988) cites several examples of managers in government agencies, unions, hospitals, law firms, and many other nonprofit organizations who have been found guilty of unethical behavior. Among his many examples are employees of the Internal Revenue Service investigated for taking bribes from a large U.S. oil company, government meat inspectors in New York indicted for taking bribes to overlook sanitary violations, FBI agents charged with misappropriating bureau funds and taking kickbacks, a postmaster for masterminding a robbery in the main post office in Atlantic City, and public officials in New York and Massachusetts for obtaining payments from companies doing business with their governments. Thus, unethical behavior may be found among managers who have the opportunity to engage in this behavior in any type of organization and not just in private business firms.

▨ CONCLUSIONS

Ethical problems in American management appear to be widespread at the present time. However, whether American managers are more or less ethical than those in other nations cannot be determined, except perhaps for certain types of ethical situations. Also, whether American managers are becoming more ethical or less ethical is an issue. Even though surveys seem to indicate that the general public is less satisfied today than in the past about the ethical behaviors of business managers, this may simply reflect higher standards of performance or greater sensitivity to this issue.

We have seen that certain American cultural characteristics in general, as well as particular occupational characteristics of managers, do contribute to the higher frequencies of certain types of ethical dilemmas that American managers often face, as compared to managers in other countries. Perhaps the most significant of these cultural characteristics is the very high degree of individualism found in the United States, as compared to that of other nations. This often leads to a low degree of concern for those outside one's own skin and especially for those outside one's immediate group. We have seen also that the amoral ethical style and the high pragmatic and utilitarian values of American managers are at the root of many of the ethical difficulties that managers fall into. Many managers take whatever course of action will best achieve their goals, irrespective of the effects of that course of action on organizational members, on the future of the organization, or on the society in which they live. In fact, there is often a complete indifference to the impact of particular courses of action on various organizational members and other so-called stakeholders because managers do not accept the concept of stakeholders in the first place. Also, a key cultural aspect affecting managerial behavior is the strong desire for material wealth in America, which has been prevalent since the nation's beginnings. Associated with this viewpoint is a feeling that only wealth that can be displayed to others in a concrete way is a sign of achievement and success for most Americans. This high need for the display of material well-being seems to be an important causal factor in many of the ethical problems that American managers create for themselves and their companies. In terms of occupational cultural characteristics, the high need for power and the power orientation of many American managers probably result in a certain amount of arrogance and moral indifference. This may also contribute to some of the gender and discriminatory problems and practices facing U.S. companies today.

▧ DISCUSSION QUESTIONS

1. Do you believe that outsiders, such as the three French observers of the United States described in this chapter, are more or less accurate than American observers? Why?

2. Analyze the nine critical incidents or cases presented in Table 7.1 from the perspective of a Japanese manager, based on your reading of Chapter 6. How would such an individual look at these situations in all likelihood?

3. Do you think that U.S. managers by and large manage all of their employees ethically? Why or why not?

4. What do you consider to be the top ethical problems of American management, based on reading this chapter? Why are these the most important problems, in your opinion?

5. Should American companies be regulated with respect to how they manage their overseas plants? Why or why not? If they should be, in what ways?

6. What is your position on the issue of the very high levels of compensation paid to many CEOs of large American companies? Why do you feel this way?

7. Do you believe that the affirmative action programs that many U.S. companies have adopted, to give some special preference to disadvantaged groups, are ethical or not ethical? Why or why not?

8

Cross-Cultural Managerial Ethical Behaviors
Continued Divergence or Toward Greater Convergence?

Training for Globalization in Italy

Fiat, the Italian automaker, has recently started an internationalization program in response to what it sees as the globalization of competition. In 1989, this large company (300,000 employees) had locations in 56 countries. The company has set out to foster an openness to other cultures and approaches among its employees. One aspect of its program is to assign employees to 2-year tours of duty in other countries. Another part of the program is to provide foreign language training to its recent college graduate hires. One English-language program provides more than 100 hours of instruction to each participant. In addition, the company added training in internationalization as part of its existing management development programs.

Audia (1991)

Foreign Ownership of American Firms

Several American firms have recently been acquired by foreign firms, especially as the exchange rate of the dollar has fallen, making such acquisitions favorable. A recent study of 225 U.S. firms, acquired in the period between 1979 and 1989, where the purchase price exceeded $10 million, found a diversity in such foreign buyers. Firms from the United Kingdom acquired the largest number (80 firms). Some other countries involved were Canada (31 firms), France (15 firms), Japan (18 firms), the Netherlands (11 firms), Switzerland (16 firms), and Germany (13 firms).

Eun, Kolodny, and Scheraga (1992)

Japan's Business Cartels Are Starting to Slowly Change

Near zero economic growth and other factors are contributing to the
unraveling of Japanese monopolistic cartels under pressure from the
government and the purchasing policies of large Japanese companies. It is
estimated that cartels cost the Japanese consumers up to $140 billion a
year through their effectiveness as trade barriers. However, business
collusion remains a deeply embedded part of Japan's economy.

Wall Street Journal ("Business Cartels Changing," 1995)

In this book, we started with an assumption that there are differences in the ethicality of managerial decisions in various societies. Of course, the issues of what is unethical behavior and which of several behaviors is the most unethical (see Item 8.1) is not really answerable. Moreover, we have tended to rely on behaviors or managerial decisions that are often perceived to be unethical, recognizing that in certain cultures and among certain individuals within a culture there may be considerable disagreement as to the ethicality of a managerial behavior or practice. We have cited a number of research studies that seem to indicate that individuals from different nations do indeed react to various ethical situations or scenarios differently. Also, we have documented significant differences in the values and beliefs of nations, and especially in their managers, which are predictors (but by no means guarantors) of later behaviors. Furthermore, we have described differences in laws, HRM practices, and organizational cultures among nations that not only help to transmit cultural values but also provide independent influences on the behavior of managers. In addition, we have cited numerous case incidents of unethical behaviors of managers within various nations, especially in the highlighted countries of Japan and the United States, and explained these incidents through the use of some documented national cultural differences. Most important, we have developed a basic model that provides an explanation of why such societal differences in managerial behaviors exist and why there is variance within cultures as well. This model identifies national cultural differences as a major explanation of differences in managerial behavior.

Our model also identifies the key societal mechanisms through which differences in cultural expectations and values are transmitted to managers. These include such primary influences as parenting styles and characteristics of the educational system. Then, when such individuals become managers, they

Item 8.1

Three purchasing agents, working for different U.S. clothing manufacturers in a country in Asia, placed separate orders with a supplier for bolts of silk that, at the time, were in short supply. All received notice that delivery would take 6 months. Agent A received a phone call, saying she could get immediate delivery if she paid a bribe; she did and shortly received the shipment. Agent B took the initiative and called up a government official known to him and offered him a cash payment if he would expedite the shipment; expediting occurred. The third purchasing agent waited 6 months for the delivery. The issue is the question of differences in ethicality between purchasing agents A and B. It can be argued that purchasing agent B's behavior is more unethical because it involves both private and public corruption and was initiated by the agent.

SOURCE: DeGeorge (1993).

are subjected to secondary influences, such as the laws of a nation, the human resource management systems to which managers are subjected, and the cultures of the organizations employing them. Also, codes of professional ethics play a role here, as we have indicated. Variations in some of these primary and secondary influences within a nation can account for the differences in managerial behaviors within each culture. Furthermore, our model also describes some fundamental root causes of differences in national cultures themselves, such as differences in history, resources, religious beliefs, relationships with other nations, and so on. We believe that we have provided thorough documentation in the book of the fact that culture influences the ethical behaviors and practices of managers. We also believe that the information presented up to this time is quite congruent with the model posed earlier.

In this chapter, we would now like to take up the new question of whether the behaviors (ethical and otherwise) of managers from different societies around the world will grow increasingly similar or different, or will remain somewhat the same as they are at present. Our model, which identifies some of most critical factors of why societal differences in managerial behaviors exist and the mechanisms through which societal values and beliefs are transmitted to managers, can be useful in this regard. By examining how the critical factors involved in creating a culture and transmitting it to its citizens may be changing, we may be able to gain some insights into what to expect of managerial ethical behaviors in various nations in the future. In doing this, we must recognize that our model posits that the ethical behaviors of managers are affected not only by culture itself but by such factors as characteristics of the legal system, the human resource management systems employed, and the informal and formal behavioral imperatives transmitted by an organization's culture. Thus, even if national cultures do not change substantially, some of these other influencing systems may change and, with this outcome, one might expect alterations in managerial behaviors.

◪ SOME ARGUMENTS FOR THE CONTINUED DIVERGENCE IN THE ETHICAL PRACTICES OF MANAGERS AMONG NATIONS

Although there are a number of similarities in how managers from different nations look at various types of managerial decisions that differ in perceived ethicality, there are also documented differences. There are arguments for the resistance to change and the continuation of such cultural differences in managerial practices. First, in terms of actual managerial behavioral differences over time, how much change has occurred over the past several decades? It could be argued that during this period of massive political and economic change in our world, changes in managerial behaviors and in the societal and organizational factors that affect them have been rather slight. Peterson (1993) takes this position: After reviewing the essays in his book on managerial behaviors in 15 nations, he states there is only very slight empirical evidence for a growing universality in managerial behavior. He points to a previous survey of managerial behaviors around the world by Harbison and Myers, published in 1959. These authors described differences in managerial behaviors around the world at that time and predicted that, as the level of industrial civilization became more similar, managerial behaviors would also become more similar. In fact, they and others argued at the time that an American model of management would be adopted by managers in many nations after exposure to it. Peterson (1993) indicates that the essays in his book seem to document the fact that managers in other countries such as France and Germany still manage differently from the way American managers do and even differently from each other (see Table 8.1). In addition, he argues that important determinants of managerial behavior, such as the human relations practices to which they are subjected, are still quite different from one nation to another. These are even different within larger regions such as Europe and Asia. When it comes to differences between Asian management and that found in the United States and in Europe, the differences are even greater, he argues.

TABLE 8.1 A Comparison of French, German, and U.S. Responses to an Ethical Scenario Dealing With Bribery (in percentages)

Rationale for Response	German	U.S.	French
A bribe is unethical	9	9	23
Is not unethical, just the price of business	55	29	14

SOURCE: Becker and Fritzsche (1987).

Other arguments for the continued diversity in managerial behaviors and the perceived ethicality of various managerial decisions focus on the difficulty in changing the fundamental behavioral influences in a society. There seems to be a basic inertia present in all social organizations and social institutions that precludes significant change in them. There are, of course, many such behavioral influences, some of which we have described at length in previous chapters. Others not mentioned extensively include differences in organizational design that reflect cultural differences (Tosi, Rizzo, & Carroll, 1994). For example, a study that compared 55 American and 51 Japanese firms (Lincoln, Hanada, & McBride, 1986) found significant differences between these two countries in the degrees of centralization and formalization of authority. A study of leadership styles of managers in the United Kingdom, Germany, and France, all European countries, found differences in degrees of delegation, interest in subordinates, and the degree to which the managers want to be informed about subordinate activities (Child, 1981). Furthermore, the degree to which group work assignments are used has been found to be quite different in Sweden, Japan, and the United States (Cole, 1989). Obviously, such factors as these can significantly influence managerial behaviors and practices, which are not likely to change unless organizational structures, leadership styles, and work assignment approaches are altered (Adler, 1991).

Perhaps more important are the cultural dimensions identified and explored by Hofstede (1980a, 1991) in a number of studies. Among these factors, the individualism-collectivism dimension seems especially important in explaining cultural differences in managerial behaviors and practices. The frequency with which certain managerial actions with ethical implications vary, such as layoffs, establishing pay for CEOs, copying intellectual property without permission, and carrying out orders without question does appear to be different from one society to another. Also, reactions to these practices by present or future managers seem to vary among cultures. And, although individualism and collectivism are important, differences in the other dimensions of power distance, masculinity-femininity, the long- versus short-term orientation, uncertainty avoidance, and others we have described previously also seem to explain variability in managerial behavior both among cultures and within cultures. The issue is, how much will these fundamental characteristics of a people vary over time? Many doubt they will vary much at all from present levels.

▨ SOME ARGUMENTS FOR A GREATER CONVERGENCE IN THE ETHICAL PRACTICES OF MANAGERS AMONG NATIONS

On the other hand, it could be argued that there are fairly recent significant changes in the societal forces affecting managerial behaviors in various countries around the world that would contribute to a growing convergence of such behaviors. Because these changes are quite recent, their effects are not apparent yet and it will take a few years until they are. These significant managerial behavioral influences include a growing body of international law governing business relationships among countries, a growing convergence in human resource management systems, and a growing convergence in certain factors influencing organizational cultures such as business strategies employed. In addition, primary influencing factors such as parenting styles, educational methods, and mass culture are becoming increasingly similar in at least the more advanced nations of the world.

Trends in International Business Law

Donaldson (1989) has discussed the dramatic expansion of external remedies in the form of international laws, agreements, and codes of conduct as they apply to the ethicality of managerial decisions around the world. Hotchkiss (1994) has documented the growth of the field of international commercial law. She shows how such laws have been created over the past several hundred years to accommodate the ever-increasing trade among nations. Furthermore, she illustrates how, in recent years, the growing influence of multinational enterprises, often very powerful organizations in their own nations, has accelerated the pressures on nations to agree on the legal foundations of conducting international business. Even on extremely contentious issues where significant cultural differences exist, such as in the area of bribery or the protection of intellectual property, the government of the United States has pressured other nations to adopt its position.

The Growth of International Trade Agreements

The recently signed General Agreement on Tariffs and Trade (GATT), which included more than 90 member countries, attempts to make the economies of its members more uniform. Government economic protections for its industrial companies and government actions against foreign firms are diminished under this act. This in itself will have an impact on ethical behavior, because, as we have already indicated, many of these now proscribed government actions were widely perceived by foreign firms to be unfair or unethical.

Changing Attitudes Toward Managerial Authority

There is some evidence that managerial authority is no longer as unquestionably accepted as it once was in the United States (Ashforth & Lee, 1989) or in Japan (Whitehill, 1991). For example, in the United States, the perceived legitimacy of managerial influence in such areas as subordinate behavior decreased between 1962 and 1987, according to a study conducted by Ashforth and Lee (1989) using samples of students, union officials, and managers themselves. Even managers seemed to deny their own subordination to higher levels to some degree, although they had a tendency to believe their own influence over subordinates was legitimate. Such results may mean that subordinates may be somewhat less susceptible to influence by higher managerial levels than was the case in past years.

Political Changes Leading to More
Privatization of Government Businesses

Obviously, Eastern Europe has been the most dramatic example of privatizing former government enterprises. Of course, this is also the case in Germany and many other countries around the world, such as Japan, Italy, and the United States, where utilities and various regulated monopolies have been privatized. Also, there are trends in this direction in the case of government services, especially in the United Kingdom and the United States.

Trends in International HRM
Systems and Organizational Cultures

There is some evidence that the human resource management systems of nations that were formerly quite diverse are now becoming somewhat more similar. Some of this change is the result of the adoption of international labor standards in the European Economic Community nations and pressures to accept them in various regional trade agreements, such as the North American Free Trade Agreement between the United States, Canada, and Mexico. However, economic and technological factors are also exerting an influence in this direction. Carroll (1992) documents some growing similarities between Japanese and U.S. HRM systems. Japan is a country in which managerial values, as compared to those of the United States, are as different as they could possibly be (Whitehill, 1991). Yet, Whitehill sees that there are fundamental recent changes occurring in seven major management practices. These are in the areas of organization and planning systems, staffing practices, leadership and career development practices, compensation systems, motivation and evaluation systems, and communication systems. Finally, he identifies changes in Japanese managerial strategic thinking. All of these differences that he and others (Carroll, 1992) describe are in the general direction of greater similarity to the practices of American companies, for example, smaller proportions of permanent core employees, less emphasis on seniority in promotion and compensation and more on merit, more opportunities for women in management, and less use of arbitrary work assignments.

Greater Similarity in Managerial Training

Increasingly, managers around the world are being exposed to the same managerial training. Foreign attendance in U.S. MBA programs has been increasing dramatically. Not only does this help foster the notion of a universal management model but the cultural contacts themselves also help to create a greater understanding of cultural differences. Of course, the degree to which this occurs in visitors to another country is a function of how closely such individuals integrate in the society (see "Training for Globalization in Italy"). In addition to receiving students from abroad, many U.S. business schools have established MBA programs in other countries, such as Dartmouth's in Japan. U.S. managerial professors have increasingly lectured on management in foreign countries. For example, we have lectured on management in a wide variety of European and Asian countries over the past several years. One of us taught a large number of Chinese professors from different parts of Mainland China, over a period of several months, how to introduce and teach a course in organizational behavior at their home universities. An example of the influence of American managerial training over time in China is provided by Stross (1990). He describes the popularity of many U.S. managerial books in

China, such as *In Search of Excellence* (Peters & Waterman, 1982), *The One Minute Manager* (Blanchard & Johnson, 1982), and *Intrapreneuring* (Pinchot, 1985). Also, the establishment of the large U.S. management style training center, on the campus of the Dalien Institute of Technology, for Chinese managers occurred in 1980. Furthermore, there are the many management programs established by U.S. business schools, such as UCLA, The Wharton School, Columbia, The University of Texas, and others, at various Chinese universities. All of this change has created a way of thinking that Stross calls "managerialism" in China, where we increasingly have a type of similar thinking on what constitutes good management practices.

Growing Awareness of Environmental Interdependence

Deresky (1994) describes the growing perception in the world today of environmental interdependence; that is, the realization that in an environmental sense we live in one world, and environmental problems in one nation have a tendency to create environmental problems in other nations as well. The meeting of world leaders in Brazil, in 1992, to discuss ecological preservation is one example of this awareness. Because many of the ethical issues and problems of managers revolve around environmental impacts of decisions, this may mean that managers all over the world will have to be more environmentally conscious than they were in the past. Actually, new international rules and treaties may force them to do this. For example, the North American Free Trade Agreement (NAFTA), which now links the United States and Mexican economies to a much greater degree than in the past, has features that will pressure Mexican managers and U.S. managers in Mexico to adopt a higher standard of environmental protection. In recent years, considerable controversy has emerged over the export of pesticides, especially by U.S. and German firms, to less-developed nations. Governments in such countries have now come under considerable pressure from their own citizens to stop this practice.

Parenting and Growing Social Class Similarities

There is some evidence that certain factors such as social class do have similar effects across cultures. For example, one study (Kâgitçibasi, 1990) found that middle-class parents from Malaysia, Austria, Canada, France, Japan, Germany, and the United States tended to behave in a similar manner in raising their children, as compared to how working-class parents raise their children. This may mean

Item 8.2

An age-old issue is the origin of moral behavior. Does it come from our genetic backgrounds and is therefore relatively immutable, or is it the product of our environments? This issue has raged for some time. A recent book by Robert Wright argues that we are slaves to our biology. He also argues that morality in human beings is shaped extensively by our fundamental biological drives. Furthermore, he argues that in a world where Darwinian natural selection is the rule, the capacity for virtue exists only if it has survival or evolutionary value.

On the other hand, there are those who argue that human nature is not immutable; they take a much more positive view of human possibilities for an ever-increasing degree of what we generally regard as high moral behavior. In fact, in this school of thought, humans are regarded as not only capable of moral improvement but actually as improving in their moral behavior over time.

SOURCES: Wright (1994); Zeldin (1994).

that as the economies of certain countries become more alike, individuals in those countries will become more similar due to having similar socialization experiences. In addition, there has been much criticism in recent years of educational systems in various countries, such as the United States and Japan (see Item 8.2), and a result of such criticism is some convergence in practices. Of course, some of this convergence raises the issue of the degree to which moral behavior is a function of such environmental factors as parenting and education, as contrasted to relatively immutable biological factors (see Item 8.2).

Growing Equality of Women in the Workforce

Although there is obviously still a long way to go in providing women in various countries around the world with equal opportunities, many countries are now aware of this issue and are attempting to change the situation (Powell, 1993). This has relevance for ethical behavior, because some of the unethical behaviors of management are in the area of unequal treatment of women. In the United States, much larger proportions of the entering classes of medical, law, business, dental, and other professional schools are now female than was the case formerly. The proportion of female managers has been rising steadily in U.S. companies for some time. In the United States, women have been admitted to the military academies and are even allowed to assume certain combat roles. Of course, not all these trends have been due to heightened societal sensitivity to this issue. Obviously, such factors as the new information technologies have served as a great gender equalizer in the world and will continue to do so in the future.

Growing Use of Codes of Ethics
in International Companies

Ethics codes help to standardize behavior within and between organizations. This is because some ethical problems arise out of a lack of sensitivity and alertness by managers (Gioia, 1991). Although there is now an ethics code gap between large U.S. firms and those in other nations, such as in Europe (Deresky, 1994), such codes are increasing in most companies. Some of the pressure for their adoption comes from the creation of many foreign subsidiaries within a country's borders. Because there appears to be some corporate modeling in the contents of such codes of ethical conduct through the institutionalization process (Martell & Carroll, 1995b), we would expect this factor alone to foster some increased uniformity in the ethical behavior of managers.

Increasing Proportion of Foreign-Owned
Subsidiary Firms in Other Nations

More than 500 Japanese companies have located in the State of California alone in the past few decades (Carroll, 1992). Many other former U.S. firms have been purchased by a variety of foreign firms (see "Foreign Ownership of American Firms"). About 900 firms from America and Europe have located in Ireland in the past decade (Hannaway, 1992). The evidence is that these foreign firms have affected the human resource management practices of domestic firms in Ireland. One such effect is to make larger Irish firms more efficiency-oriented and less protective of labor union privileges and rights. Similarly, U.S. firms locating in Taiwan (Yeh, 1986) and Mexico (Taylor, Moxon, & Beechler, 1991) have brought with them American managerial values and standards.

▨ WILL COMPANIES AND MANAGERS BECOME MORE ETHICAL IN THEIR MANAGEMENT PRACTICES IN THE FUTURE?

The various pressures on companies and managers to become more similar in terms of their managerial practices does not mean that there will be diminished frequencies of managerial unethical behaviors or practices in the future. In fact, one study of the ethical standards for managers, asking 1,408 American managers what they consider as acceptable behavior, reports that these standards had declined somewhat between 1961 and 1976 (Posner & Schmidt, 1987). Thus, there are forces and trends that could increase the frequency of unethical behaviors in companies around the world, which we will now describe.

Increased Economic Competition

One factor is certainly increased competition itself, which is occurring all over the world at both the domestic and the international levels. By itself, it may pressure managers to use unethical practices to compete successfully. Unethical behavior is, after all, a means to an end. When managers can suffer personal misfortune such as loss of bonuses, promotions, or even loss of their jobs for failure to compete successfully, they naturally will be motivated to achieve imposed end results by whatever means possible.

Some also predict that stronger international competition may increase the frequency of unethical managerial behaviors and managerial practices of large domestic U.S. firms. This is because such firms will have to lower their ethical standards to those of competitors in less-developed nations, and such nations tend to have lower environmental, labor, and other standards in general. Also, with increasing competition, companies that have been proactive in the social responsibility or corporate ethics area may find that such programs can no longer be justified. Control Data Corporation, for example, has had to stop some of its more innovative social responsibility programs (see Item 8.3).

On the other hand, who knows what the structure of industry will be in the future? It is quite possible that the large and very successful multinational companies will continue to acquire many other firms around the world, including many of their competitors. If there is a natural tendency for firms to form cartels or monopolies when they can get away with it, future economic competition may lessen rather than increase. Although this might be worse for the world's consumers, it might reduce some of the many ethical problems caused by very high competition.

New Ethical Issues Themselves

There are newer areas of managerial action that give rise to more possibilities of what will be perceived as unethical managerial behaviors. For exam-

Item 8.3

For a number of years, Control Data Corporation (CDC) followed a strategy of locating new plants in inner-city communities. William C. Norris, the chairman of the board of CDC, feels that this is the responsible thing to do because it helps these distressed communities and provides upward mobility opportunities for neighborhood residents. This activity is not without its extra costs for CDC. In one community, the company's lawyer sometimes has to bail out company workers from the city jail and also provide legal assistance to workers who get into difficulty with the law.

SOURCE: Carroll (1984, p. 33).

ple, managers today, as compared to managers in the past, have new areas of decision making such as plant closings (Millspaugh, 1990) and software piracy (Swinyard et al., 1990) to deal with. With many new products and components of products continuing to be developed, there is increased complexity in product design. More choices may mean more possibilities of making decisions that will be viewed by others as unethical.

Increasing Use of Group
Decision Making in Management

Sims (1992) has described how group decision making contributed to unethical behavior in three famous ethical cases in U.S. companies. One of these was an adulterated food product case (Beech-Nut), another an investor fraud case (E. F. Hutton), and the third a case of violation of U.S. Treasury rules in bond auctions (Salomon Brothers). In all of these cases, Sims argued that groupthink processes (Janis, 1972) operated, in which group forces led to more unethical decisions than individuals might have produced operating independently. Groupthink conditions include such factors as insularity of the group, lack of critical evaluation, and the suppression of dissent.

New Organizational Structures

Still another factor that might contribute to more unethical behavior is the new evolving network structure of organizations, in which companies divest themselves of various business functions and contract for them with outside organizations. Thus, the newer network organization is one that has elaborate and complex relationships

Item 8.4

During the investigation of the murder of a wealthy woman, an individual confessed to killing about 20 horses over a period of several years for a fee. The fee was generally $5,000 an animal but reached $40,000 for one of the animals; the method of killing was usually electrocution. The horses' owners had ordered the killings so that they could collect the insurance taken out on the horses. Those ordering the killings were socialite owners, trainers, and world-class competitive riders. As a result of this investigation, 19 individuals were indicted for ordering the killings. A U.S. attorney involved in the case said that those charged represented a "virtual Who's Who of the nation's equestrian industry."

SOURCE: Blum (1995).

with many other suppliers, customers, and partner organizations. Obviously, under this type of organizational arrangement, there is less control possible by a given company's managers over all aspects of the production process and, as a result, the opportunity for unethical behavior is greatly increased.

Environmental Degradation

An examination of the issue of environmental degradation, which often occurs as a result of managerial decisions and which can be considered as unethical, suggests that it may be more pervasive in those countries that are industrializing. Although Japan now, in some ways, is an exemplar model of a country that has attempted to control its industrial pollution, for many years as its economy was growing rapidly, it had several terrible environmental catastrophes, including a famous mercury poisoning case. There are vivid description of environmental nightmares in Mexico involving smog, pollution, chemical waste, and other problems (Denesky, 1994). However, the people who live and work there have few if any other alternatives.

Growing International Materialism

Many observers believe that materialistic goals and perspectives are a major causal factor in unethical behavior. Materialism may mean the pursuit of wealth or money, even without regard to what it can or will purchase. It may not be pursued because one is in need, and even very wealthy individuals may do many unethical things to gain even more wealth than they have (see Item 8.4). Wealth might be sought because it has been psychologically associated with happiness in a person's mind, even though ultimately it may become a "false happiness" (Solomon, 1993).

This orientation can be traced to what one writer calls "abstract greed" (Solomon, 1993). Some argue that, irrespective of their purpose or uses, materialistic values are becoming more common throughout the world, perhaps most vividly seen in China and Russia (Laaksonen, 1988). There are many newspaper accounts of the new Russian and Chinese obsessions with getting rich. Some observers feel that these new materialistic values are due in part to a mass cultural colonization from the United States through TV programs, movies, and advertising. Some governments, such as that of Singapore, have attempted to ward off this disease of materialism with government programs. In Singapore, the government proposed programs to counteract what is called "moneytheism" and they involve stressing the importance of a caring society, the introduction of moral and religious concepts (Confucian ethics) into the school curricula, and an appeal to families to emphasize traditional and family values in the upbringing of children (Chew, 1995). How well such efforts will work is in question.

Societal and Institutional Inertia

There is also the same inertia in all social systems that has existed for centuries. Machiavelli pointed out, hundreds of years ago, the difficulty in obtaining change in social systems, because all of those advantaged by the old way of doing things are motivated to resist change. Those questioning current practices and systems can often expect the same treatment that the Athenians gave Socrates. Cultural characteristics can facilitate or hinder change. For example, Tiernan (1995) has documented the successful change in culture of a quasi-government firm in Ireland, Team Aer Lingus, from a bureaucracy to a more innovative structure. The company was forced into an extensive organizational change, when much higher levels of innovation and flexibility were needed, because of a significant loss of its customer base and the loss of certain government support. She describes how some cultural characteristics of the Irish, such as a deference to authority, loyalty, and some conformism, were in conflict with other cultural characteristics, such as respect for individual strengths and characteristics, in these change efforts. Nonetheless, these factors together constituted a more flexible organization. Unfortunately, these change efforts have not necessarily resulted in an economic turnaround for the company, given the fact that no organization can control significant economic and political forces in its environments.

The Search for a Universal Code of Ethics

As we indicated in Chapter 1, there has been a search for a universal set of ethical principles for thousands of years. In a recent paper, Hosmer (1995) provides brief summaries of 10 ethical principles from various well-known philosophers or thinkers in the field of ethics over the years (see Table 8.2). He also makes a strong case for the critical importance of trust, which others also have pointed out is the essential glue that holds all societies and their components together (Smith, Carroll, & Ashford, 1995). Indeed, trust has been the historical mandatory requirement for moving very small human entities (family groups) into larger social units (villages, cities, and nations). Hosmer points out, as have others, that trust requires accepted ethical standards and thus, ethics obviously is an essential ingredient in social integration—whether it is at the level of the organization, or of the society as a whole, and perhaps now of the global community as well. As this becomes better known, we might expect that the need or functionality of a universal system of ethics for organizational, societal, and even global effectiveness will be increasingly realized by key societal groups.

Donaldson and Dunfee (1994) also present an effective argument for a universal set of normative ethical principles in the practice of business. They point out the importance of having a set of hypernorms, which are very fundamental principles for human existence; these can serve as the basis for evaluating lower-level moral norms that are often in conflict. Also, they propose an integrative social contracts theory, which establishes ethical norms and ground rules for members of various communities to relate together more effectively. Their proposals are particularly interesting because they focus directly on the difficulties of international business relationships, in which countries must face up to the problem of conflicts among national norms of conduct.

This increased interest in the creation of fundamental hypernorms on the part of various international political and trade organizations, and the growing awareness among businessmen that ethical standards can enhance economic effectiveness, seem likely to us to add pressures for establishing a list of unacceptable behaviors or actions by international firms (Jones, 1995). If organizations can then develop codes of ethics that are congruent with such

TABLE 8.2 Brief Summaries of Ten Ethical Principles[a]

Self-Interests (Protagoras and others). If we would all look after our own self-interests, without forcefully interfering with the rights of others, then society as a whole will be better off because it will be as free and productive as possible. Over the short term, this would seem to be a simple recipe for selfishness; over the long term, however, it creates a much more meaningful guide for action, because our long-term interests are usually very different from our short-term desires. The principle, then, can be expressed as "Never take any action that is not in the long-term self-interests of yourself and the organization to which you belong."

Personal Virtues (Plato and Aristotle). The lack of forceful interference with the rights of others is not enough. As we each pursue our own self-interests, even those that are good only over the long term, we have to adopt a set of standards for our fair and courteous treatment of one another. We have to be honest, open, and truthful, for example, to eliminate distrust, and we should live temperately so as not to incite envy. In short, we should be proud of our actions and of our lives. The principle, then, can be expressed as "Never take any action that is not honest, open, and truthful, and which you would not be proud to see reported widely in national newspapers and on network television."

Religious Injunctions (St. Augustine). Honesty, truthfulness, and temperance are not enough; we also have to have some degree of compassion and kindness toward others to form a truly good society. That compassion and kindness are best expressed in the Golden Rule, which is not limited to the Judeo-Christian tradition but is part of almost all the world's religions. Reciprocity—"Do unto others as you would have them do unto you"—and compassion together build a sense of community. The principle, then, can be expressed as "Never take any action that is not kind, and that does not build a sense of community, a sense of all of us working together for a commonly accepted goal."

Government Requirements (Hobbes and Locke). Compassion and kindness would be ideal if everyone would be compassionate and kind, but everyone won't be. People compete for property and for position, and some people will always take advantage of others. To restrain that competition and maintain peace within our society, we all have to agree to obey some basic rules from a central authority that has the power to enforce those rules. In a democratic nation, we think of that authority as the government and those rules as the law. The principle, then, can be expressed as "Never take any action that violates the law, for the law represents the minimal moral standards of our society."

Utilitarian Benefits (Bentham and Mill). Common obedience to basic rules would work if the people associated with the central authority did not have self-interests of their own. They do. Consequently, we need a means of evaluating the laws of the government, and that same means can be used to evaluate the justice of our own actions. A law or an act is right if it leads to greater net social benefits than social harms. This is the principle that is often summarized as the greatest good for the greatest number. A more accurate way of expressing the principle is "Never take any action that does not result in greater good than harm for the society of which you are a part."

(continued)

TABLE 8.2　Continued

Universal Rules (Kant). Net social benefit is elegant in theory, but the theory does not say anything about how we should measure either the benefits or the harms—what is your life or health or well-being worth?—nor how we should distribute those benefits and allocate those harms. What we need is a rule to eliminate the self-interest of the person who decides, and that rule must be applicable to everyone. This principle, then, can be expressed as "Never take any action that you would not be willing to see others, faced with the same or a closely similar situation, also be encouraged to take."

Individual Rights (Rousseau and Jefferson). Eliminating self-interest on the part of the decision maker isn't really possible, given what people actually are like. They are self-interested. Consequently, we need a list of agreed-upon rights for everyone that will be upheld by everyone. These rights would certainly include guarantees against arbitrary actions of the government and would ensure freedom of speech, of assembly, of religion, and so on, and would provide security against seizure of property, interference with privacy, and deprivation of liberty without due process. The principle, then, can be expressed as "Never take any action that abridges the agreed-upon rights of others."

Economic Efficiency (Adam Smith). Basic rights are meaningless without the essentials of food, clothing, and shelter. Therefore, we should maximize the output of the needed goods and services by setting marginal revenues equal to marginal costs. At this point, the economic system will be operating as efficiently as possible, and we can reach a condition known as *Pareto Optimality,* in which it is impossible to make any one person better off without harming someone else. The principle, then, is "Always act to maximize profits subject to legal and market constraints and with full recognition of external costs, for maximum profits under those conditions are the sign of the most efficient production."

Distributive Justice (Rawls). The problem with the economic efficiency argument is that the market distributes the output of needed goods and services unjustly, for it excludes those who are poor, uneducated, or unemployed. We need a rule to ensure that those people are not left out. If we did not know who among us would be rich and who poor, who educated and who uneducated, then any rule that we made for the distribution of the output goods and services could be considered just. It can be argued that under those conditions—known as the *Social Contract*—the only agreement we could make would be that the poor and uneducated and unemployed should not be made worse off. The principle, then, is "Never take any action in which the least among us are harmed in some way."

Contributing Liberty (Nozick). Perhaps liberty—the freedom to follow one's self-interests within the constraints of the law and the market—is more important than justice—the right to be included in the overall distribution of goods and services. If so, then the only agreement that would be made under the conditions of the Social Contract—in which people do not know who would be rich or poor, who active or slothful—would be that no one should interfere with the self-development of others, for personal self-development will eventually contribute to society. The principle, then, is "Never take any action that will interfere with the rights of others for self-development and self-fulfillment."

---

a. Derived from Hosmer (1994).

hypernorms and if these are implemented through the organizational sociali-zation process, very positive steps will have been taken toward a worldwide set of ethical standards. There is some evidence that organizational codes of ethics can influence the actual everyday behavior of organizational members (Weeks & Nantel, 1992) and organizational ethics training programs can do the same (Delaney & Sockell, 1992). Of course, based on the material presented in this book, we now realize that any set of such principles must be supported by a nation's educational system and its parenting processes and also by each organization's HRM practices and organizational culture. Thus some trends do support the possibility that a universal set of business ethical principles, which actually provide useful guides to managerial decisions and behaviors, might be created. However, such a set of universal principles is not likely except at the hypernorm level, with some differences in cultural norms. Also, any set of such hypernorms requires support by all of an organization's behaviors, systems, and practices.

◪ CONCLUSIONS

Information has been presented in this book in support of a model of cultural formation, cultural socialization, and transmission. We have seen that managerial ethical behaviors do reflect not only cultural differences but also other factors, such as the laws of a nation, its human resource management systems, the cultures of the organizations in which managerial work is done, and so on. Of course, many of these factors are in fact determined by cultural variables. Thus, culture can influence managerial ethical behaviors directly because managers internalize cultural values. It can also affect managerial behaviors indirectly through its impact on the characteristics of a nation's human resource management systems and the cultures of that nation's organi-zations, which, in turn, influence managerial behaviors. Due to space limita-tions, we have chosen to illustrate the model with only two cultures in depth, those of Japan and the United States; however, we have also provided many other examples. We have discussed, for example, the human resource manage-ment systems of several European and Asian countries and have presented examples of unethical managerial behaviors from a number of countries, such as China, which also represent a good contrast to conditions existing in the United States. In terms of the future, we have indicated that although some observers see little change in cultural differences in managerial behavior occurring over the years, we believe that there are forces contributing to greater future cultural similarities in managerial behavior and practices, including ethical behaviors. These include such factors as the growth of a new international law governing relationships among trading partners, a rising standard of living, an emphasis on materialism, and a growing middle class in many formerly underdeveloped nations. There also may be some wider acceptance in the future of the stakeholder concept in management, in which all nations come to show greater appreciation for the interests of groups other than stockholders (Donaldson & Preston, 1995). All in all, it appears to us more likely that managers around the world will become more ethical rather than less, given the number and strength of the forces pushing on this issue at the present time. In general, ethical behavior seems to be related to the need for trust among components of a society and across nations. There does seem to be growing awareness that we do live in a global community in which trust and cooperation among nations are urgently needed. It is difficult, however, to predict whether future incidents of managerial unethical behaviors will increase or decrease. Still, it does seem clear that the world's managers have become more similar in their ethical standards and practices, given all that we have described in this chapter and book. As this happens, international trade should be enhanced, international economic relationships should be facilitated, and progress should be the norm rather than the exception.

References

Abadinsky, H. (1991). *Law and justice.* Chicago: Nelson-Hall.

Abegglen, J. C. (1973). *Management and labor: The Japanese solution.* Tokyo: Kodansha International.

Abegglen, J. C., & Stalk, G. (1985). *Kaisha, the Japanese corporation.* New York: Basic Books.

Adler, N. J. (1991). *International dimensions of organizational behavior.* Boston: PWS-Kent.

Adler, N. J., & Izraeli, D. N. (1995). Women managers: Moving up and across borders. In O. Shenkar (Ed.), *Global perspectives of human resource management* (pp. 165-194). Englewood Cliffs, NJ: Prentice Hall.

Agar, M. (1994). *Languageshock.* New York: Morrow.

Aguilar, F. J. (1994). *Managing corporate ethics.* New York: Oxford University Press.

Ajzen, I., & Fishbein, M. (1980). *Understanding attitudes and predicting social behavior.* Englewood Cliffs, NJ: Prentice Hall.

Amadi, E. (1992). *Ethics in Nigerian culture.* Ibadan, Nigeria: Heinemann.

American Chamber of Commerce in Japan. (1973). *Doing business in Japan.* Tokyo: Author.

Anders, W. (1991, May 20). Hefty bonuses for hefty gains. *Wall Street Journal,* p. A18.

Anthony, W. P., Perrewe, P. L., & Kacmar, K. M. (1993). *Strategic human resource management.* Ft. Worth, TX: Dryden.

Araka, H., Nihei, S., Sasaki, M., Memopto, S., Yamahar, H., & Akdasaka, N. (1992, June 13-14). Japanese students' attitudes toward employment in Japanese firms and foreign subsidiary firms located in Japan. In K. Takeuchi (Ed.), *Corporate activities in the era of global economy* (pp. 173-183). Tokyo: Keizai University International Symposium.

Aram, J. D. (1993). *Presumed superior: Individualism and American business.* Englewood Cliffs, NJ: Prentice Hall.

Arkin, A. (1992a, February). At work in the powerhouse of Europe. *Personnel Management,* pp. 32-35.

Arkin, A. (1992b, March). The land of social welfare. *Personnel Management,* pp. 33-35.

Ashforth, B. E., & Lee, R. T. (1989). The perceived legitimacy of managerial influence: A twenty-five year comparison. *Journal of Business Ethics, 8*(4), 231-242.

Audia, G. (1991). *Managing internationalization at corporate level: The case study of Fiat.* Unpublished paper, Bocconi School, Milan, Italy.

Baba, M., Hanoka, M., Hara, H., & Baba, F. (1984). *Managerial behavior in Japan and the U.S.A.: A cross-cultural survey.* Tokyo: Japan Productivity Center.

Baker, J. (1985). The international infant formula controversy: A dilemma in corporate social responsibility. *Journal of Business Ethics, 4,* 181-190.

Baldwin, J. (1955). *Notes of a native son.* Boston: Beacon.

Ball, D., & McCulloch, W. (1990). *International business: Introduction and essentials* (4th ed.). Homewood, IL: BPI/Irwin.

Ball, D. A., & McCulloch, W. H., Jr. (1993). *International business.* Homewood, IL: Irwin.

Banai, M., & Gayle, D. J. (1994). Great Britain. In R. B. Peterson (Ed.), *Managers and national culture* (pp. 42-68). Westport, CT: Quorum Books.

Barnathan, J., Galuszka, P., & Del Vallue, C. (1994, June 20). Something's rotten in France, Spain.... *Business Week,* pp. 54-55.

Bartels, R. (1967). A model for ethics in marketing. *Journal of Marketing, 31,* 20-26.

Baudrillard, J. (1988). *America.* London: Verso.

Becker, H., & Fritzsche, D. (1987). A comparison of the ethical behavior of American, French, and German managers. *Columbia Journal of World Business, 22,* 87-95.

Bendix, R. (1956). *Work and authority in industry.* New York: John Wiley.

Benedict, R. (1946). *Chrysanthemum and the sword.* Boston: Houghton Mifflin.

Bennett, J. T., & DiLorenzo, T. J. (1994). *Unhealthy charities.* New York: Basic Books.

Benson, G. (1992). *Business ethics in America.* Lexington, MA: Lexington Books.

Berkhofer, R. D., Jr. (1978). Native Americans. In J. Higham (Ed.), *Ethnic leadership in America* (pp. 119-149). Baltimore: Johns Hopkins University Press.

Besse, D. (1992, August). Finding a new raison-d'être. *Personnel Management,* pp. 40-43.

Black, D. (1989). *Sociological justice.* New York: Oxford University Press.

Blanchard, K., & Johnson, S. (1982). *The one minute manager.* New York: William Morrow.

Blum, H. (1995, January). The horse murders. *Vanity Fair,* pp. 92-101, 138-140.

Blumberg, R. L. (1987). *Corporate fraud: A case study in organizations in contemporary society.* Englewood Cliffs, NJ: Prentice Hall.

Bohlman, H. M., & Dundas, M. J. (1993). *The legal, ethical and international environment of business* (2nd ed.). St. Paul, MN: West.

Boisjoly, R. P., Curtis, E. F., & Mellican, E. (1989). Roger Boisjoly and the *Challenger* disaster: The ethical dimensions. *Journal of Business Ethics, 8,* 217-230.

Bonavia, D. (1989). *The Chinese.* London: Penguin.

Bond, M., Wan, K., Leung, K., & Giacalone, R. (1985). How are responses to verbal insults related to cultural collectivism and power distance? *Journal of Cross-Cultural Psychology, 16,* 111-127.

Bottomley, G., & DeLepervanche, J. (Eds.). (1984). *Ethnicity, class and gender in Australia.* London/Sydney: Allen & Unwin.

Bowers, D. F. (1944). *Foreign influences in American life.* Princeton: Princeton University Press.

Brenkert, G. (1992). Can we afford international human rights? *Journal of Business Ethics, 11,* 515-521.

Brislin, R. (1993). *Understanding culture's influence on behavior.* Fort Worth, TX: Harcourt Brace Jovanovich.

Brouthers, L. E., & Werner, S. (1990). Are the Japanese good global competitors? *Columbia Journal of World Business, 25,* 5-11.

Burns, G., Dwyer, P., Foust, D., Glasgald, W. (1995, March 13). The lesson from Barings' strait. *Business Week,* pp. 30-32.

Burr, A. (1917). *Russell H. Conwell and his work.* Philadelphia: John C. Winston.

Byrne, J. (1994, May 9). The victim: The living hell of life on the firing line. *Business Week,* p. 68.

Cameron, K. (1994). Strategies for successful organizational downsizing. *Human Resource Management, 33*(2), 189-212.

Caplan, J. (1992, April). It's the climate that counts. *Personnel Management,* pp. 32-35.

Carroll, A. (1981). *Business and society: Managing corporate social performance.* Boston: Little, Brown.

Carroll, A. B. (1984). *Social responsibility of management, modules in management.* Chicago: Science Research Associates.

Carroll, A. B. (1987, March-April). In search of the moral manager. *Business Horizons,* pp. 7-15.

Carroll, S. J. (1987). What can HRM do to help U.S. firms cope with current change pressures? Some ideas from the Pacific Basin nations. *Human Resources Planning, 3,* 115-124.

Carroll, S. J. (1990). High technology companies and the multiple management approach. In L. R. Gomez-Mejia & M. W. Lawless (Eds.), *Organizational issues in high technology management.* New York: JAI Press.

Carroll, S. J. (1992, June). Recent trends in U.S. HRM systems: Implications for Japanese subsidiary firms in America. In K. Takeuchi (Ed.), *Corporate activities in the era of global economy* (pp. 82-97). Tokyo: Keizai University International Symposium.

Carroll, S. J., Martell, K. D., & Gupta, A. K. (1990, January). Aligning executive human resource management with innovation strategies: An empirical study of industrial firms. In M. W. Lawless & L. R. Gomez-Mejia (Eds.), *Strategic leadership in high technology organizations* (pp. 237-247). Proceedings of Second Annual Conference on Managing the High Technology Firm, Boulder, CO.

Carroll, S. J., Olian, J. D., & Giannantonio, C. M. (1987). Performance enhancement through mentoring. In C. E. Schneider, R. W. Beatty, & L. S. Baird (Eds.), *The performance management sourcebook* (pp. 3-11). Amherst, MA: Human Resource Development Press.

Carroll, S. J., & Ramamoorthy, N. (1995). *Do business students from different nations but with the same business educational experiences perceive ethical situations differently?* Working paper, College of Business and Management, University of Maryland.

Carroll, S. J., & Schneier, C. (1982). *Performance appraisal and review systems.* Chicago: Scott, Foresman.

Carroll, S. J., & Takeuchi, K. (1982). Current problems with Japanese human resource management systems. In *Symposium: Japanese management: A realistic assessment of its potential for design and management of U.S. industrial firms.* Annual Meetings, Academy of Management, New York.

Carroll, S. J., & Tosi, H. L. (1973). *Management by objectives.* New York: Macmillan.

Carroll, S. J., & Tosi, H. L. (1976). *Organizational behavior.* Chicago: St. Clair.

Cherrington, J. O., & Cherrington, D. J. (1992). A menu of moral issues: One week in the life of the Wall Street Journal. *Journal of Business Ethics, 11,* 255-266.

Chew, E. (1995, Winter). Singapore: Emerging national identity in a global city (IHJ. Bulletin 15[1]). *International House of Japan,* pp. 6-8.

Child, J. C. (1981). Culture, contingency, and capitalism in the cross-national study of organizations. In L. L. Cummings & B. M. Staw (Eds.), *Research in organizational behavior* (Vol. 3, pp. 303-356). Greenwich, CT: JAI Press.

Christopher, R. (1983). *The Japanese mind.* New York: Fawcett Columbine.

Church, G. J. (1996, January 15). Disconnected: How AT&T is planning to put 40,000 members of its workforce out of service. *Time,* pp. 44-45.

Cohen, J., Pant, L., & Sharp, D. (1992). Cultural and socioeconomic constraints on international codes of ethics: Lessons from accounting. *Journal of Business Ethics, 11,* 687-700.

Cole, R. E. (1989). *Strategies for learning: Small group activities in American, Japanese, and Swedish industry.* Berkeley: University of California Press.

Collins, D. (1992). An ethical analysis of organizational power at Salomon Brothers. *Business Ethics Quarterly, 2*(3), 367-377.

Companies receive symbolic wrist slap. (1992, May 28). *Asahi Evening News,* p. 1.

The Confucius Connection. (1987). Chinese values and the search for culture-free dimensions of culture. *Journal of Cross-Cultural Psychology, 18,* 143-164.

Crichton, M. (1994). *Disclosure.* New York: Random House.

Crystal, G. (1991, June 17). How much CEOs really make. *Fortune,* pp. 72-80.

Czander, W. M. (1993). *The psychodynamics of work and organizations.* New York: Guilford.

Daniels, R. (1978). The Japanese. In J. Higham (Ed.), *Ethnic leadership in America* (pp. 36-63). Baltimore: Johns Hopkins University Press.

Davidson, J., & Cooper, C. (1993). *European women in business and management.* London: Paul Chapman.

Davis, M. A., Johnson, N. B., & Ohmer, D. G. (1994, August). *Issue-contingent effects on ethical decision making: A cross-cultural comparison.* Proceedings of Academy of Management Meetings, Dallas, TX.

DeGeorge, R. (1986). *Business ethics* (2nd ed.). New York: Macmillan.

DeGeorge, R. (1993). *Competing with integrity in international business.* New York: Oxford University Press.

Delaney, J. T., & Sockell, D. (1992). Do company ethics training programs make a difference? An empirical analysis. *Journal of Business Ethics, 11,* 719-727.

DeMente, B. (1991). *The kata factor.* Phoenix, AZ: Phoenix Books.

Deresky, H. (1994). *International management.* New York: HarperCollins.

Dollinger, J. (1988). Confucian ethics and Japanese management practices. *Journal of Business Ethics, 4,* 575-584.

Donaldson, T. (1985). Multinational decision-making reconciling international norms. *Journal of Business Ethics, 4,* 357-366.

Donaldson, T. (1989). *The ethics of international business.* New York: Oxford University Press.

Donaldson, T., & Dunfee, T. W. (1994). Toward a unified conception of business ethics: Integrative social contracts theory. *Academy of Management Review, 19,* 252-284.

Donaldson, T., & Preston, L. E. (1995). The stakeholder theory of the corporation: Concepts, evidence and implications. *The Academy of Management Review, 20*(1), 65-91.

Dore, R., & Sako, M. (1989). *How the Japanese learn to work.* London: Routledge.

Downs, L. (1994, April 3). In Japan where mom knows best. *Washington Post Education Review,* p. 16.

Dreiser, T. (1912). *The financier.* New York: New American Library.

Duke, B. (1986). *The Japanese school: Lessons for industrial America.* New York: Praeger.

Durkheim, E. (1965). *The elementary forms of the religious life.* New York: Free Press. (Original work published 1915)

Emerson, R. W. (1936/1841). *Essays.* Reading, PA: Spencer.

England, G. (1975). *The manager and his values.* Cambridge, MA: Ballinger.

Eun, C. S., Kolodny, R., & Scheraga, C. (1992). *Cross-border acquisitions and shareholder wealth: Evidence from U.S. and foreign stock markets.* Working paper, College of Business and Management, University of Maryland.

Evans, J. M. (1976). *America: The view from Europe.* San Francisco: San Francisco Book Co.

Felicita, J. T. (1994). Negotiating with the Americans. In L. Catlin & T. White (Eds.), *International business: Cultural sourcebook and case studies* (pp. 29-31). Cincinnati, OH: Southwestern.

Fernandez, J. P. (1991). *Managing a diverse work force.* Lexington, MA: Lexington Books.

Fields, R. (1991). *The code of the warrior.* New York: Harper Perennial.

Fishbein, M., & Ajzen, I. (1975). *Belief, attitude, intention, and behavior: An introduction to theory and research.* Reading, MA: Addison-Wesley.

Fisher, G. (1988). *Mindsets.* Yarmouth, ME: Intercultural Press.

Flax, S. (1984, May 14). How to snoop on your competitor. *Fortune,* pp. 28-33.

Foulkes, F. K., & Livernash, E. R. (1989). *Human resource management: Text and cases.* Englewood Cliffs, NJ: Prentice Hall.

Franklin, B. (1936/1771). *The autobiography of Benjamin Franklin.* Reading, PA: Spencer.

Freeman, R., & Gilbert, D. (1988). *Corporate strategy and the search for ethics.* Englewood Cliffs, NJ: Prentice Hall.

Friedland, J. (1995, December 11). Did IBM unit bribe officials in Argentina to land a contract? *Wall Street Journal,* p. A1.

Friedman, L. M. (1993). *Crime and punishment in American history.* New York: Harper-Collins.

Fu, C. L. (1994, March 10). Chinese executive executed for bribery. *The Washington Post*, p. C3.

Gannon, M., & Associates. (1994). *Understanding global cultures: Metaphorical journeys through 17 countries*. Thousand Oaks, CA: Sage.

Gessel, V. C. (1993). *Three modern novelists: Soseki, Tanizaki, Kawabata*. Tokyo: Kodansha International.

Gioia, D. A. (1991). Pinto fires and personal ethics: A script analysis of missed opportunities. *The Journal of Business Ethics, 10*.

Graham, J. (1983). Foreign corrupt practices: A manager's guide. *Columbia Journal of World Business, 18*(3), 89-94.

Graham, J. (1984, Winter). The foreign corrupt practices act: A new perspective. *Journal of International Business Studies*, pp. 107-123.

Greenwald, J., & Thigpen, D. E. (1991, May 6). Whose company is this? *Time*, p. 48.

Gundling, E. (1991). Ethics and working with the Japanese: The entrepreneur and the "elite course." *California Management Review*, pp. 25-39.

Gutman, A. (1993). *EEO law and personnel practices*. Newbury Park, CA: Sage.

Hall, E. T. (1989). *Beyond culture*. Garden City, NY: Doubleday.

Hall, E., & Hall, M. (1990). *Understanding cultural differences*. Yarmouth, ME: Intercultural Press.

Hamaji, M. (1994, June 21). In Japan, bankruptcy is a moral offense. *Wall Street Journal*, p. A23.

Hamilton, D. P., & Shirouzu, N. (1992, December 22). Japan's business cartels are starting to erode but change is slow. *The Wall Street Journal*, p. A1.

Hampton-Turner, C., & Trompenaars, A. (1993). *The seven cultures of capitalism*. New York: Doubleday.

Hanami, T. (1991). *Managing Japanese workers*. Tokyo: The Japan Institute of Labor.

Hannaway, C. (1992). Why Irish firms are smiling. *Personnel Management*, pp. 38-41.

Harbison, F., & Myers, C. A. (Eds.). (1959). *Management in the industrial world*. New York: McGraw-Hill.

Hartley, R. F. (1991). *Management mistakes and successes* (3rd ed.). New York: John Wiley.

Hawthorne, N. (1992/1850). *The scarlet letter*. New York: Knopf.

Haycraft, J. (1985). *Italian labyrinth*. New York: Penguin.

Henderson, V. (1992). *What's ethical in business?* New York: McGraw-Hill.

Higham, J. (Ed.). (1978). *Ethnic leadership in America*. Baltimore: Johns Hopkins University Press.

Hill, C. W. L. (1994). *International business.* Burr Ridge, IL: Irwin.

Hofstede, G. (1980a). *Culture's consequences: International differences in work-related values.* Beverly Hills, CA: Sage.

Hofstede, G. (1980b, Summer). Motivation, leadership, and organizations: Do American theories apply abroad? *Organizational Dynamics, 2,* 42-63.

Hofstede, G. (1991). *Culture and organizations.* New York: McGraw-Hill.

Hofstede, G., & Bond, M. (1988). The Confucius connection: From cultural roots to economic growth. *Organizational Dynamics, 16,* 15-21.

Hofstede, G., Neuijen, B., Ohayv, D., & Sanders, G. (1992). Measuring organizational cultures: A qualitative and quantitative study across twenty cases. *Administrative Science Quarterly, 35,* 286-316.

Hoogendoorn, J. (1992, December). New priorities for Dutch HRM. *Personnel Management,* pp. 42-48.

Hosmer, L. T. (1994). *Moral leadership in business.* Burr Ridge, IL: Irwin.

Hosmer, L. T. (1995). Trust: The connecting link between organizational theory and philosophical ethics. *Academy of Management Review, 20,* 379-403.

Hotchkiss, C. (1993). *International law for business.* New York: McGraw-Hill.

Hotchkiss, C. (1994). *International law for business.* New York: McGraw-Hill.

Huddleston, J. N., Jr. (1990). *Gaijin kaisha, running a foreign business in Japan.* Armonk, NY: M. E. Sharpe.

Huggins, N. I. (1978). Afro-American. In J. Higham (Ed.), *Ethnic leadership in America* (pp. 91-118). Baltimore: Johns Hopkins University Press.

Hunt, S. D., & Vitell, S. (1986). A general theory of marketing ethics. *Journal of Macromarketing, 6,* 5-16.

Jacobs, M. A. (1994, June 6). Riding crop and slurs: How Wall Street dealt with a sex bias case. *Wall Street Journal,* pp. A1, A6.

James, H. (1984). *Daisy Miller.* New York: Penguin.

Janis, I. L. (1972). *Victims of groupthink.* Boston: Houghton Mifflin.

Japan's high-tech spies. (1982, July 5). *Newsweek,* pp. 47-49.

Jelinek, M., & Adler, N. (1988). Women: World-class managers for global competition. *Academy of Management Executive, 11*(1), 11-19.

Jones, T. M. (1995). Instrumental stakeholder theory: A synthesis of ethics and economics. *Academy of Management Review, 20,* 404-437.

Kagan, H., & Cohen, J. (1990). Cultural adjustment of international students. *Psychological Science, 1*(2), 133-137.

Kagitcibasi, C. (1990). Family and home based intervention. In R. Brislin (Ed.), *Applied cross-cultural psychology* (pp. 121-141). Newbury Park, CA: Sage.

Kahn, H. (1970). *The emerging Japanese superstate.* Harmondsworth, UK: Penguin.

Kanter, R. M. (1977). *Men and women of the corporation.* New York: Basic Books.

Kashima, Y., & Callan, V. J. (1994). The Japanese work group. In H. C. Triandis, M. D. Dunnette, & L. M. Hough (Eds.). *Handbook of industrial and organizational psychology* (2nd ed., Vol. 4, pp. 609-646). Palo Alto, CA: Consulting Psychologists Press.

Kato, S. (1979). *A history of Japanese literature* (3 Vols.). Tokyo: Kodansha International.

Katzenstein, G. (1989). *Funny business: An outsider's year in Japan.* New York: Prentice Hall.

Kelley, L., & Shenkar, O. (Eds.). (1993). *International business in China.* London: Routledge.

Kerr, J., & Slocum, J. W. (1987). Managing corporate culture through reward systems. *Academy of Management Executive, 1,* 99-108.

Kluckholn, F., & Strodtbeck, F. (1961). *Variations in value orientations.* Evanston, IL: Row, Peterson.

Kohls, J., & Buller, P. (1994). Resolving cross-cultural ethical conflict: Exploring alternative strategies. *Journal of Business Ethics, 13,* 31-38.

Korman, A. K. (1994). *Human dilemmas in work organizations.* New York: Guilford.

Kotkin, J. (1993). *Tribes.* New York: Random House.

Kozinski, J., & Listwan, T. (1993). Poland. In R. B. Peterson (Ed.), *Managers and national culture* (pp. 178-208). Westport, CT: Quorum Books.

Laaksonen, O. (1988). *Management in China during and after Mao in enterprises, government, and party.* New York: Walter de Gruyter.

Langlois, C., & Schlegermilch, B. (1990). Do corporate codes of ethics reflect national character? Evidence from Europe and the United States. *Journal of International Business Studies, 4,* 512-539.

Ledvinka, J., & Scarpello, V. G. (1991). *Federal regulation of personnel and human resource management.* Boston: PWS-Kent.

Lee, G. (1995, January 6). Louisiana company's officers admit fouling the Mississippi. *Washington Post,* p. A2.

LeFebvre, M., & Singh, J. (1992). The content and focus of Canadian codes of ethics. *Journal of Business Ethics, 13,* 31-38.

Leo, J. (1994, June 13). Selling the woman-child. *U.S. News & World Report,* p. 27.

Lewis, S. (1922). *Babbitt.* New York: New American Library.

Liebow, E. (1967). *Tally's corner: A study of negro streetcorner men.* Boston: Little, Brown.

Lincoln, J. (1989). Employee work attitudes and management practice in the U.S. and Japan: Evidence from a large comparative study. *California Management Review, 32*(1), 89-105.

Lincoln, J. R., Hanada, M., & McBride, K. (1986). Organizational structures in Japanese and U.S. manufacturing. *Administrative Science Quarterly, 31,* 338-364.

Lo, J. (1990). *Office ladies/factory women: Life and work at a Japanese company.* Armonk, NY: M. E. Sharpe.

Luebke, F. (1978). The Germans. In J. Higham (Ed.), *Ethnic leadership in America* (pp. 64-90). Baltimore: Johns Hopkins University Press.

Lysonski, S., & Gaidis, W. (1991). A cross-cultural comparison of the ethics of business students. *Journal of Business Ethics, 10,* 141-150.

Maccoby, M. (1976). *The gamesman.* New York: Simon & Schuster.

Machiavelli, N. (1952/1513). *The prince* (Luigi Ricci, Trans.). New York: New American Library.

March, R. M. (1992). Western manager, Japanese boss. *Intersect, 8,* 11-16.

Martell, K., & Carroll, S. J. (1995a). How strategic is HRM? *Human Resource Management, 34,* 253-267.

Martell, K., & Carroll, S. J. (1995b). Which executive human resource management practices for the top management team are associated with higher firm performance? *Human Resource Management, 34,* 497-512.

Martinez, M. N. (1995a, January). HRM update. Companies already complying with $1-million deduction cap. *HRMagazine,* p. 18.

Martinez, M. N. (1995b, January). HRM update. Mentoring with an "equality" twist. *HRMagazine,* p. 16.

Matsushita, M. (1993). *International trade and competition law in Japan.* Oxford, UK: Oxford University Press.

Mayer, D., & Cava, A. (1993). Ethics and the gender equality dilemma for U.S. multinationals. *Journal of Business Ethics, 12,* 701-708.

Mayo, M., & Marks, L. J. (1990). An empirical investigation of a general theory of marketing ethics. *Journal of the Academy of Marketing Science, 18,* 163-172.

McClelland, D. (1961). *The achieving society.* New York: Van Nostrand.

McClelland, D., & Winter, D. (1969). *Motivating economic achievement.* New York: Free Press.

McDonald, G., & Zepp, R. (1988). Ethical perceptions of Hong Kong Chinese business managers. *Journal of Business Ethics, 7,* 835-845.

Meek, C. B., & Song, Y.-H. (1993). South Korea. In R. B. Peterson (Ed.), *Managers and national culture* (pp. 287-300). Westport, CT: Quorum Books.

Miller, A. (1957). *Collected plays.* New York: Viking-Penguin.

Millspaugh, P. E. (1990). Plant closing: Ethics root in American law. *Journal of Business Ethics, 9,* 665-670.

202 ■ ETHICAL DIMENSIONS OF MANAGEMENT

Miner, J. B. (1965). *Studies in management education.* New York: Springer.

Miner, J. B. (1988). *Organizational behavior: Performance and productivity.* New York: Random House.

Morgan, T. (1988). *On becoming American.* New York: Paragon House.

Munson, R. (1995). *Intervention and reflection: Basic issues in medical ethics.* Belmont, CA: Wadsworth.

Nash, A. N., & Carroll, S. J. (1974). *The management of compensation.* Pacific Grove, CA: Brooks/Cole.

Newman, W. H. (1970, January-February). Is management exportable? *Columbia Journal of World Business,* 439-455.

O'Neill, E. (1950). *Long day's journey into night.* New Haven: Yale University Press.

O'Neill, E. (1957). *The iceman cometh.* New York: Random House.

Ott, J. S. (1989). *The organizational culture perspective.* Chicago: Dorsey.

Perdomo, R. (1990). Corruption and business in present day Venezuela. *Journal of Business Ethics, 9,* 555-566.

Peters, T. J., & Waterman, R. H. (1982). *In search of excellence.* New York: Harper & Row.

Peterson, R. B. (Ed.). (1993). *Managers and national culture: A global perspective.* Westport, CT: Quorum Books.

Peterson, R. B., & George-Falvy, J. (1993). United States. In R. B. Peterson (Ed.), *Managers and national culture: A global perspective* (pp. 14-48). Westport, CT: Quorum Books.

Pinchot, J., III. (1985). *Intrapreneuring.* New York: Harper & Row.

Posner, B. Z., & Schmidt, W. H. (1987). Ethics in American companies: A managerial perspective. *Journal of Business Ethics, 6*(5), 383-392.

Powell, G. N. (1993). *Women and men in management* (2nd ed.). Newbury Park, CA: Sage.

Pratt, C. (1991). Multinational corporate social policy process for ethical responsibility in sub-Saharan Africa. *Journal of Business Ethics, 10,* 527-541.

Preble, J. F., & Reichel, A. (1988). Attitudes towards business ethics of future managers in the U.S. and Israel. *Journal of Business Ethics, 7,* 941-949.

Prindle, T. K. (1989). *Made in Japan and other Japanese "business novels."* Armonk, NY: M. E. Sharpe.

Putnam, R. (1993). *Making democracy work: Civic traditions in modern Italy.* Princeton: Princeton University Press.

Ramamoorthy, N., & Carroll S. J. (1996). *Individualism-collectivism orientations and preferences for human resources management practices: An empirical study.* Working paper, College of Business and Management, University of Maryland.

Rand, A. (1943). *The fountainhead*. New York: Bobbs-Merrill.

Rand, A. (1957). *Atlas shrugged*. New York: Signet.

Ray, A. (1993). *International business law: Text, cases, and readings*. Englewood Cliffs, NJ: Prentice Hall.

Reading, B. (1992). *Japan: The coming collapse*. New York: Harper Business.

Reger, R. K., Gustafson, L. T., DeMarie, S. M., & Mullane, J. V. (1992). Reframing the organization: Why implementing total quality is easier said than done. *Academy of Management Review, 19,* 565-584.

Rehder, R. R. (1989). Japanese transplants: In search of a balanced and broader perspective. *Columbia Journal of World Business, 24,* 17-20.

Reischauer, E. O. (1981). *The Japanese*. Cambridge, MA: Harvard University Press.

Reischauer, E. O. (1988). *The Japanese today*. Cambridge, MA: Harvard University Press.

Rest, J. R., & Narvaez, D. (1994). *Moral development in the professions*. Hillsdale, NJ: Lawrence Erlbaum.

Rimer, J. T. (1988). *A reader's guide to Japanese literature: From the eighth century to the present*. Tokyo: Kodansha International.

Robertson, D., & Schlegermilch, B. (1993). Corporate institutionalization of ethics in the United States and Great Britain. *Journal of Business Ethics, 12,* 301-312.

Rogers, R., & Hunter, J. (1991). The impact of management by objectives on organizational productivity. *Journal of Applied Psychology, 76,* 322-336.

Rohler, L. (1995). *Ralph Waldo Emerson: Preacher and lecturer*. Westport, CT: Greenwood.

Ross, B. (1986, February). W. Edwards Deming: Shogun of quality control. *Magazine for Financial Executives*, pp. 25-31.

Rossant, J. (1993, March 1). The cleanup of Italy Inc. *Business Week*, pp. 50-51.

Salwen, K. (1992, February 13). Shareholder proposals on pay must be aired, SEC to tell 10 firms. *Wall Street Journal*, p. A1.

Sapsford, J. (1994, November 30). Destitute on paper, a Japanese tycoon is "too big to fail." *Wall Street Journal*, pp. A1, A16.

Sathe, V. (1985). *Culture and related corporate realities: Text, cases and readings on organizational entry, establishment, and change*. Homewood, IL: Irwin.

Schein, E. (1985). *Organizational culture and leadership*. San Francisco: Jossey-Bass.

Schneider, B. (1983). Interactional psychology and organizational behavior. *Research in Organizational Behavior, 5,* 1-31.

Selekman, B. M. (1949). Varieties of labor relations. *Harvard Business Review, 27,* 125.

Shaw, B. (1988). Foreign corrupt practices act: A legal and moral analysis. *Journal of Business Ethics, 7,* 789-796.

Shaw, W., & Barry, V. (1989). *Moral issues in business* (4th ed.). Belmont, CA: Wadsworth.

Shea, G. (1988). *Practical ethics* (AMA Management Briefing). New York: AMA Membership Publications Division.

Sims, R. R. (1992). Linking groupthink to unethical behavior in organizations. *Journal of Business Ethics, 11,* 651-662.

Sinclair, U. (1906). *The jungle.* New York: Bantam.

Singletary, M. (1994, March 7). When the house lights go up and the jobs are gone. *Washington Post Business,* p. 17.

Small, M. W. (1992). Attitudes toward business ethics held by Western Australian students: A comparative study. *Journal of Business Ethics, 11,* 745-752.

Smith, C. S. (1995, November 3). A beer tampering scare in China shows a peril of global marketing. *Wall Street Journal,* p. B1.

Smith, H. (1958). *The religions of man.* New York: Harper & Row.

Smith, H. (1991). *The world's religions.* San Francisco: HarperCollins.

Smith, K. G., Carroll, J. J., & Ashford, S. J. (1995). Intra and inter organizational cooperation. Toward a research agenda. *Academy of Management Journal, 39,* 7-23.

Smith, P. (1992). *Japanese fairy tales.* New York: Dover.

Sokaiya link seen in death of Fuji executive, (1994, March 2). *Japan Times,* p. 2.

Solomon, R. C. (1993). *Ethics and excellence.* New York: Oxford University Press.

Sprotzer, I., & Goldberg, I. V. (1992). Fetal protection: Law, ethics and corporate policy. *Journal of Business Ethics, 11,* 731-752.

Steidlmeier, P. (1993). The moral legitimacy of intellectual property claims: American business and developing country perspectives. *Journal of Business Ethics, 12,* 157-164.

Stewart, E. C., & Bennett, M. J. (1991). *American cultural patterns* (2nd ed.). Yarmouth, ME: Intercultural Press.

Stross, R. E. (1990). *Bulls in the China shop.* Honolulu: University of Hawaii Press.

Swinyard, W., Rinne, H., & Kau, A. (1990). The morality of software piracy: A cross-cultural analysis. *Journal of Business Ethics, 9,* 655-664.

Taka, I., & Foglia, W. (1994). Ethical aspects of "Japanese leadership style." *Journal of Business Ethics, 13,* 135-148.

Tarbell, I. M. (1904). *The history of the Standard Oil Company.* New York: Macmillan.

Tasker, P. (1987). *The Japanese: Portrait of a nation.* New York: Meridian.

Taylor, M. S., Tracy, K. B., Renard, M. K., Harrison, J. K., & Carroll, S. J. (1995). Procedural justice in performance appraisal: A field test of the due process metaphor for performance appraisal systems. *Administrative Science Quarterly, 40,* 495-523.

Taylor, S. (1993). Japan. In B. Peterson (Ed.), *Managers and national culture: A global perspective* (pp. 257-286). Westport, CT: Quorum Books.

Taylor, S., Moxon, D., & Beechler, S. (1991, August). *Human resource management in offshore manufacturing plants: A comparison of American and Japanese macquiladoras in Mexico.* Presented at Symposium: Research in Progress, Academy of Management Annual Meetings, Miami, FL.

Terborg, J. R. (1981). Interactional psychology and research on human behavior in organizations. *Academy of Management Review, 6,* 569-576.

That eye-popping executive pay. (1994, April 25). *Business Week,* pp. 52-58.

The victim: The living hell of life on the firing line. (1994, May 9). *Business Week,* p. 68.

Tiernan, S.D. (1995). *From bureaucratic to network organization: Organizational change and the outcomes of Team Aer Lingus.* Doctoral thesis, University of Limerick, Ireland.

Tobin, J., Wu, D., & Davidson, D. (1989). *Preschool in three cultures: Japan, China, and the United States.* New Haven: Yale University Press.

Tocqueville, A. de. (1945). *Democracy in America: Vol. II. The social influence of democracy.* New York: Knopf. (Original work published 1840)

Toner, J. H. (1995). *True faith and allegiance: The burden of military ethics.* Lexington: University of Kentucky Press.

Tosi, H. L., & Carroll, S. J. (1976). *Management: Contingencies, structure, and process.* Chicago: St. Clair.

Tosi, H. L., Rizzo, J. R., & Carroll, S. J. (1994). *Managing organizational behavior* (2nd ed.). New York: John Wiley.

Tosi, H. L., Rizzo, J. R., & Carroll, S. J. (1994). *Managing organizational behavior* (3rd ed.). London: Blackwell.

Toffler, B. (1986). *Tough choices: Managers talk ethics.* New York: John Wiley.

Triandis, H. C. (1994). Cross-cultural industrial and organizational psychology. In H. C. Triandis, M. D. Dunnette, & L. M. Hough (Eds.), *Handbook of industrial and organizational psychology* (2nd ed., Vol. 4, pp. 103-172). Palo Alto, CA: Consulting Psychologists Press.

Trompenaars, F. (1993). *Riding the waves of culture.* Homewood, IL: Irwin.

Trotter, R. C., Day, S. G., & Love, A. E. (1989). Bhopal, India and Union Carbide: The second tragedy. *Journal of Business Ethics, 8,* 439-454.

U.S. Department of Commerce. (1980, September). *Report of the president on expert promotion functions and retentional expert disincentive.* Washington, DC: Government Printing Office.

Varley, H. P. (1984). *Japanese culture* (3rd ed.). Honolulu: University of Hawaii Press.

Vitell, S. J., & Hunt, S. D. (1990). The general theory of marketing ethics: A partial test of the model. *Research in Marketing Annual, 10,* 237-266.

Vogel, D. (1992, Fall). The globalization of business ethics: Why America remains distinctive. *California Management Review,* pp. 30-49.

Weber, M. (1930). *The Protestant ethic and the spirit of capitalism* (T. Parsons, Trans.). New York: Scribner.

Wedenoja, W. (1995). Social and cultural psychiatry of Jamaicans. In I. Al-Issa (Ed.), *Handbook of culture and mental illness* (33-50). Madison, CT: International Universities Press.

Weeks, W. A., & Nantel, J. (1992). Corporate codes of ethics and sales force behavior: A case study. *Journal of Business Ethics, 11,* 753-760.

Whipple, T. W., & Swords, D. F. (1992). Business ethics judgements: A cross-cultural comparison. *Journal of Business Ethics, 11,* 671-678.

White, L. P., & Rhodeback, M. J. (1992). Ethical dilemmas in organization development: A cross-cultural analysis. *Journal of Business Ethics, 6,* 289-295.

White, M. (1987). *The Japanese educational challenge: A commitment to children.* New York: Free Press.

Whitehill, A. M. (1991). *Japanese management: Tradition and transition.* London: Routledge.

Wilke, J. R., O'Brien, T. L., & Shirouzu, N. (1995, November 3). U.S. bars Daiwa Bank and indicts institution. *Wall Street Journal,* p. A1.

Williams, W. (1985, June 9). White collar crime: Booming again. *New York Times,* p. 4.

Wilson, J. Q. (1994). *The moral sense.* New York: Free Press.

Woronoff, J. (1990). *Japan as anything but number one.* Armonk, NY: M. E. Sharpe.

Wright, R. (1994). *The moral animal: Evolutionary psychology and everyday life.* New York: Pantheon.

Yeh, R. S. (1986). Values and interorganizational influence: A comparative study of Taiwanese, Japanese, and American firms in Taiwan (Doctoral dissertation, Temple University). *University Microfilms International.*

Yin, R. (1989). *Case study research: Design and methods.* London: Sage.

Yukl, G. A. (1989). *Leadership in organizations* (2nd ed.). Englewood Cliffs, NJ: Prentice Hall.

Young, M. K. (1988). Foreign lawyers in Japan: A case study in transnational dispute resolution and marginal reform. *Law in Japan, 21,* 84-21. pp. 84-91.

Zabid, A., & Alsagoff, S. (1993). Perceived ethical values of Malaysian managers. *Journal of Business Ethics, 12,* 331-337.

Zeldin, T. (1994). *An intimate history of humanity.* New York: HarperCollins.

Name Index

Subject Index

Achievement, 95
  American beliefs in, 65, 137, 145
  Japan and, 104
  judging based on, 48
Action:
  reasoned, 7
  responsibility for one's own, 59
ADAPSO, 26
Advertising, deceptive, 24-25
Affective managers, 45
African countries, bribery and, 20-21
Agreements, international, 178
A.H. Robbins Company, 132
Altruism, America and, 137
Amae, 17, 60
America, *see* United States
Analyzing, integrating versus, 47, 48-49
Anti-intellectualism, America and, 137
Armstrong World Industries, 152
Artifacts, 38
Ascribed status, 48, 49-50
Asian countries:
  bribery and, 20
  copyrights and, 27
  economic growth and, 73
  intellectual property protection and, 84-85
  software piracy, 26
  wage systems, 91
Asians:
  emotional unpredictability and, 60
  parenting styles, 58

primary motivation of, 59
religious influences, 69
utilitarian ethic in making moral
  decisions, 27
Assumptions, value, 38
Australia:
  gender inequality and, 31
  managerial values, 46
Authority:
  acceptance of, 53
  changing attitudes toward, 178
  U.S. managers and, 158-159, 178
Autocratic management, in Japan, 112-113
Autonomy, U.S. managers and, 144
Avoidant orientation, 97

Baksheesh, 22
Bamboo ceiling case, 121-122
Barings, 76
Beech-Nut, 184
Behavior:
  acceptable, 2
  fundamental societal influences on, 175
  homogeneity of, 95
  individual characteristics, 7
  interactional perspective on, 7
  modeling, 152
  predicting, 7
  primary influences on, 10-11
  secondary influences on, 11-12

About the Authors

Stephen J. Carroll completed his BA at UCLA and his MA and PhD at the University of Minnesota. He is author or coauthor of more than 12 books and monographs and more than 100 published papers. The books and monographs include *Management by Objectives, The Management of Compensation, Management: Contingencies, Structure and Process, Managing Organziational Behavior, Performance Appraisal and Review Systems, Management, Human Resource Management in the 1980s, Cases in Management, Development of Management Performance,* and *The Design and Implementation of Pension Plans.* The papers have been published in many outlets including *Administrative Science Quarterly, Academy of Management Journal, Academy of Management Review, Californial Management Review, Human Resource Management, Industrial Relations, Journal of Applied Psychology, Journal of Business, Personnel Psychology,* and *Public Opinion Quarterly.* He has been a consultant to more than 40 business or government organizations. He has been elected a fellow in the Academy of Management, The American Psychological Association, and the American Psychological Society. His professional and administrative experience includes positions as chairman, Personnel/Human Resources Division of the Academy of Management; Chair Faculty of Management and Organization, University of Maryland; co-director, Center for Innovation, University of Maryland; Distinguished Scholar-Teacher, University of Maryland; Fulbright Research Professor in Japan; and editorial board, *Academy of Management Journal.*

Martin J. Gannon, who received his PhD from Columbia University, is Professor of Management, College of Business and Management, University of

Maryland at College Park. In this college he has also served as Associate Dean for Academic Affairs, chairperson of the Faculty of Management and Organization, and co-director of the Small Business Development Center. He has also been the Senior Research Fulbright Professor at the Center for Higher Education and Work in West Germany; the John F. Kennedy/Fulbright Professor at Thammasat University, Bangkok; and a visiting faculty member at the London Business School, Bocconi University (Italy), University College Dublin, and the University of Kassel (Germany). He has written 75 articles that have been published in journals such as the *Academy of Management Journal, The Academy of Management Review, Journal of Applied Psychology, California Management Review, International Journal of Management, Industrial Relations,* and several others. His 10 authored or coauthored books include *Managing Without Traditional Methods: International Innovations in Human Resource Management; Understanding Global Cultures: Metaphorical Journeys Through 17 Countries; The Dynamics of Competitive Strategy; Management; Strategic Management Skills;* and *Organizational Behavior.* He is a past president and fellow, Eastern Academy of Management. He has also been past chairperson of the Human Resource Division of the Academy of Management. Throughout his career, he has served as a management trainer and consultant to a number of private firms and government agencies, including Chemical Bank, The Upjohn Company, U.S. Office of Personnel Management, American Federation of Government Employees, and the U.S. General Accounting Office, and has taught managers and students in Europe and Asia.